1000 Recipes
Quick & Easy

igloo books

Published in 2013
by Igloo Books Ltd
Cottage Farm
Sywell
NN6 0BJ
www.igloobooks.com

SHE001 0313
2 4 6 8 10 9 7 5 3 1
ISBN 978-1-78197-173-4

Food photography and recipe development: PhotoCuisine UK
Front and back cover images © PhotoCuisine UK

Printed and manufactured in China

1000 Recipes

Quick & Easy

CONTENTS

STARTERS AND SIDES

SERVES 4

Pork and Courgette Gremolata Kebabs

PREPARATION TIME 25 MINUTES

COOKING TIME 8 MINUTES

....

INGREDIENTS

4 cloves garlic, chopped
50 g / 1 ¾ oz flat leaf parsley, finely chopped
1 lemon, zest and juice
3 tbsp olive oil
900 g / 2 lb / 6 cups pork shoulder, cubed
3 courgettes (zucchini), cubed

- Put 12 wooden skewers in a bowl of water and leave to soak for 20 minutes.
- Meanwhile, put all of the ingredients in a large freezer bag and massage together. Leave to marinate for 20 minutes.
- Preheat the grill to its highest setting.
- Thread alternate chunks of pork and courgette onto the skewers and spread them out on a large grill tray.
- Grill the kebabs for 4 minutes on each side or until they are golden brown and cooked through.
- Serve with a green salad.

Pork and Courgette Pesto Kebabs

2

- For an even speedier alternative, replace the garlic, parsley and lemon zest with 4 tbsp pesto.

SERVES 4

Chicken, Peach and Fennel Kebabs

PREPARATION TIME 30 MINUTES

COOKING TIME 8 MINUTES

....

INGREDIENTS

½ tsp white peppercorns
½ tsp fennel seeds
½ tsp chilli flakes
1 clove garlic, crushed
3 tbsp olive oil
6 boneless skinless chicken thighs, cubed
2 small bulbs fennel, cut into chunks
3 peaches, cut into eighths

- Put 12 wooden skewers in a bowl of water and leave to soak for 20 minutes.
- Meanwhile, grind the peppercorns, fennel seeds and chilli flakes together in a pestle and mortar, then add the garlic and oil and pound into a paste.
- Scrape the paste into a large freezer bag, add the rest of the ingredients and massage together. Leave to marinate for 20 minutes.
- Preheat the grill to its highest setting.
- Thread alternate chunks of chicken, fennel and peach onto the skewers and spread them out on a large grill tray.
- Grill the kebabs for 4 minutes on each side or until they are golden brown and cooked through.

Lamb, Apricot and Fennel Kebabs

4

- Replace the peaches with fresh apricots and the chicken with 450 g cubed lamb shoulder.

5

MAKES 6 Prosciutto and Quail's Egg Crostini

- Preheat the grill to its highest setting.
- Spread the baguette slices out on a grill tray and toast for 2 minutes on each side or until golden brown.
- Rub the crostini with the halved garlic clove and brush with half of the olive oil.
- Heat the rest of the oil in a large frying pan and break in the quails eggs. Fry the eggs for 2 minutes or until the whites are set.
- Lay a slice of prosciutto on top of each crostini and top each one with a fried quails egg.

PREPARATION TIME 2 MINUTES

COOKING TIME 6 MINUTES

INGREDIENTS

6 slices baguette
½ clove garlic
2 tbsp olive oil
6 quail's eggs
6 slices prosciutto

Goats' Cheese and Prosciutto Crostini

6

- Replace the quail's eggs with 6 slices of goats' cheese. Grill the crostini for 2 minutes to melt the cheese.

7

SERVES 4 Lamb Koftas

- Put 12 wooden skewers in a bowl of water to soak.
- Meanwhile, cook the lentils in boiling water for 20 minutes, then drain well.
- While the lentils are cooking, fry the onion and chilli in the oil for 5 minutes then add the garlic and spices and cook for 2 more minutes. Season with salt and pepper.
- Put the lentils in a food processor with the lamb, coriander and spiced onion mixture and pulse.
- Squeeze a handful of the kofta mixture around each skewer, then chill in the fridge for 30 minutes.
- To make the dip, put the cucumber in a sieve and squeeze out as much liquid as possible then stir it into the yoghurt with the mint, sugar and salt and pepper.
- Preheat the grill to its highest setting.
- Grill the koftas for 4 minutes on each side or until they are golden brown and cooked through.

PREPARATION TIME 40 MINUTES

COOKING TIME 35 MINUTES

INGREDIENTS

50 g / 1 ¾ oz / ⅓ cup red lentils
2 onions, finely chopped
1 red chilli, finely chopped
2 tbsp rapeseed oil
2 cloves garlic, crushed
2 tsp ground cumin
1 tsp ground mixed spice
450 g / 1 lb / 3 cups lamb mince
a small bunch coriander (cilantro), chopped

FOR THE DIP

100 g / 3 ½ oz / ⅔ cup cucumber, coarsely grated
200 ml / 7 fl. oz / ⅘ cup Greek yoghurt
1 tbsp garden mint, chopped
½ tsp caster (superfine) sugar

Meatball Pitas

8

- Shape the kofta mixture into small balls and fry for 10 minutes, then serve in warm pita with a little tzatziki spooned over.

SERVES 4

Goats' Cheese Potato Cakes

Goats' Cheese and Chorizo Potato Cakes

10

- Fry 100 g cubed chorizo in 2 tbsp olive oil before adding it to the potato and goat's cheese mixture.

Feta and Cumin Potato Cakes

11

- Replace the goat's cheese with crumbled Feta and replace the chives with ½ tsp ground cumin.

PREPARATION TIME 15 MINUTES

COOKING TIME 8 MINUTES

INGREDIENTS

300 g / 10 ½ oz / 2 cups left over boiled potatoes, cold
1 egg yolk
100 g / 3 ½ oz / ⅔ cup fresh goats' cheese, cubed
2 tbsp fresh chives, chopped
1 tbsp flat leaf parsley, chopped
50 g / 1 ¾ oz / ⅓ cup panko breadcrumbs
4 tbsp olive oil

TO SERVE

1 beefsteak tomato
28 g / 1 oz rocket leaves
a few sprigs parsley and chives
1 tbsp olive oil

- Mash the potato with the egg yolk and plenty of salt and pepper then knead in the goats' cheese and herbs.
- Divide the mixture into 4 and shape it into patties. Dip the potato cakes in the breadcrumbs to coat.
- Heat the oil in a large frying pan and fry the potato cakes for 4 minutes on each side or until golden brown.
- Meanwhile, cut 4 large slices from the middle of the tomato and cut the ends into cubes.
- Put a tomato slice in the centre of each plate and arrange the rocket, cubed tomato and herbs round the outside.
- Drizzle the salad with oil then position a potato cake on top of each tomato slice.

12
SERVES 4
Cheese Goujons

- Cut the cheese into fingers with a sharp knife.
- Put the flour, egg and panko breadcrumbs in 3 separate bowls.
- Dip the cheese first in the flour, then in egg, then in the breadcrumbs.
- Heat the oil in a deep fat fryer, according to the manufacturer's instructions, to a temperature of 180°C.
- Lower the goujons in the fryer basket and cook for 4 – 5 minutes or until crisp and golden brown.
- Line a large bowl with a thick layer of kitchen paper and when they are ready, tip them into the bowl to remove any excess oil.
- Sprinkle with a little sea salt to taste and serve immediately.

PREPARATION TIME 15 MINUTES

COOKING TIME 4-5 MINUTES

INGREDIENTS

400 g / 14 oz / 3 ½ cups Emmental or young Gouda
4 tbsp plain (all-purpose) flour
1 egg, beaten
75 g / 2 ½ oz / ½ cup panko breadcrumbs
2 - 3 litres / 3 ½ pints – 5 pints / 8-12 cups sunflower oil

Deep-fried Camembert
13

- Replace the cheese fingers with wedges of Camembert. Serve with redcurrant sauce.

14
SERVES 4
Sautéed Potatoes with Cumin and Thyme

- Boil the potatoes in salted water for 8 minutes then drain well and leave to steam dry for 2 minutes.
- Heat the oil in a large sauté pan.
- Sprinkle the potatoes with cumin, thyme and plenty of salt and pepper then fry for 10 minutes, shaking the pan and stirring occasionally.

PREPARATION TIME 2 MINUTES

COOKING TIME 18 MINUTES

INGREDIENTS

800 g / 1 lb 12 oz / 5 ⅓ cups charlotte potatoes
4 tbsp olive oil
1 tsp ground cumin
2 tbsp fresh thyme leaves

Sautéed Potatoes with Garlic and Rosemary
15

- Break 1 bulb of garlic into cloves and boil in their skins with the potatoes before sautéing. Leave out the cumin and replace the thyme with chopped fresh rosemary.

16

SERVES 2

Cheese, Tomato and Mustard Sandwich

PREPARATION TIME 2 MINUTES

COOKING TIME 18 MINUTES

INGREDIENTS

2 tbsp butter, softened
4 slices white bread
150 g / 5 ½ oz / 1 cup Reblochon cheese
1 medium tomato, thinly sliced
3 tbsp crème fraiche
2 tsp wholegrain mustard
2 tsp chives, chopped

- Preheat a sandwich press.
- Butter the bread on both sides and top two of the pieces with the cheese and tomato slices.
- Mix the crème fraiche with the mustard and chives and spread it over the other two slices, then close the sandwiches and transfer them to the sandwich press.
- Toast the sandwiches for 4 minutes or until the bread is golden and the cheese has melted inside.

Cheese, Ham and Mustard Toasties

17

- Replace the tomatoes with 4 thin slices of Parma ham.

18

SERVES 4

Ham and Cucumber Tortilla Wraps

PREPARATION TIME 4 MINUTES

INGREDIENTS

4 flour tortillas
200 g / 7 oz / 2 cups / 1 ⅓ cups cooked ham, cut into strips
½ cucumber, peeled and sliced
handful of bean sprouts
2 tbsp pine nuts, toasted

FOR THE DRESSING
4 tbsp Greek yoghurt
1 tbsp lemon juice
1 shallot, finely grated
1 tbsp fresh chives, chopped

- Lay out the tortillas and arrange the ham, cucumber, bean sprouts and pine nuts on top.
- Mix the yoghurt with the lemon juice and season with salt and pepper then stir in the shallot and chives.
- Spoon the dressing over the tortillas then fold up and serve.

Chicken and Avocado Tortilla Wraps

19

- Fill the tortillas with strips of cooked chicken and chunks of avocado instead of the ham and vegetables, before spooning over the shallot and yoghurt dressing.

20

SERVES 4

Chicken and Lemon Leaf Kebabs

Chicken and Lime Leaf Kebabs

21

- Replace the lemon leaves with kaffir lime leaves and replace the paprika with 2 tbsp Thai green curry paste. Replace the lemon in the salsa with lime.

Chicken and Bay Leaf Kebabs

22

- Replace the lemon leaves with bay leaves and serve with mustard mayonnaise instead of the lemon salsa.

PREPARATION TIME 20 MINUTES

COOKING TIME 8 MINUTES

....

INGREDIENTS

1 tsp smoked paprika
2 tbsp olive oil
6 skinless chicken breasts, cubed
3 red peppers, cubed
32 lemon leaves

FOR THE LEMON SALSA
1 lemon
1 red chilli, finely chopped
1 tbsp coriander (cilantro) leaves, finely chopped
2 tbsp olive oil

- Put 12 wooden skewers in a bowl of water and leave to soak for 20 minutes.
- Meanwhile, stir the paprika into the oil and toss it with the chicken and peppers.
- Leave to marinate for 20 minutes.
- Meanwhile, make the salsa. Cut the rind off the lemon then cut out each segment, leaving the pith behind. Use your fingers to shred the segments into small pieces. Stir in the chilli, coriander and oil then spoon the mixture into a ramekin or hollowed out lemon.
- Preheat the grill to its highest setting.
- Thread alternate chunks of chicken, pepper and lemon leaves onto the skewers and spread them out on a large grill tray.
- Grill the kebabs for 4 minutes on each side or until they are golden brown and cooked through.

23

SERVES 4

Stuffed Mushrooms

PREPARATION TIME 4 MINUTES

COOKING TIME 15 MINUTES

....

INGREDIENTS

8 anchovy fillets
100 g / 3 ½ oz / ⅔ cup mascarpone
1 clove garlic, crushed
1 tbsp chives, chopped
1 tbsp flat leaf parsley, chopped
4 large mushrooms, destalked

- Preheat the oven to 200°C (180° fan), 390 F, gas 6.
- Finely chop 4 of the anchovy fillets and mix them with the mascarpone, garlic and half the herbs.
- Divide the mixture between the mushroom cavities and top each one with a whole anchovy fillet and some more herbs.
- Spread the mushrooms out on a baking tray and bake for 15 minutes or until the mushroom has softened and the topping is golden brown and bubbling.

Bacon Stuffed Mushrooms

24

- Replace the anchovies with 4 rashers of crispy streaky bacon.

25

SERVES 4

Oven-Baked Vegetables

PREPARATION TIME 2 MINUTES

COOKING TIME 45 MINUTES

....

INGREDIENTS

4 baby artichokes, trimmed and halved
½ cauliflower, broken into florets
1 stick of celery, chopped
1 courgette (zucchini) (zucchini), cut into batons
8 mushrooms, sliced
4 tomatoes, cubed
2 tbsp fresh thyme leaves
2 cloves garlic, unpeeled and bruised
4 tbsp olive oil

- Preheat the oven to 200°C (180° fan), 390 F, gas 6.
- Mix all the vegetables with the thyme, garlic and olive oil and layer in a baking dish.
- Season well with salt and pepper then bake for 45 minutes, stirring every 15 minutes.

Baked Chicken and Vegetables

26

- Add 4 chicken thigh quarters to the vegetables and cook as before.

27

MAKES 12 # Mini Herb Frittatas

- Preheat the oven to 180°C (160° fan), 355 F, gas 4.
- Lightly beat the eggs and mix them with the onion and herbs then season well with salt and pepper.
- Pour the mixture into a 12-hole silicone cupcake mould and bake in the oven for 15 – 20 minutes or until the frittatas are set in the centre.
- Serve warm or at room temperature.

PREPARATION TIME 2 MINUTES

COOKING TIME 15-20 MINUTES

INGREDIENTS

6 eggs
½ red onion, finely chopped
2 tbsp flat leaf parsley, finely chopped
2 tbsp chives, finely chopped
2 tbsp basil, finely chopped

Mini Breakfast Frittatas

28

- Chop 2 cooked rashers of streaky bacon and 1 cooked sausage and stir them into the eggs in place of the onions and herbs.

29

SERVES 4 # Fresh Broad Bean Salad

- Put the shallots in a bowl with the vinegar, sugar and a big pinch of salt and leave to macerate for 10 minutes.
- Meanwhile, blanch the broad beans in boiling water for 5 minutes then drain and refresh in cold water. Drain well.
- Whisk the olive oil into the shallot vinegar and taste for seasoning then stir in the chervil and broad beans.

PREPARATION TIME 10 MINUTES

COOKING TIME 5 MINUTES

INGREDIENTS

2 shallots, finely chopped
3 tbsp sherry vinegar
2 tsp caster (superfine) sugar
600 g / 1 lb 5 oz / 5 ½ cups fresh broad beans, podded weight
4 tbsp extra virgin olive oil
a small bunch chervil, chopped

Green Bean salad

30

- Replace the broad beans with 400 g of trimmed green beans.

SERVES 4

Vegetable Kebabs

Haloumi and Vegetable Kebabs

32

- Marinate 300 g of cubed Haloumi cheese with the vegetables.

Spicy Vegetable Kebabs

33

- Replace the herbs de Provence with 1 tbsp harissa paste.

PREPARATION TIME 20 MINUTES

COOKING TIME 8 MINUTES

....

INGREDIENTS

1 tbsp dried herbs de Provence
3 tbsp olive oil
1 red pepper, cubed
1 green pepper, cubed
1 large courgette (zucchini), thickly sliced
½ aubergine, cubed
100 g / 3 ½ oz / 1 ⅓ cups button mushrooms, thickly sliced
4 salad onions, halved

FOR THE DIP

1 tbsp lemon juice
½ tsp cracked black pepper
4 tbsp mayonnaise

- Put 12 wooden skewers in a bowl of water and leave to soak for 20 minutes.
- Meanwhile, stir the herbs into the oil and toss it with the vegetables.
- Leave to marinate for 20 minutes.
- Meanwhile, make the dip by stirring the lemon juice and black pepper into the mayonnaise.
- Preheat the grill to its highest setting.
- Thread alternate vegetables onto the skewers and spread them out on a large grill tray.
- Grill the kebabs for 4 minutes on each side or until they are golden brown and cooked through.

MAKES 6

Warm Scotch Eggs

- Put 6 of the eggs in a pan of cold water then bring to a simmer and cook for 5 minutes.
- Cool, then peel off the shells.
- Skin the sausages and divide the meat into 6. Flatten a portion of sausage meat onto your hand and put an egg in the centre, then squeeze the meat round the outside to coat. Repeat with the other 5 eggs.
- Put the flour, remaining egg and panko breadcrumbs in 3 separate bowls.
- Dip the scotch eggs first in the flour, then in egg, then in the breadcrumbs.
- Heat the oil in a deep fat fryer, according to the manufacturer's instructions, to a temperature of 180°C.
- Lower the scotch eggs in the fryer basket and cook for 4 – 5 minutes or until crisp and golden brown.
- Sprinkle with a little sea salt and serve immediately.

PREPARATION TIME 30 MINUTES

COOKING TIME 10 MINUTES

INGREDIENTS

7 small eggs
4 good quality pork sausages
4 tbsp plain (all-purpose) flour
75 g / 2 ½ oz / ½ cup panko breadcrumbs
2 - 3 litres / 3 ½ pints – 5 pints / 8-12 cups sunflower oil

Black Pudding Scotch Eggs   35

- Halve the quantity of sausages and mix with 200 g of crumbled black pudding.

SERVES 4

Ham and Mushroom Savoury Pancakes

- Preheat the oven to 200°C (180° fan), 390 F, gas 6.
- Melt the butter in a large saucepan and fry the mushrooms with a pinch of salt for 5 minutes.
- Stir in the flour then gradually incorporate the milk, stirring continuously to avoid any lumps forming.
- When the mixture starts to bubble, stir in the ham and a grind of black pepper then take the pan off the heat.
- Lay the pancakes out on the work surface and divide the mushroom mixture between them.
- Roll the pancakes up and transfer them to a baking tray then bake for 10 minutes or until golden brown.

PREPARATION TIME 4 MINUTES

COOKING TIME 20 MINUTES

INGREDIENTS

50 g / 1 ¾ oz / ¼ cup butter
200 g / 7 oz / 2 cups / 2 ⅔ cups button mushrooms, chopped
1 tbsp plain (all-purpose) flour
300 ml / 10 ½ fl. oz / 1 ⅓ cups milk
100 g / 3 ½ oz / ⅔ cup ham, chopped
8 ready-made pancakes

Three Cheese Savoury Pancakes   37

- Replace the ham and mushrooms with 75 g each of cubed Mozzarella, finely grated Parmesan and cubed Gorgonzola.

MAKES 20

Goats' Cheese and Hazelnut Canapés

PREPARATION TIME 10 MINUTES

INGREDIENTS

250 g / 9 oz / 1 ⅔ cups soft goats' cheese
55 g / 2 oz / ⅓ cup hazelnuts (cobnuts), chopped

- Divide the goats' cheese into 20 pieces and roll them into balls with your hands.
- Roll the balls in the chopped hazelnuts to coat in an even layer then chill in the fridge until needed.

Goat's Cheese, Pear and Walnut Canapés
39

- Finely chop a ripe pear and mix it with the goat's cheese. Replace the hazelnuts with chopped walnuts for rolling.

SERVES 4

Salmon Kebabs with Balsamic Glaze

PREPARATION TIME 25 MINUTES

COOKING TIME 8 MINUTES

INGREDIENTS

2 tbsp balsamic vinegar
2 tbsp runny honey
1 tbsp olive oil
a few bay leaves
450 g / 1 lb / 3 cups salmon fillet, cubed
300 g / 10 ½ oz / 2 cups pancetta, in large cubes

- Put 12 wooden skewers in a bowl of cold water and leave to soak for 20 minutes.
- Meanwhile, whisk together the vinegar, honey and oil and stir in the bay leaves. Pour it into a large freezer bag, add the salmon and pancetta pieces and massage it all together. Leave to marinate for 20 minutes.
- Preheat the grill to its highest setting.
- Thread alternate chunks of salmon and pancetta onto the skewers and spread them out on a large grill tray.
- Grill the kebabs for 8 minutes, turning and basting with left over marinade half way through.

Salmon Kebabs with Honey and Soy
41

- Replace the balsamic vinegar with soy sauce and replace the bay leaves in the marinade with 3 whole star anise.

42

SERVES 2

Prawn and Tomato Risotto

Crab, Chilli and Tomato Risotto

43

- Fry 1 finely chopped red chilli with the onions and replace the prawns with 150 g cooked fresh crab meat.

Mozzarella and Tomato Risotto

44

- Replace the prawns with 150 g cubed mozzarella, letting it turn stringy and melted in the heat of the pan.

PREPARATION TIME 5 MINUTES

COOKING TIME 35 MINUTES

....

INGREDIENTS

500 ml / 17 ½ fl. oz / 2 cups fish stock
500 ml / 17 ½ fl. oz / 2 cups tomato passata
2 tbsp olive oil
1 onion, finely chopped
2 cloves of garlic, crushed
150 g / 5 ½ oz / 1 cup risotto rice
100 g / 3 ½ oz / ⅔ cup cooked king prawns (shrimps), peeled
2 tbsp crème fraiche
2 tbsp coriander (cilantro) leaves

- Heat the stock and passata together in a saucepan.
- Heat the olive oil in a sauté pan and gently fry the onion for 5 minutes without colouring.
- Add the garlic and cook for 2 more minutes then stir in the rice.
- When it is well coated with the oil, add 2 ladles of the hot stock.
- Cook, stirring occasionally, until most of the stock has been absorbed before adding the next 2 ladles.
- Continue in this way for around 15 minutes or until the rice is just tender.
- Stir in the prawns and crème fraiche, then cover the pan and take off the heat to rest for 4 minutes.
- Uncover the pan and season well with salt and pepper, then spoon into warm bowls.
- Scatter over the coriander and serve.

SERVES 4 — 45

Spicy Prawn and Green Bean Salad

PREPARATION TIME 5 MINUTES

COOKING TIME 4 MINUTES

INGREDIENTS

200 g / 7 oz / 2 cups green beans, trimmed
1 clove garlic, crushed
½ tsp Cayenne pepper
3 tbsp olive oil
12 raw king prawns (shrimps), peeled leaving tails intact
1 tbsp lemon juice
30 g / 1 oz / ⅓ cups Parmesan shavings
4 sprigs coriander (cilantro)

- Preheat the grill to its highest setting.
- Blanch the beans in boiling salted water for 4 minutes or until al dente. Plunge into cold water and drain well.
- Meanwhile, mix the garlic and Cayenne with 1 tablespoon of the oil and massage the paste into the prawns.
- Spread the prawns out on a grill tray and grill for 2 minutes on each side or until only just opaque.
- Mix the rest of the oil with the lemon juice and season well with salt and pepper.
- Toss the dressing with the beans then top with the prawns.
- Use a vegetable peeler to shave some Parmesan over the top and garnish with coriander.

Prawn and Bean Salad — 46

- Omit the Parmesan. Make a dressing using 1 tbsp caster (superfine) sugar, 1 tbsp fish sauce and juice of 1 lime. Stir in ½ tsp of finely chopped garlic and ½ tsp red chilli before dressing.

47

SERVES 4

Melon, Feta and Mint Salad

PREPARATION TIME 5 MINUTES

INGREDIENTS

1 small white-fleshed melon, halved
1 small orange-fleshed melon, halved
100 g / 3 ½ oz / ⅔ cup Feta, finely cubed
4 tbsp mint leaves, shredded
4 tbsp extra virgin olive oil

- Use a melon baller to scoop small bowls out of the melons and toss them with the Feta and mint.
- Drizzle with olive oil then sprinkle with sea salt and freshly ground black pepper.

Melon, Goat's Cheese and Basil Salad — 48

- Replace the Feta with an equal quantity of goat's cheese and replace the mint with shredded basil.

49

SERVES 2

Feta and Cherry Tomato Salad

- Arrange the lettuce leaves on 2 plates and top with the Feta, tomatoes and olives.
- Drizzle with olive oil and sprinkle with pink peppercorns.

PREPARATION TIME 5 MINUTES

INGREDIENTS

6 large lettuce leaves
100 g / 3 ½ oz / ⅔ cup Feta, cubed
6 cherry tomatoes, quartered
a few kalamata olives
4 tbsp extra virgin olive oil
½ tsp pink peppercorns, crushed

Greek Salad   50

- Cut half a cucumber into cubes and toss with the Feta, olives and tomatoes.

51

SERVES 2

Potato and Antipasti Salad

- Boil the potatoes in salted water for 12 minutes or until tender in the middle, then plunge into cold water to stop the cooking and drain well.
- Toss the potatoes with the vegetable antipasti and dress with 2 tablespoons of the oil.
- Use a vegetable peeler to shave over some Parmesan and garnish with basil.

PREPARATION TIME 2 MINUTES

COOKING TIME 12 MINUTES

INGREDIENTS

300 g / 10 ½ oz / 2 cups Maris Piper potatoes, peeled and thickly sliced
1 jar mixed vegetable antipasti in oil, drained and oil reserved
30 g / 1 oz / ⅓ cups Parmesan
a few sprigs basil

Potato and Preserved   52
Octopus Salad

- Replace the mixed antipasti with 200 g canned octopus pieces in oil. Squeeze the juice of a lemon over the finished salad before serving.

SERVES 4

Couscous with Sultanas and Almonds

Couscous with Apricots and Pistachios   54

- Leave out the peppers and replace the sultanas and almonds with equal quantities of chopped dried apricots and pistachio nuts.

Couscous with Tomatoes and Basil   55

- Replace the sultanas with chopped sundried tomatoes and replace the mint with shredded basil.

PREPARATION TIME 5 MINUTES

COOKING TIME 5 MINUTES

....

INGREDIENTS

300 g / 10 ½ oz / 1 ¾ cups couscous
1 red pepper, cubed
1 green pepper, cubed
75 g / 3 oz / ½ cup sultanas
75 g / 3 oz / ¾ cup flaked (slivered) almonds
2 tbsp mint, chopped

FOR THE DRESSING
1 tsp runny honey
½ lemon, juiced
3 tbsp olive oil

- Put the couscous in a large serving bowl and pour over 300 ml of boiling water.
- Cover the bowl with clingfilm and let it stand for 5 minutes then fluff up the grains with a fork.
- Stir through the peppers, sultanas, almonds and mint.
- Whisk the honey with the lemon juice then whisk in the olive oil.
- Pour the dressing over the couscous and serve.

56

SERVES 4

Tuna and Couscous Salad

- Put the couscous in a large serving bowl and pour over 300 ml of boiling water.
- Cover the bowl with clingfilm and let it stand for 5 minutes then fluff up the grains with a fork.
- Stir through the peppers, sweetcorn and tuna.
- Whisk the honey with the lime juice then whisk in the olive oil.
- Pour the dressing over the couscous and garnish with the chives.

PREPARATION TIME 5 MINUTES

COOKING TIME 5 MINUTES

INGREDIENTS

300 g / 10 ½ oz / 1 ¾ cups couscous
1 red pepper, cubed
100 g / 3 ½ oz / 1 cup canned sweetcorn, drained
100 g / 3 ½ oz / ⅔ cup canned tuna, drained
a few chives to garnish

FOR THE DRESSING
1 tsp runny honey
1 lime, juiced
3 tbsp olive oil

Crab and Couscous Salad 57

- Replace the canned tuna with an equal quantity of fresh cooked crab meat.

58

SERVES 4

Sundried Tomato and Prosciutto Salad

- Toss together all of the salad ingredients and divide between 4 plates.
- Whisk the oil and lemon juice together and drizzle over the salad.

PREPARATION TIME 5 MINUTES

INGREDIENTS

12 thin slices prosciutto
1 jar sundried tomatoes in oil, drained, oil reserved
1 yellow pepper, cubed
1 ball mozzarella, cubed
50 g / 1 ¾ oz / ⅓ cup kalamata olives, pitted
50 g / 1 ¾ oz / 1 cup rocket (arugula) leaves
2 tbsp toasted pine nuts
a small bunch basil, torn

FOR THE DRESSING
2 tbsp oil from the tomato jar
½ lemon, juiced

Artichoke and Prosciutto Salad 59

- Replace the sundried tomatoes with a jar of preserved baby artichokes in oil.

60

SERVES 4

Sweetcorn Salad

PREPARATION TIME 5 MINUTES

INGREDIENTS

1 round lettuce, separated into leaves
1 can sweetcorn, drained
1 can pimento-stuffed green olives, drained and sliced
1 green pepper, quartered and sliced
4 cherry tomatoes, halved

FOR THE DRESSING
1 lemon, juiced
3 tbsp olive oil

- Line a large salad bowl with lettuce leaves.
- Mix the sweetcorn with the olives, pepper and tomatoes and spoon on top of the lettuce.
- Put the lemon juice and oil in a jar with a pinch of salt and pepper and shake to emulsify.
- Drizzle the dressing over the salad and serve immediately.

Sweetcorn and Avocado Salad   61

- Replace the green pepper with 2 ripe avocados that have been peeled, stoned and cubed.

62

SERVES 4

Farfalle with Peppers, Feta and Lemon

PREPARATION TIME 2 MINUTES

COOKING TIME 12 MINUTES

INGREDIENTS

400 g / 14 oz / 5 cups farfalle pasta
4 tbsp olive oil
4 cloves garlic, crushed
2 yellow peppers, thinly sliced
1 small preserved lemon, quartered and thinly sliced
100 g / 3 ½ oz / ⅔ cup Feta, cubed
a small bunch of basil, leaves only

- Cook the farfalle in boiling salted water according to the packet instructions or until al dente.
- While the pasta is cooking, heat the olive oil in a large frying pan and cook the garlic and peppers for 8 minutes, stirring occasionally.
- Reserve 1 ladle of the pasta water and drain the rest then stir the pasta into the peppers with the preserved lemon and Feta. Add a little of the cooking water if it looks too dry.
- Chop half the basil and stir it into the pan, reserving the rest for garnish.
- Divide the pasta between 4 warm bowls and scatter over the basil leaves.

Farfalle with Olives and Preserved Lemon   63

- Replace the Feta with 75 g of stoned kalamata olives.

64

SERVES 4

Asparagus and Parmesan Salad

Asparagus, Feta and Pea salad

65

- Replace the tomatoes with 200 g cooked peas and replace the Parmesan with 75 g of crumbled Feta cheese.

Asparagus and Smoked Salmon Salad

66

- Omit the Parmesan and olives and add 150 g of thinly sliced smoked salmon to the salad.

PREPARATION TIME 5 MINUTES

COOKING TIME 6 MINUTES

....

INGREDIENTS

200 g / 7 oz / 2 cups / 1 cup asparagus, trimmed
100 g / 3 ½ oz / 2 cups mixed salad leaves
100 g / 3 ½ oz / ⅔ cup cherry tomatoes, quartered
8 baby spring onions (scallions), halved lengthways
75 g / 2 ½ oz / ½ cup kalamata olives
2 tbsp sesame seeds
30 g / 1 oz / ⅕ Parmesan
a few sprigs flowering thyme to garnish

FOR THE DRESSING
1 tbsp mayonnaise
1 tbsp natural yoghurt
1 tbsp lemon juice
1 tsp fresh thyme leaves, chopped

- Blanch the asparagus in boiling salted water for 6 minutes or until al dente. Plunge into cold water and drain well.
- Divide the leaves between 4 plates and top with the asparagus, tomatoes, onions and olives.
- Sprinkle over the sesame seeds and use a vegetable peeler to shave over some Parmesan.
- Mix the dressing ingredients together and drizzle over the salad, then garnish with flowering thyme.

67

SERVES 4

Fusilli with Mixed Vegetables

PREPARATION TIME 2 MINUTES

COOKING TIME 12 MINUTES

INGREDIENTS

400 g / 14 oz / 5 cups fusilli pasta
4 tbsp olive oil
4 cloves garlic, crushed
1 red pepper, cubed
½ head broccoli, broken into small florets
1 carrot, shredded
1 courgette (zucchini), shredded

- Cook the fusilli in boiling salted water according to the packet instructions or until al dente.
- While the pasta is cooking, heat the olive oil in a large frying pan and cook the garlic, peppers and broccoli for 5 minutes, stirring occasionally.
- Add the shredded carrot and courgette to the pan and cook for 2 more minutes.
- Reserve 1 ladle of the pasta cooking water and drain the rest then stir the pasta into the frying pan.
- If it looks a bit dry, add some of the cooking water and shake the pan to emulsify.
- Divide the pasta between 4 warm bowls and serve.

68

SERVES 4

Fusilli with Olives and Artichokes

PREPARATION TIME 2 MINUTES

COOKING TIME 12 MINUTES

INGREDIENTS

400 g / 14 oz / 5 cups fusilli pasta
4 tbsp olive oil
4 cloves garlic, crushed
1 red pepper, cubed
1 jar preserved baby artichokes, drained
75 g / 3 oz / ½ cup green olives, pitted
75 g / 3 oz / ½ cup black olives, pitted and sliced

- Cook the fusilli in boiling salted water according to the packet instructions or until al dente.
- While the pasta is cooking, heat the olive oil in a large frying pan and cook the garlic and peppers for 5 minutes, stirring occasionally.
- Stir in the artichokes and olives and warm through.
- Reserve 1 ladle of the pasta cooking water and drain the rest then stir the pasta into the frying pan.
- If it looks a bit dry, add some of the cooking water and shake the pan to emulsify.
- Divide the pasta between 4 warm bowls and serve.

SERVES 4

Couscous Salad

- Put the couscous in a large serving bowl and pour over 300 ml of boiling water.
- Cover the bowl with clingfilm and let it stand for 5 minutes then fluff up the grains with a fork.
- Stir through the peppers, tomato and mint.
- Whisk the honey with the lemon juice then whisk in the olive oil.
- Pour the dressing over the couscous and serve.

PREPARATION TIME 5 MINUTES

COOKING TIME 5 MINUTES

INGREDIENTS

300 g / 10 ½ oz / 1 ¾ cup couscous
1 red pepper, cubed
1 green pepper, cubed
1 tomato, deseeded and cubed
2 tbsp mint, chopped

FOR THE DRESSING
1 tsp runny honey
½ lemon, juiced
3 tbsp olive oil

70

SERVES 4

Salad Niçoise

PREPARATION TIME 5 MINUTES

COOKING TIME 12 MINUTES

INGREDIENTS

400 g / 14 oz / 2 ⅔ cup charlotte potatoes, halved
1 oak leaf lettuce, leaves separated
1 jar white tuna in olive oil, drained
and cubed
6 tomatoes, quartered
75g / 2 ½ oz / ½ cup black olives, pitted
4 tbsp extra virgin olive oil
a few sprigs chervil to garnish

- Boil the potatoes in salted water for 12 minutes or until tender, then drain well.
- Arrange the lettuce on 4 serving plates and arrange the tuna, potatoes, tomatoes and olives on top.
- Drizzle with olive oil and garnish with chervil.

71

SERVES 4

Chef's Salad

PREPARATION TIME 8 MINUTES

INGREDIENTS

1 lettuce, separated into leaves
½ cucumber, peeled and sliced
2 tomatoes, cut into wedges
1 stick celery, chopped
1 hard-boiled egg, quartered
100 g / 3 ½ oz / 1 cupEmmental, cut
into sticks
1 cooked chicken breast, strips
100 g / 3 ½ oz / ⅔ cup ham, cubed

FOR THE DRESSING
1 tsp Dijon mustard
1 tsp runny honey
1 lemon, juiced
3 tbsp olive oil

- Line 4 serving bowls with lettuce leaves and arrange the cucumber, tomato and celery on top.
- Add a boiled egg quarter to each bowl and divide the cheese, chicken and ham between them.
- Put the dressing ingredients in a jar with a pinch of salt and pepper and shake to emulsify.
- Drizzle the dressing over the salad and serve immediately.

72

SERVES 4

Roast Chicken and Boiled Egg Salad

PREPARATION TIME 8 MINUTES

INGREDIENTS

a small bunch of radishes, trimmed
1 lettuce, separated into leaves
½ cucumber, sliced
2 tomatoes, cut into wedges
1 stick celery, chopped
2 hard-boiled eggs, quartered
75 g / 3 oz / ½ cup black olives, pitted
2 skin-on roasted chicken breasts, sliced
mayonnaise, to serve

- Slit the ends of the radishes and put them in a bowl of iced water for 5 minutes to fan out.
- Line a large serving bowl with lettuce leaves and arrange the cucumber, tomato and celery on top.
- Add a ring of boiled egg quarters and radishes round the outside and put the chicken in the middle.
- Scatter over the olives and serve with a bowl of mayonnaise on the side.

Poached Salmon and Boiled Egg Salad

 73

- Replace the chicken with 300 g cold flaked poached salmon fillet.

74

SERVES 4

Imam Bayildi

PREPARATION TIME 2 MINUTES

COOKING TIME 30 MINUTES

INGREDIENTS

6 tbsp olive oil
1 onion, finely chopped
4 cloves garlic, crushed
1 tbsp sesame seeds
3 tomatoes, skinned, deseeded and finely chopped
1 tbsp mint, finely chopped
1 tbsp flat leaf parsley, finely chopped
2 aubergines (eggplant)(eggplants), sliced

- Heat 2 tablespoon of the oil in a sauté pan and fry the onion for 5 minutes. Add the garlic and sesame seeds and cook for 2 more minutes.
- Stir in the tomatoes, mint and parsley and simmer gently for 15 minutes, adding a little water if it gets too dry.
- Meanwhile, brush the aubergines with 4 tablespoons of the oil and season with salt and pepper.
- Fry them in batches for 3 minutes on each side or until golden brown and tender. Keep the cooked aubergines warm in a low oven while you cook the rest.
- Divide the aubergines between 4 plates and layer up with the tomato sauce.

Aubergine with Preserved Lemon

75

- Cut 1 lemon into quarters and remove the flesh. Finely chop the rind and stir it into the tomato sauce before layering with the aubergine slices.

76

SERVES 2

Marinated Anchovies with Tomato Salsa

- Score a cross in the top of the tomatoes and blanch in boiling water for 30 seconds. When the skin of the tomatoes starts to curl up, remove them with a slotted spoon and dunk in a bowl of cold water.
- Peel off and discard the skins then cut them in half and remove the seeds. Chop the tomato flesh into small cubes.
- Mix the herbs with the olive oil, a pinch of salt and plenty of freshly ground black pepper.
- Arrange the anchovy fillets on 2 plates and spoon some of the herb oil on top.
- Stir the rest of the herb oil into the chopped tomatoes and divide between the 2 plates.

PREPARATION TIME 10 MINUTES

COOKING TIME 1 MINUTE

INGREDIENTS

2 medium tomatoes
1 tbsp fresh basil leaves, chopped
1 tbsp flat leaf parsley, chopped
1 tsp fresh young rosemary, finely chopped
4 tbsp extra virgin olive oil
16 marinated anchovy fillets

Grilled Sardines
with Tomato Salsa

77

- This salsa also works really well with fresh sardines. Brush 6 sardines with olive oil and

78

SERVES 4

Cucumber Salad

- Crush the peppercorns and chilli flakes with a pestle and mortar then add the garlic and a pinch of salt and grind to a paste.
- Add the lemon juice, stirring with the pestle, followed by the oil, then stir in the yoghurt.
- Spoon the mixture into a serving bowl and toss with the cucumber and herbs.

PREPARATION TIME 5 MINUTES

INGREDIENTS

½ tsp mixed peppercorns
a pinch chilli flakes
½ clove garlic
1 tbsp lemon juice
2 tbsp olive oil
3 tbsp Greek yoghurt
1 cucumber, cut into batons
a small bunch chives, chopped
a small bunch flat leaf parsley, chopped

Cucumber and Beetroot Salad

79

- Cut 3 small cooked and peeled beetroots into batons and combine with the cucumber and dressing.

Bulgur Wheat Salad

80

SERVES 4

Bulgur Wheat and Caper Salad

81

- Stir 2 tbsp of baby capers into the salad just before serving.

Bulgur Wheat and Pumpkin Salad

82

- Replace the cucumber and tomatoes with 300 g roasted pumpkin cubes and stir through 2 tbsp pumpkin seeds before serving.

PREPARATION TIME 4 MINUTES

COOKING TIME 18 MINUTES

INGREDIENTS

150 g / 5 ½ oz / 1 cup bulgur wheat
1 cucumber, peeled and cubed
4 tomatoes, deseeded and chopped
3 tbsp flat leaf parsley, roughly chopped
1 tbsp basil, roughly chopped
½ lemon, juiced
2 tbsp extra virgin olive oil

- Put the bulgur wheat in a bowl and pour over enough boiling water to just cover it. Cover the bowl tightly and leave to soak for 15 minutes.
- Tip the bulgur wheat into a sieve and run it under the cold tap to cool. Drain well.
- Stir the cucumber, tomato and herbs into the bulgur and dress with the lemon juice and olive oil.
- Taste for seasoning and adjust with sea salt and black pepper.

83

SERVES 4

Radish and Coriander Salad

- Thinly slice the radishes with a sharp knife or mandolin and mix them with the coriander.
- Stir the fish sauce and lime juice into the sugar until it dissolves then pour the dressing over the salad.
- Wait for 10 minutes for the flavours to amalgamate before serving.

PREPARATION TIME 15 MINUTES

INGREDIENTS

200 g / 7 oz / 2 cups / 2 cups radishes
a small bunch fresh coriander (cilantro), roughly chopped
1 tbsp fish sauce
2 limes, juiced
1 tbsp caster (superfine) sugar

Radish and Cucumber Salad 84

- Add half a thinly sliced cucumber to the radishes before dressing.

85

SERVES 4-6

Caponata with Boiled Eggs

- Heat the oil in a large sauté pan and cook the aubergine until golden brown. Remove from the pan with a slotted spoon and leave to drain in a sieve.
- Fry the celery in the same way and leave to drain with the aubergine, followed by the peppers.
- Fry the onion and chilli for 5 minutes or until starting to caramelise then add the red wine vinegar and bubble away almost to nothing.
- Add the tomatoes to the pan with their juice and cook for 5 minutes.
- Return the fried vegetables to the pan and simmer together for another 5 minutes. Season to taste with salt and black pepper.
- Spoon the caponata into a serving dish and top with the olives and egg quarters. Serve warm or at room temperature.

PREPARATION TIME 5 MINUTES

COOKING TIME 40 MINUTES

INGREDIENTS

100 ml / 3 ½ fl. oz / ½ cup olive oil
1 aubergine (eggplant) (eggplant), diced
2 sticks celery, diced
2 red peppers, diced
1 onion, finely chopped
1 red chilli, finely chopped
3 tbsp red wine vinegar
3 tomatoes, finely chopped
50 g / 1 ¾ oz / ⅓ cup black olives
1 hard-boiled egg, quartered

Caponata Bruschetta 86

- Toast 6 large slices of sourdough bread and top with the caponata mixture before dotting over the olives.

SERVES 4

Tuna and Red Pepper Salad

PREPARATION TIME 5 MINUTES

INGREDIENTS

2 little gem lettuces, leaves separated
2 jars tuna in olive oil, drained and flaked
1 red pepper, diced
½ red onion, thinly sliced
50 g / 1 ¾ oz / ⅓ cup mixed olives
1 tbsp basil, chopped
4 tbsp extra virgin olive oil
2 hard-boiled eggs, halved

- Arrange the lettuce on 4 serving plates and arrange the tuna, peppers, onion and olives on top.
- Scatter over the basil and dress with olive oil then garnish each plate with half a boiled egg.

Salmon and Red Pepper Salad   88

- Replace the tuna with 200 g of flaked canned red salmon.

89

SERVES 4

Broccoli, Tomato and Coriander Salad

PREPARATION TIME 5 MINUTES

COOKING TIME 10-12 MINUTES

INGREDIENTS

1 small head broccoli, broken into small florets
1 tsp coriander seeds
3 tomatoes, cut into wedges
a small bunch fresh coriander (cilantro), leaves only
½ lemon, juiced
3 tbsp extra virgin olive oil

- Blanch the broccoli in boiling salted water for 3 – 4 minutes or until just tender. Drain well.
- Meanwhile, dry fry the coriander seeds until fragrant, shaking the pan regularly.
- Toss the drained broccoli with the tomatoes and coriander leaves and split between 4 serving plates.
- Sprinkle over the coriander seeds and dress with the lemon juice and olive oil.
- Season with salt and pepper just before serving.

Cauliflower, Tomato and Coriander Salad   90

- Substitute the broccoli with cauliflower florets and proceed as above.

91

SERVES 4

Strawberry and Ciliegine Salad

Tomato and Ciliegine Salad

92

- Replace the strawberries with 200 g of halved cherry tomatoes.

Melon, Prosciutto and Ciliegine Salad

93

- Replace the strawberries with 200 g melon balls and tear 4 thin slices of prosciutto into strips.

PREPARATION TIME 5 MINUTES

INGREDIENTS

200 g / 7 oz / 2 cupsstrawberries, halved
200 g / 7 oz / 2 cups / 1 ⅓ cups mozzarella balls
a few sprigs of fresh young thyme
4 tbsp extra virgin olive oil

- Mix the strawberries with the ciliegine and thyme and divide between 4 plates.
- Dress with the olive oil and season well with sea salt and freshly ground black pepper.

Tuna Koftas

94

SERVES 4

PREPARATION TIME 35 MINUTES

COOKING TIME 8 MINUTES

INGREDIENTS

2 onions, finely chopped
1 red chilli, finely chopped
2 tbsp olive oil
2 cloves garlic, crushed
2 tsp ground coriander
450 g / 1 lb / 2 cups fresh tuna, chopped
1 tbsp coriander leaves (cilantro), chopped

- Put 16 wooden kebab skewers in a bowl of water and leave to soak for 20 minutes.
- Meanwhile, fry the onion and chilli in the oil for 5 minutes then add the garlic and ground coriander and cook for 2 more minutes. Season with salt and pepper.
- Put the tuna in a food processor with the coriander leaves and spiced onion mixture and pulse until evenly mixed.
- Squeeze a handful of the kofta mixture around each skewer, then chill in the fridge for 25 minutes or until firm.
- Preheat the grill to its highest setting.
- Grill the koftas for 4 minutes on each side or until they are golden brown and cooked through.

Salmon Koftas

95

- Replace the tuna with 450 g of fresh skinless salmon fillet.

Pork and Turnip Kebabs

96

SERVES 4

PREPARATION TIME 30 MINUTES

COOKING TIME 15 MINUTES

INGREDIENTS

250 g / 9 oz / 1 ½ cup baby turnips
450 g / 1 lb / 3 cups pork belly, cut into cubes
3 tbsp soy sauce
1 tbsp runny honey
1 tsp sesame oil
2 tbsp sesame seeds
2 tbsp poppy seeds

- Put 12 wooden skewers in a bowl of cold water and leave to soak for 20 minutes.
- Meanwhile, cook the turnips in boiling salted water for 10 minutes or until tender. Drain well.
- While the turnips are cooking, mix the soy sauce, honey and sesame oil together and use ¾ of the mixture to marinade the pork for 15 minutes.
- Preheat the grill to its highest setting.
- Thread the cooked turnips onto 4 of the skewers and brush them with the remaining marinade.
- Thread the pork onto the final 8 skewers. Sprinkle 4 of the pork skewers with sesame seeds and the other 4 with poppy seeds.
- Grill the kebabs for 4 minutes on each side or until the pork is cooked through.

Pork and Jerusalem Artichoke Kebabs

97

- Substitute the turnips with an equal quantity of Jerusalem Artichokes.

SERVES 2

Goats' Cheese and Courgette Ciabatta

- Preheat a griddle pan until smoking hot.
- Brush the courgette slices with half of the oil and season with salt and pepper.
- Griddle the courgettes for 2 minutes on each side or until nicely marked.
- Toast the ciabatta halves then brush them with the rest of the oil.
- Arrange the courgette slices on top with the tomatoes and goat's cheese then sprinkle with pink peppercorns and garnish with parsley.

PREPARATION TIME 10 MINUTES

COOKING TIME 4MINUTES

INGREDIENTS

1 courgette (zucchini), sliced lengthways
2 tbsp olive oil
1 ciabatta roll, halved
4 tomatoes, halved
60 g / 2 oz / ⅓ cup fresh goats' cheese
½ tsp pink peppercorns, crushed
2 sprigs flat leaf parsley

Bruschetta with Griddled Aubergines

99

- Replace the courgette with a sliced aubergine and griddle for 1 more minute on each side.

100

SERVES 2

Prosciutto, Gruyère and Thyme Toasts

- Preheat the grill to its highest setting.
- Toast the sourdough on one side under the grill.
- Turn them over and top each one with a slice of prosciutto, the cheese and a sprinkle of thyme.
- Grill for 2 more minutes or until the cheese is bubbling and the bread is toasted at the edges.

PREPARATION TIME 5 MINUTES

COOKING TIME 5 MINUTES

INGREDIENTS

4 slices sourdough bread
4 slices prosciutto
100 g / 3 ½ oz / 1 cup Gruyere cheese, grated
1 tbsp fresh thyme leaves

Prosciutto, Brie and Thyme Toasts

101

- Replace the Gruyere with 4 thick slices of Brie.

102

SERVES 4

Prosciutto-Wrapped Halloumi Kebabs

Prosciutto-Wrapped Chicken Kebabs

103

- Replace the Haloumi with 300 g cubed skinless chicken breast.

Prosciutto-Wrapped Salmon Kebabs

104

- Replace the Haloumi with 300 g cubed skinless salmon fillet.

PREPARATION TIME 20 MINUTES

COOKING TIME 8 MINUTES

....

INGREDIENTS

300 g / 10 ½ oz / 2 ½ cup Halloumi, cubed
150 g / 5 ½ oz / 1 cup prosciutto
28 cherry tomatoes
2 shallots, quartered
12 bay leaves, halved

- Put 12 wooden skewers in a bowl of water and leave to soak for 20 minutes.
- Preheat the grill to its highest setting.
- Wrap each Halloumi cube in prosciutto then thread them onto the skewers with the tomatoes, shallots and bay leaves.
- Grill the kebabs for 4 minutes on each side or until they are golden brown and cooked through.

105

SERVES 2

Griddled Courgettes

- Preheat a griddle pan until smoking hot.
- Brush the courgette slices with half of the oil and griddle for 2 minutes on each side or until nicely marked.
- Transfer the courgettes to 2 warm serving plates, drizzle with the rest of the olive oil and sprinkle with sea salt. Garnish with oregano.

PREPARATION TIME 2 MINUTES

COOKING TIME 4 MINUTES

INGREDIENTS

2 courgettes (zucchini), sliced lengthways
2 tbsp olive oil
2 sprigs oregano

Griddled Aubergine

106

- Substitute the courgettes with a sliced aubergine.

107

SERVES 4

Chicken and Fruit a la Plancha

- Put 12 wooden skewers in a bowl of water and leave to soak for 20 minutes.
- Meanwhile, stir the spices into the oil and toss with the chicken and fruit.
- Leave to marinate for 20 minutes.
- Preheat a plancha (cast iron skillet) to its highest setting.
- Thread the chicken pieces onto the skewers spread them out on the plancha. Arrange the fruit around the sides and cook everything for 4 minutes on each side or until the chicken is cooked through.

PREPARATION TIME 20 MINUTES

COOKING TIME 8 MINUTES

INGREDIENTS

½ tsp ground white pepper
½ tsp ground coriander
4 tbsp olive oil
6 skinless chicken breasts, cubed
½ pineapple, skin on, cut into wedges
2 red apples, cut into chunks

Prawns and Mango a la Plancha

108

- Replace the chicken breasts with 300 g raw king prawns and marinate as above. Substitute the fruit with a large mango that has been peeled, stoned and cut into fingers.

109

SERVES 4

Gnocchetti with Cherry Tomatoes

PREPARATION TIME 5 MINUTES

COOKING TIME 20 MINUTES

INGREDIENTS

300 g / 10 oz / 1 ¼ cups cherry
tomatoes
1 tbsp olive oil
500 g / 1 lb / 2 cups gnocchetti pasta
Handful basil
2 tbsp Parmesan, grated to serve

- Preheat the oven to 200°C / 400F / gas 6.
- Place the cherry tomatoes in a roasting tin and drizzle
  with oil. Season and roast in the oven for at least 20
  minutes or until starting to blacken.
- Meanwhile cook the pasta in boiling salted water
  according to packet instructions
- Drain the pasta.
- Toss the pasta with the tomatoes and their roasting
  juices and chopped basil.
- Adjust the seasoning and serve with Parmesan.

Gnocchetti with Balsamic Tomatoes

110

- Add 1 tbsp balsamic to the tossed pasta.

111

SERVES 4

Potato Wedges with Thyme

PREPARATION TIME 5 MINUTES

COOKING TIME 40-45 MINUTES

INGREDIENTS

4 tbsp olive oil
800 g / 1 lb 12 oz / 6 cup maris piper
potatoes, cut into wedges
2 tbsp fresh thyme leaves

- Preheat the oven to 220°C (200° fan), 430 F, gas 7.
- Put the oil in a large roasting tin and heat in the oven
  for 5 minutes.
- Carefully tip the potato wedges into the pan and turn
  to coat in the oil, then sprinkle with thyme leaves and
  season well with salt and black pepper.
- Bake the wedges for 40 – 45 minutes, turning them
  every 15 minutes.

Potato Wedges with Paprika and Cumin

112

- Sprinkle the potatoes with 1 tsp of smoked paprika
  and 1 tsp of ground cumin instead of the thyme.

113

SERVES 4

Mushrooms and Butterbeans Bresaola

Mushrooms with Prosciutto

114

- Omit the butterbeans and replace the bresaola with prosciutto.

Mushrooms with Beans and Anchovies

115

- Replace the bresaola with 8 anchovy fillets in oil.

PREPARATION TIME 1 MINUTE

COOKING TIME 12 MINUTES

....

INGREDIENTS

4 large portabella mushrooms
50 g / 1 ¾ oz / ¼ cup butter
200 g / 7 oz / 2 cups / 2 ⅔ cup wild mushrooms, cleaned
2 cloves garlic, crushed
100 ml / 3 ½ fl. oz / ½ cup double cream
100 g / 3 ½ oz / ⅔ cup canned butterbeans, drained
2 tbsp chives, chopped
4 slices bresaola
extra whole chives to garnish

- Preheat the oven to 200⁰C (180⁰ fan), 390 F, gas 6.
- Remove the stalks from the portabella mushrooms and arrange cut side up in a baking dish.
- Add 1 teaspoon of the butter to the centre of each and roast for 20 minutes.
- Heat the rest of the butter in a frying pan and cook wild mushrooms for 6 minutes.
- Add the garlic and continue to cook for 2 minutes, then add the cream and butterbeans and bring to a simmer.
- Season to taste with salt and pepper then stir in the chives.
- Put a portabella mushroom on each plate and spoon over the wild mushroom mixture. Top each one with a slice of bresaola and decorate with a few whole chives.

116

SERVES 4

Baked Potatoes with Crispy Prosciutto

PREPARATION TIME 5 MINUTES

COOKING TIME 45 MINUTES

....

INGREDIENTS

4 medium baking potatoes
8 prosciutto slices
4 tbsp soured cream
2 tbsp chives, chopped

- Preheat the oven to 220°C (200° fan), 430 F, gas 7.
- Prick the potatoes and cook them in a microwave on high for 5 minutes.
- Wrap the potatoes in foil and bake in the oven for 40 minutes or until cooked through.
- Meanwhile, dry fry the prosciutto slices in batches until crisp – this should take 1 – 2 minutes per batch.
- Reserve 4 whole slices and crumble the rest into the soured cream.
- When the potatoes are ready, carefully unwrap the foil and split in half. Add a dollop of soured cream and a slice of crisp prosciutto to each one then sprinkle with chives.

Baked Potatoes
with Stilton Dressing

117

- Omit the prosciutto and stir 100 g of crumbled Stilton into the soured cream.

118

SERVES 4

Potatoes with Mushrooms and Feta

PREPARATION TIME 10 MINUTES

COOKING TIME 30 MINUTES

....

INGREDIENTS

4 medium baking potatoes
25 g / 1 oz butter
200 g / 7 oz / 2 cups / 2 ⅔ cup button mushrooms, sliced
2 cloves garlic, chopped
100 g / 3 ½ oz / ⅔ cup Feta, crumbled

TO SERVE

2 tbsp pesto
a few sprigs parsley

- Preheat the oven to 220°C (200° fan), 430 F, gas 7.
- Prick the potatoes and cook them in a microwave on high for 8 minutes.
- Cut them in half and scoop out the centres and arrange, cut side up, in a roasting tin.
- Bake the potatoes for 20 minutes or until cooked through.
- Meanwhile, melt the butter in a frying pan and fry the mushrooms with a pinch of salt for 10 minutes or until any juices that come out have evaporated and they start to colour.
- Crumble in the feta and season well with freshly ground black pepper.
- When the potatoes are ready, spoon the mushroom and Feta mixture into the cavities and serve 2 halves per person with a drizzle of pesto and a sprig of parsley.

Potatoes Stuffed
with Chicken and Brie

119

- Stuff the potatoes with 150 g chopped, cooked chicken breast and 150 g cubed brie, then return them to the oven for 10 minutes to melt the cheese.

120

SERVES 2 # Roasted Mushrooms with Garlic

- Preheat the oven to 200°C (180° fan), 390 F, gas 6.
- Remove the stalks from the mushrooms and arrange cut side up in a baking dish.
- Brush the mushrooms with oil and roast for 20 minutes.
- Heat the butter in a small frying pan and cook the garlic until it just starts to turn golden, then quickly spoon the garlic butter over the mushrooms and sprinkle with parsley.

PREPARATION TIME 1 MINUTE

COOKING TIME 12 MINUTES

INGREDIENTS

4 large mushrooms
2 tbsp olive oil
25 g / 1 oz butter
4 cloves garlic, chopped
2 tbsp flat leaf parsley, chopped

Roasted Mushrooms with Gremolata   121

- Add the grated zest of a lemon to the garlic and stir the parsley into the pan before spooning the mixture over the mushrooms.

122

SERVES 6 # Meatloaf with Onion Gravy

- Preheat the oven to 200°C (180° fan), 390 F, gas 6 and line a baking tray with greaseproof paper.
- Put the grated onion, minced beef and breadcrumbs in a mixing bowl with salt and pepper and squidge it all together until it is really well mixed.
- Shape the stuffing into a long loaf on the baking tray and bake for 40 minutes or until the top is golden and the centre is cooked.
- Meanwhile, fry the sliced onion in the butter for 10 minutes or until starting to caramelise.
- Add the Madeira and a pinch of salt and bubble away almost to nothing.
- Add the beef stock and simmer gently until reduced and slightly thickened.
- Slice the meatloaf and serve with a spoonful of gravy.

PREPARATION TIME 5 MINUTES

COOKING TIME 40 MINUTES

INGREDIENTS

1 small onion, finely grated
450 g / 1 lb / 3 cups minced beef
50 g / 1 ¾ oz / ⅓ cup fresh white breadcrumbs

FOR THE GRAVY
1 large onion, sliced
2 tbsp butter
2 tbsp Madeira
250 ml / 9 fl. oz / 1 cup good quality beef stock

Burgers with Onion Gravy   123

- If you're really short of time, you can shape the meatloaf mixture into burgers and grill them for 4 minutes on each side instead.

124

SERVES 4

Mediterranean Vegetable Salad

Mediterranean Steak Salad

125

- Griddle a large sirloin steak for 3 minutes on each side then cut into thin slices and toss with the rest of the salad ingredients.

Mediterranean Snapper Salad

126

- Brush 12 red snapper fillets with olive oil and cook on a hot griddle for 2 minutes on each side, then toss with the rest of the salad ingredients.

PREPARATION TIME 2 MINUTES

COOKING TIME 15 MINUTES

INGREDIENTS

2 courgettes (zucchini), cut into batons
1 jar preserved artichokes in oil, drained
1 jar mixed roasted peppers in oil, drained, oil reserved
8 cherry tomatoes, quartered
50 g / 1 ¾ oz / ⅓ cup kalamata olives, pitted
50 g / 1 ¾ oz / 1 cup rocket (arugula) leaves

FOR THE DRESSING
2 tbsp oil from the pepper jar
½ lemon, juiced

- Toss all of the vegetables together and divide between 4 plates.
- Whisk the pepper oil with the lemon juice and season to taste then spoon it over the salad.

127

SERVES 4 Mustard Chicken with Spinach and Feta

- Preheat the grill to its highest setting.
- Mix together the mustard, oil and rosemary with a pinch of salt and pepper and rub it over the chicken breasts.
- Grill the chicken for 5 minutes on each side or until cooked through.
- Meanwhile, toss together the spinach, onion, Feta and pine nuts and divide between 4 plates.
- Put the dressing ingredients in a jar and shake to emulsify, then put the jar on the table so people can help themselves.
- Serve the chicken alongside the salad on the plates.

PREPARATION TIME 5 MINUTES

COOKING TIME 10 MINUTES

INGREDIENTS

2 tbsp grain mustard
1 tbsp olive oil
1 tsp rosemary, finely chopped
4 chicken breasts

FOR THE SALAD

75 g / 2 ½ oz / 1 cup baby spinach leaves
1 small red onion, sliced
100 g / 3 ½ oz / ⅔ cup Feta, cubed
30 g / 1 oz pine nuts

FOR THE DRESSING

1 tsp runny honey
1 tsp wholegrain mustard
2 tbsp white wine vinegar
4 tbsp olive oil

Peppered Mackerel Salad   128

- When you're really short of time, omit the chicken and flake 2 peppered smoked mackerel fillets over the salad instead.

129

SERVES 2 Tomatoes and Broccoli Conchiglie

- Preheat the oven to 220°C (200° fan), 430 F, gas 7.
- Coat the broccoli, tomatoes and garlic with oil and spread them out in a roasting tin. Roast for 15 minutes or until the tomatoes are starting to burst and the broccoli is tender inside.
- Meanwhile, cook the conchiglie in boiling salted water according to the packet instructions or until al dente.
- Reserve a ladle of pasta water and drain the rest.
- Stir the pasta into the roasting tin with the reserved cooking water and the capers and stir to coat in the juices.
- Divide between 2 warm bowls and serve.

PREPARATION TIME 4 MINUTES

COOKING TIME 15 MINUTES

INGREDIENTS

100 g / 3 ½ oz / 1 cup broccoli, broken into small florets
100 g / 3 ½ oz / ⅔ cup cherry tomatoes
1 clove garlic, halved
4 tbsp olive oil
200 g / 7 oz / 2 cups / 2 ⅔ cup conchiglie pasta
2 tbsp baby capers

Conchiglie with   130
Broccoli and Anchovies

- Omit the tomatoes and stir 6 finely chopped anchovy fillets into the pasta when you add the capers.

131

SERVES 4

Lamb's Liver Kebabs with Tomato Sauce

PREPARATION TIME 20 MINUTES

COOKING TIME 30 MINUTES

INGREDIENTS

1 tbsp rosemary, finely chopped
2 tbsp olive oil
450 g / 1 lb / 3 cups lamb's liver, cubed
1 green pepper, cubed
1 red pepper, cubed
1 yellow pepper, cubed

FOR THE SAUCE

4 tbsp olive oil
1 onion, sliced
2 cloves garlic, crushed
400 g / 14 oz / 2 ⅓ cup canned tomatoes, chopped

- Put 8 wooden skewers in a bowl of water and leave to soak for 20 minutes.
- Meanwhile, stir the rosemary into the oil and toss it with the liver and peppers.
- Leave to marinate for 20 minutes.
- Meanwhile, heat the oil in a sauté pan and fry the onion for 5 minutes to soften. Add the garlic and cook for 2 more minutes, then stir in the tomatoes. Simmer for 15 minutes.
- Preheat the grill to its highest setting.
- Thread alternate chunks of liver and pepper onto the skewers and spread them out on a large grill tray.
- Sprinkle with salt and grill for 4 minutes on each side or until they are golden brown and cooked through.
- Serve 2 skewers per person with a small bowl of tomato sauce.

Lamb's Kidney and Mushroom Kebabs · 132

- Substitute the liver with an equal weight of kidney and the peppers with 250 g button mushrooms.

133

SERVES 4

Griddled Vegetables on Toast

PREPARATION TIME 5 MINUTES

COOKING TIME 6 MINUTES

INGREDIENTS

1 courgette (zucchini), sliced lengthways
1 aubergine (eggplant) (eggplant), sliced lengthways
4 tbsp olive oil
8 slices sourdough bread
8 sundried tomatoes in oil, drained
a few sprigs basil

- Preheat a griddle pan until smoking hot.
- Brush the courgette and aubergine slices with the oil and season with salt and pepper.
- Griddle the vegetables for 3 minutes on each side or until nicely marked.
- Toast the sourdough and divide the slices between 4 plates.
- Arrange the vegetables on top with the sundried tomatoes and garnish with basil.

Griddled Vegetables and Haloumi on Toast · 134

- Cut a 200 g block of Haloumi into slices and griddle with the vegetables before arranging on top of the toast.

135

SERVES 4

Goats' Cheese, Tomato and Basil Crostini

Goat's Cheese, Peach and Basil Crostini

136

- Replace the sliced tomatoes with wedges of fresh peach.

Goat's Cheese and Prosciutto Crostini

137

- Replace the tomato with thin slices of prosciutto and replace the basil with fresh young thyme leaves.

PREPARATION TIME 5 MINUTES

COOKING TIME 10 MINUTES

INGREDIENTS

12 slices wholemeal baguette
4 tbsp olive oil
200 g / 7 oz / 2 cups/ 1 ⅓ cups fresh goats' cheese
2 tbsp basil, finely chopped
2 tomatoes, sliced
12 sprigs basil

- Preheat the oven to 200⁰C (180⁰ fan), 390 F, gas 6.
- Brush the baguette slices with half of the oil and spread them out on a baking tray. Bake for 10 minutes or until crisp.
- Meanwhile, put the goats' cheese, chopped basil and the rest of the oil in a bowl with plenty of freshly ground black pepper. Mash it to a paste with a fork.
- When the crostini are ready, spread them with the goat's cheese mixture and top each one with a slice of tomato and a sprig of basil.

Potatoes Stuffed with Chicken Curry

138

SERVES 6

PREPARATION TIME 2 MINUTES

COOKING TIME 20 MINUTES

INGREDIENTS

6 large charlotte potatoes, peeled
1 tbsp vegetable oil
1 tbsp Thai red curry paste
2 chicken breasts, skinned and chopped
6 sprigs fresh coriander (cilantro)

- Put the potatoes in a pan of cold, salted water and bring to the boil. Cook for 12 – 15 minutes or until just tender in the middle.
- Meanwhile, heat the oil in a wok and add the curry paste. Cook for 1 minute then add the chicken and stir-fry for 4 minutes.
- Add 100 ml water to the wok and simmer the chicken for 2 minutes or until the liquid has reduced to a thick sauce.
- Use washing up gloves to handle the hot potatoes and carefully remove the middles with a sharp paring knife.
- Take a small slice off the other end to create a flat base and stand them upright on a serving plate.
- Spoon the chicken curry into the cavities and garnish with coriander leaves.

Creamy Mashed Potato

139

SERVES 4

PREPARATION TIME 2 MINUTES

COOKING TIME 15 MINUTES

INGREDIENTS

900 g / 2 lb / 6 cup potatoes, peeled and cubed
250 ml / 9 fl. oz / 1 cup whole milk
150 g / 5 ½ oz / ⅔ cup butter, cubed

- Put the potatoes in a pan of cold, salted water and bring to the boil.
- Cook the potatoes for 10 minutes or until tender all the way through.
- Tip the potatoes into a colander and leave to drain.
- Put the saucepan back on the heat and add the milk and butter.
- Heat until the milk starts to simmer then return the potatoes to the pan.
- Take the pan off the heat and mash with a potato masher until smooth.
- Season to taste with salt and pepper and serve immediately.

140

SERVES 4

Sautéed New Potatoes with Oregano

- Boil the potatoes in salted water for 8 minutes then drain well and leave to steam dry for 2 minutes.
- Heat the oil in a large sauté pan then fry the potatoes for 10 minutes or until golden on all sides.
- Add the oregano to the pan with a big scrunch of sea salt flakes and stir well before serving.

PREPARATION TIME 2 MINUTES

COOKING TIME 20 MINUTES

INGREDIENTS

800 g / 1 lb 12 oz / 5 ⅓ cup baby new potatoes
4 tbsp olive oil
2 tbsp fresh oregano leaves

141

SERVES 4

Potatoes with Madeira Gravy

PREPARATION TIME 2 MINUTES

COOKING TIME 20 MINUTES

INGREDIENTS

800 g / 1 lb 12 oz / 5 ⅓ cup potatoes, cut into thick rounds
4 tbsp olive oil

FOR THE GRAVY

1 large onion, finely chopped
2 tbsp butter
2 tbsp Madeira
250 ml / 9 fl. oz / 1 cup beef stock

- Boil the potatoes in salted water for 12 minutes then drain well and leave to steam dry for 2 minutes.
- Heat the oil in a large frying pan then colour the ends for 3 minutes on each side.
- Meanwhile, fry the onion in the butter for 10 minutes or until starting to caramelise.
- Add the Madeira and a pinch of salt and bubble away almost to nothing.
- Add the beef stock and simmer gently until reduced and slightly thickened.
- Strain the gravy through a sieve to get rid of the onions then spoon it over the potatoes.

142

SERVES 4

Potatoes with Tomato

PREPARATION TIME 2 MINUTES

COOKING TIME 20 MINUTES

INGREDIENTS

800 g / 1 lb 12 oz / 5 ⅓ cup potatoes, cut into thick rounds
4 tbsp olive oil

½ small jar sundried tomato paste
fresh thyme flowers to garnish

- Boil the potatoes in salted water for 12 minutes then drain well and leave to steam dry for 2 minutes.
- Heat the oil in a large frying pan then colour the ends for 3 minutes on each side.
- Transfer the potatoes to 4 warm serving plates and top each slice with some tomato paste and a thyme flower.

SERVES 4

Pea and Potato Purée with Croutons

PREPARATION TIME 2 MINUTES

COOKING TIME 15 MINUTES

....

INGREDIENTS

600 g / 1 lb 5 ½ oz / 4 cups potatoes, peeled and cubed
400 g / 14 oz / 4 cups frozen peas, defrosted
250 ml / 9 fl. oz / 1 cup whole milk
150 g / 5 ½ oz / ⅔ cup butter, cubed
a few sprigs chervil to garnish

FOR THE HALOUMI CROUTONS

200 g / 7 oz / 2 cups Halloumi, cubed
½ tsp ground cumin
½ tsp ground coriander seeds
2 tbsp olive oil

- Put the potatoes in a pan of cold, salted water and bring to the boil.
- Cook for 10 minutes then add the peas. Continue to cook until the potatoes are tender all the way through.
- Tip the vegetables into a colander and leave to drain.
- Put the saucepan back on the heat and add the milk and butter.
- Heat until the milk starts to simmer then return the potatoes and peas to the pan.
- Take the pan off the heat and purée with an emersion blender then season to taste with salt and pepper.
- Meanwhile, toss the Halloumi with the spices and fry in the oil for 2 minutes on each side or until golden brown.
- Remove the Halloumi from the pan with a slotted spoon and sprinkle over the puree with the chervil.

Minted Pea and Potato Purée

144

- Add 1 tbsp of chopped fresh mint leaves to the pan before pureeing.

145

SERVES 4

Red Cabbage and Orange Salad

PREPARATION TIME 15 MINUTES

....

INGREDIENTS

2 oranges
½ lemon, juiced
3 tbsp olive oil
½ red cabbage, shredded
50 g / 1 ¾ oz / ⅓ cup roasted cashew nuts

- Cut a slice off the end of each orange, then stand them on end and slice off and discard the peel in strips.
- Use a sharp knife to cut out each individual segment, leaving the pith behind like the pages of a book.
- Reserve the orange segments and squeeze the pith into a bowl to collect the juices. Discard the pith.
- Add the lemon juice to the bowl and whisk in the olive oil with a good pinch of salt and pepper.
- Add the red cabbage to the bowl and toss well to coat. Leave to stand for 10 minutes to soften the cabbage slightly then stir again.
- Combine the cabbage with the orange segments and cashews and serve immediately.

Red Cabbage and Grapefruit Salad

146

- Substitute the oranges with grapefruits and use walnuts in place of the cashews.

147

SERVES 4

Red Cabbage and Apple Salad

- Whisk together the lemon juice, olive oil and coriander seeds and toss with the cabbage.
- Leave to stand for 10 minutes for the cabbage to soften then stir in the apple slices.

PREPARATION TIME 12 MINUTES

INGREDIENTS

1 lemon, juiced
4 tbsp olive oil
1 tsp coriander seeds, crushed
½ red cabbage, shredded
1 apple, cored and very thinly sliced

Red Cabbage, Pear and Stilton Salad

148

- Replace the apples with pears and crumble in 100 g of Stilton at the end.

149

SERVES 2

Broccoli and Bacon Salad

- Heat 1 tablespoon of the oil in a frying pan and fry the bacon for 3 minutes on each side or until crisp.
- Meanwhile, blanch the broccoli in boiling salted water for 3 – 4 minutes or until just tender. Drain well.
- While the bacon and broccoli are cooking, whisk the honey and mustard into the vinegar with a pinch of salt then incorporate the rest of the oil.
- Toss the drained broccoli with the dressing and split between 2 serving plates.
- Lay 2 rashers of bacon on top of each plate and use a vegetable peeler to shave over some Parmesan.

PREPARATION TIME 2 MINUTES

COOKING TIME 12 MINUTES

INGREDIENTS

3 tbsp olive oil
4 rashers streaky bacon
1 small head broccoli, broken into small florets
1 tsp runny honey
1 tsp Dijon mustard
1 tbsp balsamic vinegar
30 g / 1 oz / ½ cup Parmesan

Broccoli, Chilli and Anchovy Salad

150

- Omit the bacon and add 4 chopped anchovy fillets and a finely chopped red chilli to the dressing.

151

SERVES 4

Chicken Salad Wraps

Prawn and Avocado Wraps

152

- Replace the chicken with 150 g cooked, peeled prawns and a chopped avocado.

Chicken and Bacon Wraps

153

- Add 4 slices of chopped crispy bacon to the chicken mixture.

PREPARATION TIME 5 MINUTES

INGREDIENTS

1 cooked chicken breast, diced
1 red pepper, diced
2 tomatoes, diced
¼ cucumber, diced
1 tbsp capers
50 g / 1 ¾ oz / 1 cup lamb's lettuce
4 tbsp mayonnaise
4 flour tortillas

- Mix the chicken with the vegetables, capers and half of the lamb's lettuce and stir in the mayonnaise.
- Divide the mixture between the tortillas and roll them up.
- Cut each wrap in half and secure with cocktail sticks.
- Serve with the rest of the lambs lettuce on the side.

154

SERVES 2 # Roasted Pepper Salad

- Preheat the oven to 220°C (200° fan), 430 F, gas 7.
- Rub the peppers with half of the oil and season well with salt and pepper then spread them out in a large roasting tin. Roast for 30 minutes, turning half way through.
- Whisk the rest of the oil with the honey and lemon juice and use it to dress the peppers.
- Serve warm or at room temperature.

PREPARATION TIME 2 MINUTES

COOKING TIME 30 MINUTES

INGREDIENTS

1 green pepper, cut into wedges
1 red pepper, cut into wedges
1 yellow pepper, cut into wedges
4 tbsp olive oil
1 tsp runny honey
1 tbsp lemon juice

Roasted Asparagus Salad

155

- Replace the peppers with 200 g asparagus spears and reduce the cooking time to 18 minutes.

156

SERVES 4 # Corn with Garlic and Parsley Butter

- Mix the butter with the garlic and parsley and season with salt and pepper. Shape it into 4 small pats and chill for 20 minutes.
- Meanwhile, bring a large saucepan of water to the boil with a teaspoon of salt and cook the sweetcorn for 8 minutes. Drain well.
- Heat a griddle pan until smoking hot then griddle the corn cobs for 8 minutes, turning occasionally.
- Stick a fork in each butter pat and serve with the sweetcorn.

PREPARATION TIME 20 MINUTES

COOKING TIME 16 MINUTES

INGREDIENTS

100 g / 3 ½ oz / ½ cup butter, softened
1 clove garlic, crushed
2 tbsp flat leaf parsley, finely chopped
4 sweetcorn cobs

Corn on the Cob with Chilli Butter

157

- Add 1 finely chopped chilli to the garlic butter and replace the parsley with chopped fresh coriander leaves.

158

SERVES 2

Brie and Tomato Toasts

PREPARATION TIME 10 MINUTES

COOKING TIME 10-12 MINUTES

....

INGREDIENTS

4 slices sourdough bread
8 slices Brie
1 tomato, thinly sliced
1 tbsp fresh thyme leaves
a handful rocket (arugula) leaves
olive oil, to drizzle

- Preheat the grill to its highest setting.
- Toast the slices of sourdough on one side under the grill.
- Turn them over and top each one with the brie, tomatoes and a sprinkle of thyme.
- Grill for 2 more minutes or until the cheese is bubbling and the bread is toasted at the edges.
- Serve 2 toasts per plate with some rocket on the side. Drizzle some olive oil over the rocket and sprinkle everything with freshly ground black pepper.

Brie and Roasted Pepper Toasts   **159**

- Replace the tomatoes with a jar of roasted peppers in oil and use some of the oil from the jar to dress the rocket.

160

SERVES 4

Sole and Mushroom Skewers with Rice

PREPARATION TIME 20 MINUTES

COOKING TIME 26 MINUTES

....

INGREDIENTS

200 g / 7 oz / 2 cups / 1 cup mixed basmati, red and wild rice
450 g / 1 lb / 3 cups sole, filleted and cut into strips
200 g / 7 oz / 2 cups / 2 ⅔ cups button mushrooms, halved
2 tbsp olive oil
fresh coriander (cilantro) sprigs to garnish

- Put 16 wooden skewers in a bowl of water and leave to soak for 20 minutes.
- Meanwhile, put the rice in a saucepan and add enough water to cover it by 1 cm.
- Bring the pan to the boil then cover and turn down the heat to its lowest setting.
- Cook for 10 minutes then turn off the heat and leave to stand, without lifting the lid, for 10 minutes.
- Preheat the grill to its highest setting.
- Roll up the sole fillets and thread them onto the skewers with the mushrooms. Brush the skewers with oil and spread them out on a large grill tray.
- Sprinkle with salt and grill for 3 minutes on each side or until they are golden brown and cooked through.
- Fluff up the rice with a fork then divide it between 4 warm plates then top with the kebabs and coriander.

Sole and Prawn Skewers with Rice   **161**

- Replace the mushrooms with 150 g of raw peeled king prawns.

162

SERVES 3

Bacon-Wrapped Scallop Kebabs

Scallop, Bacon and Tomato Kebabs

163

- Substitute the mushrooms with cherry tomatoes and garnish with parsley instead of coriander.

Bacon-wrapped Monk Fish Kebabs

164

- Replace the scallops with a cubed monkfish tail.

PREPARATION TIME 20 MINUTES

COOKING TIME 8 MINUTES

....

INGREDIENTS

12 scallops
6 thin slices streaky bacon, halved
12 button mushrooms
1 lime, cut into wedges
fresh coriander (cilantro) leaves to garnish

- Put 6 wooden skewers in a bowl of water and leave to soak for 20 minutes.
- Preheat the grill to its highest setting.
- Wrap the scallops in bacon then thread them onto the skewers with the mushrooms.
- Grill the kebabs for 4 minutes on each side or until they are golden brown and garnish with lime and coriander.

165

SERVES 4

Spiced Mango Salad

PREPARATION TIME 12 MINUTES

INGREDIENTS

1 onion, thinly sliced
2 tbsp olive oil
1 tsp black mustard seeds
½ tsp red chilli flakes
2 mangoes, peeled, stoned and cubed
2 tbsp natural yoghurt
2 green chillies, 1 sliced and 1 finely chopped

- Fry the onion, mustard seeds and chilli flakes in the oil for 15 minutes or until starting to caramelise. Put the mango in a serving bowl and toss with the yoghurt and fried onion mixture.
- Scatter over the green chilli and serve.

Spiced Mango and Prawn Salad   166

- Add 150 g raw peeled king prawns to the onion mixture and fry until just opaque before tossing with the mango and yoghurt.

167

SERVES 2

Steamed Skate Wings with Leeks

PREPARATION TIME 2 MINUTES

COOKING TIME 30 MINUTES

INGREDIENTS

1 large leek, halved and sliced lengthways
1 skate wing, skinned and halved
1 tomato, seeded and cubed
1 tsp pink peppercorns
1 lemon
1 tbsp olive oil
a few sprigs flat leaf parsley

- Put a large steamer on to heat.
- Separate the leeks into individual strands and arrange them on a plate.
- Put the skate wings on top and sprinkle over the tomato and peppercorns.
- Juice half of the lemon and mix it with the olive oil and a pinch of salt then pour it over the skate.
- Cover the plate with foil and transfer it to the steamer. Cook for 10 minutes or until the skate is just cooked in the centre.
- Cut the other half of the lemon into wedges and use to garnish the plate with the parsley.

Baked Skate with Leek   168

- Prepare the recipe as above, but arrange the ingredients in a roasting tin. Cover the tin with foil and bake for 15 minutes at 180°C or until the skate is just cooked in the centre.

169

SERVES 4 King Prawn and Fennel Salad

- Mix the fennel and fennel tops with the mayonnaise and lemon juice and season well with salt and pepper.
- Use a ring mould or pastry cutter to shape the salad onto the plates and top each one with 3 prawns.
- Garnish with chives and fennel tops.

PREPARATION TIME 5 MINUTES

INGREDIENTS

1 fennel bulb, finely chopped
1 tbsp fennel tops, chopped plus extra for garnishing
3 tbsp mayonnaise
1 tbsp lemon juice
12 cooked king prawns (shrimps), peeled leaving tails intact
a small bunch chives

King Prawn and Cucumber Salad 170

- Replace the fennel with half a finely chopped cucumber and use chopped dill instead of the fennel tops.

171

SERVES 4 Warm Vegetable and Tuna Salad

- Season the vegetables with salt and pepper then steam for 15 minutes or until al dente.
- Meanwhile, make the dressing. Whisk the honey and mustard into the vinegar then incorporate the oil. Season to taste with salt and pepper.
- Mix the vegetables with the tuna, olives, gherkins and parsley then spoon over the dressing.

PREPARATION TIME 2 MINUTES

COOKING TIME 15 MINUTES

INGREDIENTS

2 small celery hearts, quartered
20 baby carrots, peeled
16 baby leeks, trimmed
150 g / 5 ½ oz / 1 cup Chinese artichokes, cleaned
250 g / 9 oz / 1 ⅔ cup tuna in olive oil, drained
50 g / 1 ¾ oz / ⅓ cup green olives, pitted
50 g / 1 ¾ oz / ⅓ cup gherkins, sliced
a small bunch flat leaf parsley, leaves only

FOR THE DRESSING
1 tsp runny honey
1 tsp wholegrain mustard
2 tbsp white wine vinegar
4 tbsp olive oil

Warm Vegetable Salad 172

- For a vegetarian version of this salad, omit the tuna or replace with butterbeans.

173
SERVES 4

Duck and Mango Salad

Chilli Duck and Mango Salad

174

- Add a finely chopped red chilli and a crushed clove garlic to the dressing before spooning it over the salad.

Duck and Pineapple Salad

175

- Replace the mango with half a diced fresh pineapple.

PREPARATION TIME 10 MINUTES

COOKING TIME 5 MINUTES

INGREDIENTS

1 large skinless duck breast, cut into thin strips
2 tbsp peanuts
1 tbsp vegetable oil
¼ Chinese cabbage, chopped
1 under-ripe mango, julienned
a small bunch of mint, leaves only
4 spring onions (scallions), sliced

FOR THE DRESSING
1 tbsp caster (superfine) sugar
1 tbsp fish sauce
2 limes, juiced
1 tsp sesame oil

- Stir-fry the duck and peanuts in the vegetable oil for 5 minutes or until cooked through.
- Toss the duck with the cabbage, mango, mint and spring onions.
- Mix together the dressing ingredients and spoon them over the top.

176

SERVES 2

Chicory and Ham Salad

- Toss the chicory leaves with the radishes, melon, ham, cheese and nuts.
- Whisk the orange juice and olive oil together with a pinch of salt and pepper and drizzle it over the salad.

Chicory and Roquefort Salad 177

- Omit the ham and radishes and replace the Gouda with Roquefort.

PREPARATION TIME 12 MINUTES

INGREDIENTS

2 heads chicory (endive), separated into leaves
4 radishes, sliced
¼ white-fleshed melon, peeled and sliced
50 g / 1 ¾ oz / ⅓ cup cooked ham, cut into matchsticks
50 g / 1 ¾ oz / ½ cup Gouda, cubed
50 g / 1 ¾ oz / ⅓ cup walnuts, chopped

FOR THE DRESSING
½ orange, juiced
1 tbsp olive oil

178

SERVES 4

Lentil, Green Bean and Asparagus Salad

- Cook the lentils in simmering, unsalted water for 20 - 30 minutes or until tender, but still holding their shape.
- Drain well and plunge into cold water to stop the cooking. Drain well.
- While the lentils are cooking, blanch the green beans in boiling salted water for 4 minutes or until al dente. Plunge into cold water and drain well.
- Meanwhile, make the dressing. Whisk the honey into the lemon juice then incorporate the oil. Season to taste with salt and pepper, then stir in the basil.
- Top the lentils with the beans and asparagus tips then spoon over the dressing.

Puy Lentil and Asparagus Salad 179

- Replace the red lentils with Puy lentils. Use 200 g of fresh asparagus instead of the jar – brush it with olive oil and griddle for 6 minutes, turning occasionally.

PREPARATION TIME 2 MINUTES

COOKING TIME 30 MINUTES

INGREDIENTS

400 g / 14 oz / 2 ⅔ cup red lentils
100 g / 3 ½ oz / ⅔ cup green beans
1 jar green asparagus tips, drained

FOR THE DRESSING
1 tsp runny honey
2 tbsp lemon juice
4 tbsp olive oil
2 tbsp basil leaves, shredded

180

SERVES 4

Watermelon, Feta and Basil Salad

PREPARATION TIME 5 MINUTES

INGREDIENTS

½ small watermelon, deseeded and cut into chunks
100 g / 3 ½ oz / ⅔ cup Feta, cubed
4 tbsp basil leaves, shredded
4 tbsp extra virgin olive oil

- Mix the watermelon with the Feta and divide between 4 plates.
- Scatter over the basil and drizzle with olive oil then sprinkle with sea salt.

Watermelon, Feta and Mint Salad

181

- Replace the basil with shredded fresh mint leaves and squeeze over the juice of half a lemon at the end.

182

SERVES 4

Smoked Mackerel and Olive Salad

PREPARATION TIME 5 MINUTES

INGREDIENTS

4 smoked mackerel fillets
8 spring onions (scallions), sliced lengthways
50 g / 1 ¾ oz / ⅓ cup green olives
50 g / 1 ¾ oz / ⅓ cup black olives
1 orange, juiced
2 tbsp olive oil

- Arrange the mackerel, onions and olives on 4 plates.
- Whisk the orange juice and oil together with a pinch of salt then drizzle it over the salad.

Smoked Mackerel and Fennel Salad

183

- Replace half the spring onions with a sliced fennel bulb and substitute the olives with 2 tbsp of capers.

184

SERVES 4

Asparagus with Dolcelatte Cream

Asparagus with Mustard Cream

185

- Replace the Dolcelatte with 1 tbsp Dijon mustard.

Asparagus with Lemon Cream

186

- Omit the Dolcelatte and stir the zest and juice of a lemon into the hot cream just before serving.

PREPARATION TIME 10 MINUTES

COOKING TIME 4-5 MINUTES

INGREDIENTS

400 g / 14 oz / 4 cups fresh asparagus
100 g / 3 ½ oz / 1 cup Dolcelatte, cubed
300 ml / 10 ½ fl. oz / 1 ½ cup double cream

- Snap the woody ends off the asparagus and cut the spears in half. Steam the asparagus for 5 minutes or until tender.
- Meanwhile, put the Dolcelatte in a small saucepan with the cream and some freshly ground black pepper.
- Bring to a gentle simmer, stirring constantly, then take off the heat.
- Divide the asparagus between 4 warm plates and spoon over the sauce.

187

SERVES 4

Moroccan Chicken Salad

PREPARATION TIME 35 MINUTES

INGREDIENTS

½ tsp ground turmeric
½ tsp ground cumin
½ tsp ground cinnamon
2 tsp runny honey
2 tbsp lemon juice
4 tbsp olive oil
2 cooked chicken breasts, cut into chunks
200 g / 7 oz / 2 cups / 1 ⅓ cup boiled potatoes, cooled
2 baby preserved lemons, halved
12 green olives
8 cherry tomatoes, halved

- Whisk the spices, honey and lemon juice into the oil.
- Mix the chicken with the potatoes, preserved lemons, olives and tomatoes and pour over the dressing.
- Leave to infuse for 30 minutes then divide between 4 bowls and serve.

Moroccan Squash Salad

188

- For a vegetarian version of this dish, replace the chicken with 300 g of roasted butternut squash chunks.

189

SERVES 4

Rice Salad with Orange and Figs

PREPARATION TIME 5 MINUTES

COOKING TIME 20 MINUTES

INGREDIENTS

200 g / 7 oz / 2 cups / 1 ¼ cup long grain rice
½ cucumber, sliced
1 orange, peeled and sliced
4 dried figs, chopped
6 dried apricots, sliced
1 tbsp pistachios, chopped
2 tbsp chives, chopped

FOR THE DRESSING
1 tsp runny honey
½ lemon, juiced
3 tbsp olive oil

- Put the rice in a saucepan and add enough water to cover it by 1 cm.
- Bring the pan to the boil then cover and turn down the heat to its lowest setting.
- Cook for 10 minutes then turn off the heat and leave to stand, without lifting the lid, for 10 minutes.
- Whisk the honey with the lemon juice then whisk in the olive oil.
- When the rice is ready, combine it with the rest of the ingredients and dressing and season well with salt and pepper.
- Serve warm or at room temperature.

Rice Salad with Grapefruit and Dates

190

- Replace the orange segments with grapefruit segments and replace the figs with chopped, stoned dates.

191

SERVES 4

Chicken, Tomato and Nasturtium Salad

- Arrange the chicken, tomatoes and spring onions on 4 plates and sprinkle over the thyme.
- Drizzle with olive oil and season with salt and pepper then garnish with the nasturtiums.

PREPARATION TIME 5 MINUTES

INGREDIENTS

2 cooked chicken breasts, sliced
200 g / 7 oz / 2 cups / 1 ⅓ cup cherry tomatoes, halved
200 g / 7 oz / 2 cups / 1 ⅓ cup yellow cherry tomatoes, halved
4 spring onions (scallions), sliced lengthways
2 tbsp thyme leaves
4 tbsp extra virgin olive oil
a handful of nasturtium flowers

Mozzarella, Tomato and Nasturtium Salad

192

- Replace the chicken with 2 sliced mozzarella balls and replace the thyme with shredded basil leaves.

193

SERVES 4

Prawn and Grapefruit Stir Fry

- Stir the chilli, garlic and coriander into the oil then pour it over the prawns and leave to marinate for 15 minutes.
- Heat a wok until smoking hot then add the prawns, mange tout and peas and stir-fry until the prawns turn opaque.
- Stir in the soy sauce and pink grapefruit and serve immediately.

PREPARATION TIME 5 MINUTES

COOKING TIME 4 MINUTES

INGREDIENTS

1 red chilli, finely chopped
1 clove garlic, crushed
1 tbsp coriander (cilantro) leaves, finely chopped
3 tbsp olive oil
20 raw king prawns (shrimps), peeled leaving tails intact
200 g / 7 oz / 2 cups / 2 cups mange tout, trimmed
100 g / 3 ½ oz / 1 cup frozen peas (snow peas), defrosted
1 tbsp soy sauce
1 pink grapefruit, cut into segments

Prawn, Broccoli and Grapefruit Stir Fry

194

- Replace the mange tout with ½ a head of broccoli, broken into small florets.

195

SERVES 4

Green Bean, Bacon and Cheese Salad

Green Bean, Bacon and Chicken Salad

196

- Omit the cheese and fry 1 cubed chicken breast with the bacon until cooked through.

Green Bean, Bacon and Caper Salad

197

- Replace the cheese with 1 tbsp of capers.

PREPARATION TIME 5 MINUTES

COOKING TIME 6 MINUTES

....

INGREDIENTS

200 g / 7 oz / 2 cups / 2 cups green beans, trimmed
6 rashers smoked bacon, sliced
2 tbsp olive oil
2 tbsp white wine vinegar
150 g / 5 ½ oz / 1 ½ cup mild Cheddar, cubed

- Blanch the beans in boiling salted water for 4 minutes or until al dente. Plunge into cold water and drain well.
- Meanwhile, fry the bacon in the oil for 4 minutes or until crisp.
- While the bacon is cooking, toss the cheese with some freshly ground black pepper.
- When the bacon is ready, remove it from the pan with a slotted spoon and toss it with the beans and cheese.
- Add the vinegar to the pan to deglaze and spoon it over the salad as a dressing.

198

SERVES 6

Provençal Anchovy Salad

- Boil the potatoes in salted water for 12 minutes or until tender, then drain well.
- Meanwhile, blanch the beans in boiling salted water for 4 minutes then plunge into cold water and drain well.
- Toss the potatoes, beans, cucumber, peppers and shallots with 8 of the boiled egg quarters and the tuna.
- Arrange the anchovies on top and scatter over the olives then arrange the tomato wedges and remaining boiled egg quarters round the outside.
- Whisk the oil and vinegar together with a good grind of salt and pepper and drizzle it over the salad just before serving.

PREPARATION TIME 10 MINUTES

COOKING TIME 12 MINUTES

INGREDIENTS

400 g / 14 oz / 2 ⅔ cup charlotte potatoes, peeled and sliced
200 g / 7 oz / 2 cups / 2 cups green beans, halved
½ cucumber, sliced
1 yellow pepper, sliced
1 shallot, thinly sliced
3 hard-boiled eggs, quartered
50 g / 1 ¾ oz / ⅓ cup white tuna in olive oil, drained and flaked
50 g / 1 ¾ oz / ⅓ cup anchovy fillets in olive oil, drained
50 g / 1 ¾ oz / ⅓ cup black olives, pitted
1 tomato, cut into wedges
4 tbsp extra virgin olive oil
2 tbsp white wine vinegar

Provencal Steak Salad
199

- Brush a large sirloin steak with olive oil and cook in a hot griddle pan for 3 minutes on each side, then slice thinly and mix with the rest of the salad ingredients.

200

SERVES 2

Asparagus with Scrambled Egg and Feta

- Snap the woody ends off the asparagus and cut the spears in half. Steam the asparagus for 5 minutes or until tender.
- Heat the olive oil in a large sauté pan and add the eggs. Stir continuously until they start to scramble then add the asparagus to the pan and stir-fry for 2 more minutes.
- Stir in the Feta and sesame seeds then serve immediately, garnished with basil.

PREPARATION TIME 5 MINUTES

COOKING TIME 10 MINUTES

INGREDIENTS

200 g / 7 oz / 2 cups / 2 cups fresh asparagus
4 tbsp olive oil
2 eggs, beaten
100 g / 3 ½ oz / ⅔ cup Feta, cubed
1 tbsp sesame seeds
a few sprigs basil

Asparagus with Feta and Sesame Dressing
201

- Follow the recipe above but omit the scrambled eggs.

202

SERVES 4

Spring Garden Salad

PREPARATION TIME 10 MINUTES

COOKING TIME 4-5 MINUTES

....

INGREDIENTS

400 g / 14 oz / 4 cups asparagus
spears, peeled
100 g / 3 ½ oz / 1 cup fresh peas
1 bunch of radishes with leaves
200 g / 7 oz / 2 cups / 1 ⅓ cup cherry
tomatoes, quartered
2 tbsp fresh chervil, chopped

FOR THE DRESSING

3 tbsp extra virgin olive oil
1 tbsp white wine vinegar
1 tsp runny honey
1 tsp Dijon mustard
½ clove garlic, crushed

- Steam the asparagus and peas for 5 minutes or until tender.
- Separate the leaves from the radishes and wash them well. Thinly slice the radishes and mix them with the leaves, tomatoes, peas and chervil.
- Transfer the salad to a serving plate and arrange the asparagus on the side.
- Put the dressing ingredients in a jar with a good pinch of salt and pepper and shake well to emulsify.
- Drizzle the dressing over the salad just before serving.

Chicken Garden Salad

203

- Poach a chicken breast in gently simmering water with a squeeze of lemon juice for 10 minutes, then slice it and add to the salad before dressing.

204

SERVES 4

Sweetcorn and Pepper Salad

PREPARATION TIME 5 MINUTES

....

INGREDIENTS

4 iceberg lettuce leaves
400 g / 14 oz / 4 cups canned
sweetcorn, drained
1 red pepper, cubed
1 green pepper, cubed
¼ cucumber, cubed
2 hard-boiled eggs, halved
1 tomato, quartered
4 black olives

FOR THE DRESSING

1 lemon, juiced
3 tbsp olive oil

- Line 4 bowls with the lettuce leaves.
- Mix the sweetcorn with the peppers and cucumber and divide between the bowls.
- Top each one with half a boiled egg, a wedge of tomato and an olive.
- Put the lemon juice and oil in a jar with a pinch of salt and pepper and shake to emulsify.
- Drizzle the dressing over the salads and serve immediately.

Pea and Pepper Salad

205

- Replace the sweetcorn with 350 g frozen peas that have been boiled for 2 minutes, then drained and cooled.

206

SERVES 4

Spring Vegetables with Herb Cream

Steamed Vegetables with Crab Cream

207

- Add 100 g of fresh brown crab meat to the cream and bring back to a simmer before stirring in the herbs and lemon juice.

Steamed Vegetables with Pesto Cream

208

- Stir 2 tbsp of pesto into the hot cream instead of the herbs and lemon juice.

PREPARATION TIME 5 MINUTES

COOKING TIME 6 MINUTES

INGREDIENTS

100 g / 3 ½ oz / 1 cup asparagus spears
6 baby celery hearts
100 g / 3 ½ oz / 1 cup green beans
100 g / 3 ½ oz / ⅔ cup baby carrots
100 g / 3 ½ oz / 1 cup fresh peas
300 ml / 10 ½ fl. oz / 1 ½ cup double cream
1 tbsp lemon juice
2 tbsp dill, chopped
2 tbsp coriander (cilantro) leaves, chopped
2 tbsp flat leaf parsley, chopped

- Steam the vegetables for 6 minutes or until tender.
- Meanwhile, heat the cream in a small saucepan until almost at a simmer then take off the heat and stir in the lemon juice and herbs. Season to taste with salt and white pepper.
- Arrange the vegetables on 4 warm plates and spoon over the cream.

65

209

SERVES 4

Celery, Cambozola and Cashew Salad

PREPARATION TIME 5 MINUTES

INGREDIENTS

50 g / 1 ¾ oz / ⅓ cup cashew nuts
8 celery sticks, cut into 8 cm lengths
150 g / 5 ½ oz / 1 ½ cup Cambozola, sliced
8 cherry tomatoes, quartered
4 tbsp olive oil

- Chop half of the cashews and leave the rest whole. Mix them with the celery, Cambozola and tomatoes and divide between 4 bowls.
- Drizzle with olive oil and sprinkle with salt and pepper before serving.

210

SERVES 4

Cucumber, Radish and Baby Corn Salad

PREPARATION TIME 10 MINUTES

INGREDIENTS

1 cucumber, thinly sliced
a small bunch of mint, leaves only
150 g / 5 ½ oz / 1 ½ cup radishes, thinly sliced
100 g / 3 ½ oz / 1 cup baby sweetcorn, thinly sliced

FOR THE DRESSING
1 tsp miso soup paste
1 tsp caster (superfine) sugar
1 tbsp rice wine vinegar

- First make the dressing. Mix the miso soup paste with 4 tbsp boiling water and stir in the sugar and vinegar to dissolve. Leave to cool.
- Mix the cucumber with the mint, radish and baby corn slices and drizzle over the dressing.

211

SERVES 4

Preserved Artichoke and Onion Salad

- Mix all of the ingredients together in a bowl and sprinkle with salt and pepper.
- Leave for 30 minutes for the flavours to infuse then divide between 4 plates and serve.

PREPARATION TIME 30 MINUTES

INGREDIENTS

400 g / 14 oz / 2 ⅔ cup canned artichoke hearts in water, drained
100 g / 3 ½ oz / ⅔ cup pickled silverskin onions
100 g / 3 ½ oz / ⅔ cup cherry tomatoes, quartered
1 tbsp chives, chopped
4 tbsp extra virgin olive oil
a few sprigs curly parsley

Vietnamese Prawn Salad

212

SERVES 4

PREPARATION TIME 10 MINUTES

INGREDIENTS

12 cooked king prawns (shrimps), peeled leaving tails intact
½ cucumber, julienned
½ red pepper, julienned
4 spring onions (scallions), sliced
¼ Chinese cabbage, shredded

FOR THE DRESSING
1 tbsp caster (superfine) sugar
1 tbsp fish sauce
1 lime, juiced
1 clove garlic, crushed
1 red chilli, finely chopped

- To make the dressing, stir the caster (superfine) sugar into the fish sauce and lime juice to dissolve, then stir in the garlic and chilli.
- Mix the cucumber, peppers, spring onion and cabbage together and divide between 4 bowls.
- Arrange the prawns on top then spoon over the dressing.

Aubergine and Oyster Sauce

213

SERVES 4

PREPARATION TIME 5 MINUTES

COOKING TIME 12 MINUTES

INGREDIENTS

4 tbsp vegetable oil
2 aubergines (eggplant)(eggplants), cubed
3 tbsp oyster sauce

1 tbsp sweet chilli sauce
2 spring onions (scallions), quartered and cut into short lengths
coriander (cilantro), to garnish

- Heat the oil in a large wok and stir-fry the aubergine for 5 minutes or until golden.
- Add the oyster sauce, chilli sauce and 2 tablespoons of water to the pan and cook for another 5 minutes or until almost all of the sauce has been absorbed.
- Add the spring onions and stir fry for 1 more minute then garnish with coriander and serve.

214

SERVES 4

Baby Octopus and Pepper Salad

PREPARATION TIME 30 MINUTES

COOKING TIME 8 MINUTES

INGREDIENTS

3 tbsp olive oil
1 red pepper, diced
1 orange pepper, diced
1 yellow pepper, sliced
1 green pepper, diced
2 cloves garlic, finely chopped
300 g / 10 ½ oz baby octopus, cleaned
2 tbsp flat leaf parsley, chopped

FOR THE DRESSING
2 tbsp olive oil
2 tbsp double cream
1 lemon, juiced
2 tsp Dijon mustard
1 tsp runny honey

- Put all of the dressing ingredients in a jar and shake well to emulsify.
- Heat the oil in a large sauté pan and fry the peppers with the garlic for 5 minutes or until softened.
- Add the octopus and parsley and cook for 2 minutes over a very high heat until just opaque.
- Pour over the dressing and turn off the heat.
- Leave for 30 minutes for the octopus to cool and absorb the flavour of the dressing before serving.

Baby Octopus and Red Onion Salad

215

- Replace the peppers with 2 sliced red onions. Fry with the garlic for 10 minutes before adding the octopus.

216

SERVES 4

Curry Fried Potatoes

PREPARATION TIME 2 MINUTES

COOKING TIME 18 MINUTES

INGREDIENTS

800 g / 1 lb 12 oz / 5 ⅓ cup charlotte potatoes, peeled and sliced
4 tbsp olive oil
1 onion, sliced
3 tsp mild curry powder
lime slices and coriander (cilantro) leaves, to garnish

- Boil the potatoes in salted water for 8 minutes then drain well and leave to steam dry for 2 minutes.
- Heat the oil in a large sauté pan and fry the onion for 4 minutes.
- Add the potatoes and curry powder and stir-fry for 4 minutes or until golden.
- Transfer to a hot serving plate and garnish with lime and coriander.

Curry Fried Sweet Potato

217

- Replace the potatoes with sweet potatoes, but reduce the boiling time to 6 minutes.

218

SERVES 2

Sautéed Potatoes, Courgettes and Feta

- Boil the potatoes in salted water for 8 minutes then drain well and leave to steam dry for 2 minutes.
- Heat 4 tbsp of the oil in a large sauté pan.
- Season the potatoes with plenty of salt and pepper then fry for 10 minutes, shaking the pan and stirring occasionally.
- Add the courgette slices and stir-fry for 2 more minutes then stir in the Feta and chives and serve immediately.

PREPARATION TIME 2 MINUTES

COOKING TIME 25 MINUTES

INGREDIENTS

6 tbsp olive oil
400 g / 14 oz / 2 ⅔ cup charlotte potatoes, peeled and cubed
1 courgette (zucchini), halved and thinly sliced
100 g / 3 ½ oz / ⅔ cup Feta, cubed
a small bunch chives, chopped

Sautéed Potatoes, Peppers and Feta

219

- Omit the courgette and add 2 julienned red peppers when you start frying the potatoes.

220

SERVES 4

Tuna Sashimi and Tomato Salad

- Score a cross in the top of the tomatoes and blanch them in boiling water for 30 seconds. When the skin of the tomatoes starts to curl up, remove them with a slotted spoon and dunk in a bowl of cold water.
- Peel off and discard the skins then finely chop the tomato flesh. Mix together the mirin, vinegar, sugar and sesame oil and use it to dress the tomatoes.
- Use a sharp knife to trim the tuna into 6 cm x 3 cm fillets, then cut it across the grain into 1 cm slices.
- Slice the avocado and onion and arrange everything on 4 serving plates.

PREPARATION TIME 20 MINUTES

COOKING TIME 30 SECONDS

INGREDIENTS

200 g / 7 oz / 2 cups / 1 ⅓ cup sushi-grade tuna loin
1 avocado, peeled and stoned
1 red onion, peeled and halved

FOR THE TOMATO SALAD
6 tomatoes
1 tbsp rice wine vinegar (mirin)
1 tbsp rice vinegar
1 tsp caster (superfine) sugar
1 tsp sesame oil

Sashimi Medley

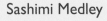

221

- Follow the method above to cut sushi-grade salmon and sea bass into sashimi as well.

SERVES 2

Almond and Olive Tapenade Crostini

222

Salsa Verde Crostini

223

- Omit the almonds and add 3 tbsp each of chopped flat leaf parsley and basil.

Black Olive Tapenade Crostini

224

- Omit the almonds and mint and replace the green olives with stoned kalamata olives.

PREPARATION TIME 10 MINUTES

COOKING TIME 4 MINUTES

INGREDIENTS

2 tbsp blanched almonds
100 g / 3 ½ oz / ⅔ cup green olives, pitted
3 tbsp capers
1 clove garlic, crushed
2 tbsp mint leaves, torn
2 tbsp olive oil
2 slices white bread, halved diagonally
sundried tomatoes and basil, to serve

- Put the almonds, olives and capers on a chopping board and chop them all together until coarsely chopped and evenly mixed.
- Scrape the mixture into a bowl and stir in the garlic, mint and oil then season to taste with salt and pepper.
- Toast the bread then spread the tapenade on top.
- Serve with some sundried tomatoes and basil on the side.

225

SERVES 2 # Pear, Brie and Hazelnut Toasts

- Preheat a griddle pan until smoking hot.
- Brush the bread with oil then toast it in the griddle pan for 4 minutes, turning every minute.
- Meanwhile, melt the butter in a frying pan and fry the pear slices for 4 minutes or until softened and golden.
- Arrange the pears on top of the toast and top with the Brie and hazelnuts. Sprinkle over a little cinnamon and serve immediately.

PREPARATION TIME 5 MINUTES

COOKING TIME 4 MINUTES

INGREDIENTS

1 slice wholemeal bread, halved diagonally
2 tbsp olive oil
1 tbsp butter
1 pear, peeled, cored and sliced
2 slices ripe Brie
2 tbsp hazelnuts (cob nuts), roughly chopped
½ tsp ground cinnamon

Pear and Brioche Toasts 226

- For a sweet version of this dish, replace the bread with brioche and omit the brie in favour of a drizzle of honey.

227

SERVES 4 # Smoked Scamorza Toasts

- Preheat the grill to its highest setting.
- Toast the slices of sourdough on one side under the grill.
- Turn them over and top each one with the Scamorza and a sprinkle of thyme.
- Grill for 2 more minutes or until the cheese is bubbling and the bread is toasted at the edges.

PREPARATION TIME 2 MINUTES

COOKING TIME 4 MINUTES

INGREDIENTS

4 slices sourdough bread
200 g / 7 oz / 2 cups / 2 cups smoked Scamorza
½ tsp dried thyme

Smoked Scamorza 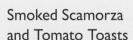 228
and Tomato Toasts

- Mix 6 quartered cherry tomatoes with the cheese and thyme before arranging on top of the bread.

229

SERVES 4

Mushroom and Spring Greens Stir Fry

PREPARATION TIME 5 MINUTES

COOKING TIME 8 MINUTES

INGREDIENTS

3 tbsp vegetable oil
2 cloves garlic, finely chopped
1 tbsp root ginger, finely chopped
200 g / 7 oz / 2 cups / 2 ⅔ cup
mushrooms, sliced
1 spring green cabbage, shredded
6 spring onions (scallions), sliced
diagonally
2 tbsp rice wine or dry sherry
1 tsp caster (superfine) sugar
1 tbsp light soy sauce

- Heat the oil in a large wok and fry the garlic, ginger and onion for 30 seconds.
- Add the mushrooms and cabbage and stir-fry for 4 minutes then add the spring onions and stir fry for 2 minutes.
- Mix the rice wine, sugar and soy together and add it to the wok.
- Stir-fry for 1 more minute then serve immediately.

Mushroom and Chinese Cabbage Stir Fry
230

- Replace the spring greens with Chinese cabbage and continue as above.

231

SERVES 4

Stir-Fried Spring Vegetables

PREPARATION TIME 2 MINUTES

COOKING TIME 8-10 MINUTES

INGREDIENTS

1 small cauliflower, broken into
florets
1 small head broccoli, broken into
florets
100 g / 3 ½ oz / 1 cup green beans
2 tbsp olive oil
1 clove garlic, crushed
1 tbsp root ginger, finely chopped
100 g / 3 ½ oz / 1 cup mange tout
(snow peas), sliced
1 carrot, coarsely grated
2 tbsp chopped coriander (cilantro)
2 tbsp light soy sauce
1 tsp sesame oil

- Steam the cauliflower, broccoli and green beans for 5 minutes or until tender.
- Heat the oil in a large wok and fry the garlic and ginger for 30 seconds.
- Add all the vegetables to the wok and stir-fry for 3 minutes then stir in the coriander, soy and sesame oil.
- Serve immediately.

Stir-Fried Pork with Spring Vegetables
232

- Add 100 g of very thinly sliced pork tenderloin to the wok after adding the garlic and ginger.

Tomato and Bacon Open Sandwich

233

SERVES 2

Tomato and Smoked Salmon Open Sandwich

234

- Omit the bacon and arrange 75 g of cold smoked salmon with the tomatoes.

Bacon and Egg Open Sandwich

235

- Omit the tomatoes. Mash 2 hard-boiled eggs with 2 tbsp of mayonnaise and spoon on to the bread before topping with the crispy bacon.

PREPARATION TIME 5 MINUTES

COOKING TIME 6 MINUTES

INGREDIENTS

4 rashers smoked streaky bacon
2 slices sourdough bread
2 tomatoes
½ clove garlic
2 tbsp olive oil
a handful of rocket (arugula) leaves

- Preheat the grill to its highest setting.
- Grill the bacon and sourdough for 3 minutes on each side or until the bread is toasted and the bacon is crisp.
- Meanwhile, cut the tomatoes in half then scrape out and discard the seeds. Cut the flesh into strips.
- When the bread is ready, rub it with garlic and drizzle with olive oil then arrange the bacon, tomatoes and rocket on top.

236

SERVES 4

Stir-Fried Noodles with Vegetables

PREPARATION TIME 5 MINUTES

COOKING TIME 15 MINUTES

INGREDIENTS

200 g / 7 oz / 2 cups / 2 ⅔ cup thin egg noodles
3 tbsp vegetable oil
1 courgette (zucchini), halved and sliced
½ aubergine (eggplant), sliced
½ jar sundried tomatoes in oil, drained
2 cloves garlic, crushed
flat leaf parsley, to garnish

- Cook the noodles in boiling salted water according to the packet instructions or until al dente, then drain well.
- Heat the oil in a large wok and fry the courgette and aubergine for 5 minutes or until browned.
- Add the sundried tomatoes and garlic and stir-fry for 2 minutes then add the drained noodles and stir-fry for a final minute.
- Divide between 4 warm bowls and serve, garnished with parsley.

Stir-Fried Noodles with Oyster Sauce

237

- Omit the tomatoes and add a sliced red pepper to the wok when you fry the courgette and aubergine. Add 3 tbsp of oyster sauce to the wok when you add the noodles.

238

SERVES 4

Cherry Tomato Gratin

PREPARATION TIME 10 MINUTES

COOKING TIME 30 MINUTES

INGREDIENTS

2 slices stale sourdough bread
1 clove garlic, finely chopped
½ tsp smoked paprika
a small bunch parsley, leaves only
400 g / 14 oz / 2 ⅔ cup cherry tomatoes
3 tbsp olive oil

- Preheat the oven to 200°C (180° fan), 390 F, gas 6.
- Tear the bread into chunks and put it in a food processor with the garlic, paprika and half of the parsley.
- Pulse until roughly chopped then season with salt and pepper.
- Arrange the tomatoes in a baking dish and sprinkle the breadcrumb mixture over the top.
- Drizzle with olive oil then bake for 30 minutes or until golden brown.
- Divide between 4 warm bowls and scatter over the rest of the parsley.

Tomato and Mozzarella Gratin

239

- Add 150 g of cubed mozzarella to the cherry tomatoes before sprinkling over the breadcrumbs.

240

SERVES 4 Red Mullet and Coppa Crostini

- To make the vinaigrette, stir the grapefruit, shallot and parsley together then whisk in the oil. Season to taste with salt and pepper.
- Heat the oil in a large frying pan. Season the red mullet fillets with salt and pepper and wrap each one in half a sheet of Coppa.
- Fry the fish, skin side down, for 2 minutes.
- Turn the fillets over then turn off the heat and leave them to cook in the heat of the pan for 1 minute.
- While the fish is cooking, toast the bread.
- Arrange the mullet on top of the crostini and drizzle over the vinaigrette. Garnish with mixed salad leaves.

PREPARATION TIME 10 MINUTES

COOKING TIME 4 MINUTES

INGREDIENTS

2 tbsp olive oil
8 red mullet fillets
4 slices Coppa ham, halved
8 slices baguette
mixed salad leaves to serve

FOR THE SALSA

4 grapefruit segments, skinned and chopped
1 shallot, finely chopped
1 tbsp flat leaf parsley, finely chopped
2 tbsp extra virgin olive oil

Sea Bass and Prosciutto Crostini 241

- Replace the red mullet with 4 sea bass fillets, cut in half diagonally. Replace the coppa with prosciutto.

242

SERVES 2 Pickled Herring and Vegetables

- Toast the ciabatta slices and top with the sundried tomatoes and aubergine then lay a herring fillet on top of each one.
- Mix the garlic and chervil with the vinegar and oil and drizzle it over the top, then garnish with chervil sprigs.

PREPARATION TIME 2 MINUTES

COOKING TIME 4 MINUTES

INGREDIENTS

4 slices ciabatta
4 pickled herring fillets
1 jar sundried tomatoes in oil, drained
1 jar preserved aubergines (eggplants) in oil, drained
½ clove garlic, crushed
1 tbsp chervil, finely chopped, plus extra sprigs to garnish
1 tsp white wine vinegar
1 tbsp olive oil

Pickled Herring and Coleslaw Toasts 243

- Replace the preserved vegetables and dressing with 4 tbsp of coleslaw.

244

SERVES 4

Spinach and Walnut Bruschetta

Spinach and Stilton Bruschetta

245

- Replace the goat's cheese with an equal quantity of Stilton.

Florentine Bruschetta

246

- Omit the goat's cheese and walnuts and add a poached egg to the top of each bruschetta.

PREPARATION TIME 4 MINUTES

COOKING TIME 4 MINUTES

....

INGREDIENTS

100 g / 3 ½ oz / 1 ⅓ cups baby leaf spinach
4 slices walnut bread
1 clove garlic, halved
2 tbsp walnut oil
50 g / 1 ¾ oz / ⅓ cup goats' cheese, cubed
2 tbsp walnuts, roughly chopped

- Heat a saucepan on the hob and wash the spinach, then put it in the pan and cover with a lid.
- Let it steam for 2 minutes, then tip it into a sieve to drain off any excess liquid.
- Toast the walnut bread then rub with the halved garlic clove and drizzle with walnut oil.
- Arrange the hot spinach on top and dot over the cheese and walnuts.

247

SERVES 4

Yakitori Chicken

- Put 16 wooden skewers in a bowl of water and leave to soak for 20 minutes.
- Meanwhile, mix together the mirin, sake, soy and sugar and massage it into the chicken pieces.
- Leave to marinate for 20 minutes.
- Prepare a barbeque or heat a griddle pan until smoking hot.
- Thread the chicken onto the skewers then cook them for 4 minutes on each side or until they are golden brown and cooked through.

PREPARATION TIME 20 MINUTES

COOKING TIME 8 MINUTES

INGREDIENTS

1 tbsp rice wine vinegar (mirin)
1 tbsp sake
1 tbsp soy sauce
2 tsp caster (superfine) sugar
8 boneless chicken thighs, cubed

Yakitori Pork Belly

248

- Replace the chicken thighs with 450 g of cubed skinless pork belly.

249

SERVES 4

Coddled Eggs with Bacon and Shallots

- Preheat the oven to 180°C (160° fan), 355 F, gas 4.
- Fry the bacon and shallot in the oil for 2 minutes then stir in the tarragon and crème fraiche.
- Divide half the mixture between 4 ramekin dishes and crack an egg into each one, then top with the rest of the crème fraiche mixture.
- Put the ramekins in a roasting tin and add enough boiling water to the tin to come half way up the side of the ramekins.
- Bake for 15 minutes or until the eggs are cooked to your liking, then serve immediately.

PREPARATION TIME 5 MINUTES

COOKING TIME 18 MINUTES

INGREDIENTS

2 rashers smoked streaky bacon, thinly sliced
1 shallot, halved and thinly sliced
1 tbsp olive oil
1 tbsp tarragon, chopped
150 g / 5 ½ oz / ⅔ cup crème fraiche
4 large eggs

Coddled Eggs with Smoked Salmon

250

- Omit the bacon and shallots and add 75 g of chopped smoked salmon when you stir in the tarragon.

251

SERVES 4

Surimi and Sweetcorn Salad

PREPARATION TIME 5 MINUTES

INGREDIENTS

8 surimi or crab sticks, sliced
400 g / 14 oz / 4 cups canned
sweetcorn, drained
1 green pepper, cubed
4 cherry tomatoes, diced

FOR THE DRESSING

1 lemon, juiced
3 tbsp olive oil

- Mix the surimi with the sweetcorn and peppers and divide between the bowls.
- Top each one with a sliced cherry tomato.
- Put the lemon juice and oil in a jar with a pinch of salt and pepper and shake to emulsify.
- Drizzle the dressing over the salads and serve immediately.

Surimi and Sweetcorn Mayonnaise

252

- Replace the dressing with 2 tbsp of mayonnaise and stir to coat the surimi and vegetables.

253

SERVES 2

Courgette and Goats' Cheese Omelette

PREPARATION TIME 5 MINUTES

COOKING TIME 8 MINUTES

INGREDIENTS

1 courgette (zucchini), coarsely
grated
4 large eggs, beaten
50 g / 1 ¾ oz / ⅓ cup goats' cheese,
crumbled
2 tbsp olive oil
flat leaf parsley, to garnish

- Wrap the grated courgette in a clean tea towel and squeeze to get rid of any excess moisture.
- Stir it into the eggs with the goat's cheese and season well with salt and pepper.
- Heat half the oil in a frying pan and pour in half the egg mixture.
- Shake the pan over a medium heat until the eggs set into a thin omelette.
- Use a palette knife to transfer the omelette to a warm plate and cook the second one in the same way.
- Garnish with flat leaf parsley and serve immediately.

Courgette, Feta and Mint Omelette

254

- Replace the goat's cheese with cubes of Feta and add 1 tbsp thinly sliced mint leaves.

255

SERVES 4

Tuna, Green Pepper and Tomato Salad

Tuna and White Asparagus Salad

256

- Replace the green pepper with 200 g of canned white asparagus.

Tuna, Olive and Tomato Salad

257

- Replace the green pepper with 75 g of stoned kalamata olives.

PREPARATION TIME 5 MINUTES

INGREDIENTS

1 lettuce, leaves separated
2 jars white tuna in olive oil, drained and flaked
1 green pepper, thinly sliced
4 tomatoes, skinned and cut into wedges
2 tbsp olive oil
1 tbsp lemon juice
½ tsp cracked black pepper

- Arrange the lettuce in 4 serving bowls and arrange the tuna, peppers and tomatoes on top.
- Whisk together the oil and lemon juice with the cracked black pepper and a pinch of salt then drizzle it over the salads.

Haloumi and Parsley Omelette

258

SERVES 1

PREPARATION TIME 1 MINUTES

COOKING TIME 4 MINUTES

....

INGREDIENTS

3 large eggs
2 tbsp flat leaf parsley
1 tbsp butter
50 g / 1 ¾ oz / ½ cup Haloumi, cubed
½ tsp pink peppercorns, crushed

- Break the eggs into a jug with a pinch of salt and pepper and beat them gently to break up the yolks.
- Stir in the parsley and Haloumi.
- Heat the butter in a non-stick frying pan until sizzling then pour in the eggs.
- Cook over a medium heat until the eggs start to set around the outside. Use a spatula to draw the sides of the omelette into the centre and tilt the pan to fill the gaps with more liquid egg.
- Repeat the process until the top of the omelette is just set then sprinkle over the pink peppercorns.

Tofu and Parsley Omelette

259

- Replace the Haloumi with cubed firm tofu that has been fried until golden in a little olive oil.

Creamy Tomato Soup

260

SERVES 4

PREPARATION TIME 10 MINUTES

COOKING TIME 30 MINUTES

....

INGREDIENTS

400 g / 14 oz / 2 ½ cup tomatoes
2 tbsp olive oil
1 onion, finely chopped
2 cloves garlic, crushed
1 tbsp tomato puree
1 litre / 1 pint 15 fl. oz / 4 cups
vegetable stock
2 tbsp crème fraiche
2 tbsp flat leaf parsley, chopped

- Score a cross in the top of the tomatoes and blanch them in boiling water for 30 seconds.
- Plunge them into cold water then peel off the skins.
- Cut the tomatoes in half and remove the seeds, then cut the flesh into small cubes.
- Heat the oil in a saucepan and fry the onion for 5 minutes or until softened. Add the garlic and cook for 2 more minutes then stir in the tomatoes and tomato puree.
- Pour in the vegetable stock and bring to the boil.
- Simmer for 20 minutes then stir in the crème fraiche and blend until smooth with an emersion blender.
- Try the soup and adjust the seasoning with salt and pepper.
- Stir in the parsley then ladle into warm bowls.

Tomato and Basil Soup

261

- Replace the parsley with a small bunch of roughly chopped basil.

262
SERVES 4 Beetroot and Tomato Soup

- Heat the oil in a saucepan and fry the onion for 5 minutes or until softened. Add the garlic and cook for 2 more minutes then stir in the tomatoes and beetroot.
- Pour in the vegetable stock and bring to the boil.
- Simmer for 10 minutes then blend until smooth with an emersion blender.
- Try the soup and adjust the seasoning with salt and pepper.
- Ladle into warm bowls and serve immediately.

PREPARATION TIME 5 MINUTES

COOKING TIME 20 MINUTES

INGREDIENTS

2 tbsp olive oil
1 onion, finely chopped
2 cloves garlic, crushed
200 g / 7 oz / 2 cups / 1 cup canned tomatoes, chopped
250 g / 9 oz / 1 cup cooked beetroot, cubed
500 ml / 18 fl. oz / 2 cups vegetable stock

Beetroot, Tomato and Feta Soup   263

- Add 100 g of Feta cheese to the soup in small cubes just before serving.

264
SERVES 4 Nettle Soup

- Heat the oil in a saucepan and fry the onion for 5 minutes or until softened. Add the garlic and cook for 2 more minutes then stir in the nettles.
- Pour in the vegetable stock and bring to the boil, then add salt and pepper to taste.
- Ladle into 4 warm bowls and serve immediately.

PREPARATION TIME 5 MINUTES

COOKING TIME 10 MINUTES

INGREDIENTS

2 tbsp olive oil
1 onion, finely chopped
2 cloves garlic, crushed
150 g / 5 ½ oz / 5 cups stinging nettles, chopped
1 litre / 1 pint 16 fl. oz / 4 cups vegetable stock

Watercress Soup   265

- Replace the nettles with an equal weight of watercress and blend with an emersion blender before serving.

266

SERVES 4

Spring Vegetable Soup

Creamy Spring Vegetable Soup

267

- Double the amount of crème fraiche and blend the soup to a smooth puree with an emersion blender.

Ham and Spring Vegetable Soup

268

- Replace the vegetable stock with ham stock and add 100 g of finely shredded cooked ham when you stir in the crème fraiche.

PREPARATION TIME 5 MINUTES

COOKING TIME 25 MINUTES

....

INGREDIENTS

2 tbsp olive oil
1 onion, finely chopped
2 cloves garlic, crushed
4 small new potatoes, quartered
100 g / 3 ½ oz / 1 cup asparagus spears, chopped
100 g / 3 ½ oz / 1 cup mange tout (snow peas), chopped
100 g / 3 ½ oz / 1 cup cabbage, shredded
100 g / 3 ½ oz / ⅔ cup fresh peas
1 litre / 1 pint 16 fl. oz / 4 cups vegetable stock
2 tbsp crème fraiche
2 tbsp flat leaf parsley, chopped
lemon wedges, to serve

- Heat the oil in a saucepan and fry the onion for 5 minutes or until softened. Add the garlic and cook for 2 more minutes then stir in the vegetables.
- Pour in the vegetable stock and bring to the boil.
- Simmer for 15 minutes then stir in the crème fraiche and parsley.
- Try the soup and adjust the seasoning with salt and pepper.
- Ladle the soup into 4 warm bowls and serve each one with a lemon wedge for squeezing over.

269

SERVES 4

Speedy Fish Soup

- Heat the oil in a saucepan and fry the onion for 5 minutes or until softened. Add the garlic and cook for 2 more minutes then stir in the tomato puree and Pernod.
- Add the mullet fillets to the pan, pour in the vegetable stock and bring to a simmer.
- Simmer for 3 minutes, then remove a few of the mullet fillets from the pan with a slotted spoon and reserve.
- Stir in the crème fraiche and blend until smooth with an emersion blender.
- Try the soup and adjust the seasoning with salt and pepper then return the whole fillets to the pan.
- Ladle into 4 warm bowls and garnish with thyme and bay leaves.

PREPARATION TIME 10 MINUTES

COOKING TIME 30 MINUTES

INGREDIENTS

2 tbsp olive oil
1 onion, finely chopped
2 cloves garlic, crushed
2 tbsp tomato puree
2 tbsp Pernod
250 g / 9 oz / 1 ½ cup red mullet fillets
1 litre / 1 pint 16 fl. oz / 4 cups fish stock
4 tbsp crème fraiche
thyme and bay leaves, to garnish

Speedy Crab Soup   270

- Replace the red mullet with an equal quantity of fresh crab meat and reduce the simmering time to 1 minute.

271

SERVES 4

Chicken and Coconut Milk Soup

- Heat the oil in a wok and fry the curry paste and lime leaves for 1 minute.
- Pour in the coconut milk and stock and bring to the boil.
- Add the chicken and cabbage and simmer for 5 minutes.
- Season to taste with the caster (superfine) sugar and fish sauce,
  then ladle into warm bowls.

PREPARATION TIME 2 MINUTES

COOKING TIME 8 MINUTES

INGREDIENTS

2 tbsp vegetable oil
1 tbsp Thai yellow curry paste
2 fresh or frozen lime leaves, shredded
400 ml / 14 fl. oz / 1 ⅔ cups coconut milk
400 ml / 14 fl. oz / 1 ⅔ cups chicken stock
2 skinless chicken breasts, cut into chunks
½ Chinese cabbage, cut into chunks
1 tsp caster (superfine) sugar
1 tbsp fish sauce

Salmon and Coconut Milk Soup   272

- Substitute the chicken with 200 g skinless salmon fillet, cut into cubes, and reduce the simmering time to 2 minutes.

273

SERVES 4

Carrot Soup with Beetroot Crisps

PREPARATION TIME 5 MINUTES

COOKING TIME 40 MINUTES

....

INGREDIENTS

2 tbsp olive oil
1 onion, finely chopped
400 g / 14 oz / 2 ¾ cup carrots, peeled and chopped
2 cloves garlic, crushed
1 litre / 1 pint 16 fl. oz / 4 cups vegetable stock
2 tbsp crème fraiche
25 g / 1 oz / 1 cup beetroot crisps

- Heat the oil in a saucepan and fry the onion and carrot for 10 minutes.
- Add the garlic and cook for 2 more minutes then pour in the vegetable stock and bring to the boil.
- Simmer for 25 minutes then stir in the crème fraiche and blend until smooth with an emersion blender.
- Try the soup and adjust the seasoning with salt and pepper, then ladle into warm bowls.
- Crush some of the beetroot crisps and sprinkle on top, then garnish with a few whole crisps.

Carrot and Coriander Soup

274

- Fry 1 tsp of crushed coriander seeds with the onions and stir in 2 tbsp chopped fresh coriander leaves after the soup has been pureed.

275

SERVES 4

Provencal Pistou Soup

PREPARATION TIME 10 MINUTES

COOKING TIME 18 MINUTES

....

INGREDIENTS

2 tbsp olive oil
1 onion, finely chopped
2 cloves garlic, crushed
75 g / 2 ½ oz / ½ cup green beans
75 g / 2 ½ oz / ¾ cup mange tout (snow peas), chopped
75 g / 2 ½ oz / ½ cup celery hearts, sliced
75 g / 2 ½ oz / ½ cup fresh peas
75 g / 2 ½ oz / ½ cup fresh broad beans, podded weight
200 g / 7 oz / 2 cups / ½ cup canned butter beans, drained
1 litre / 1 pint 16 fl. oz / 4 cups vegetable stock

FOR THE PISTOU

1 clove garlic, peeled
50 g / 1 ¾ oz / 1 ½ cup basil leaves, chopped
4 tbsp olive oil

- Heat the oil in a saucepan and fry the onion for 5 minutes or until softened. Add the garlic and cook for 2 more minutes then stir in the vegetables and butter beans.
- Pour in the vegetable stock and bring to the boil.
- Turn down the heat and simmer for 10 minutes.
- Meanwhile, crush the garlic with a mortar and pestle, then add the basil and a pinch of salt and pound to a paste. Stir in the olive oil then divide the pistou between 4 small bowls
- Try the soup and adjust the seasoning with salt and pepper.
- Ladle the soup into 4 warm bowls and serve each one with a portion of pistou for stirring in at the table.

Tuna and Pistou Soup

276

- Omit the butterbeans and add 200 g of cubed fresh tuna steak to the pan 2 minutes before the end of cooking time.

277

SERVES 4

Bacon and Onion Gratin

Mushroom and Onion Gratin

278

- Replace the bacon with 100 g of sliced button mushrooms.

Bacon and Leek Gratin

279

- Replace the onions with 2 thinly sliced leeks.

PREPARATION TIME 5 MINUTES

COOKING TIME 30 MINUTES

INGREDIENTS

600 ml / 1 pint / 2 ½ cups whole milk
3 tbsp butter
1 tbsp plain (all-purpose) flour
75 g / 2 ½ oz / ¾ cup Cheddar, grated
8 rashers of smoked bacon
1 large onion, halved and thinly sliced

- Preheat the oven to 190⁰C (170⁰ fan), 375 F, gas 5 and bring the milk to a simmer.
- Heat the butter in a small saucepan then stir in the flour and cook for 1 minute.
- Gradually incorporate the hot milk, stirring continuously to avoid any lumps forming.
- Continue to stir until it starts to bubble then stir in the cheese and season with salt and pepper.
- Arrange the bacon and onions in 4 small gratin dishes then spoon over the sauce.
- Cook the gratins in the oven for 20 minutes or until the onions are cooked.

280

SERVES 6

Chilled Cucumber and Mint Soup

PREPARATION TIME 5 MINUTES

INGREDIENTS

2 cucumbers, peeled and chopped
½ clove garlic, crushed
a small bunch mint, chopped
500 ml / 18 fl. oz / 2 cups vegetable stock
100 g / 3 ½ oz / 1 cup Feta, cubed

- Put the cucumber, garlic, mint and vegetable stock in a liquidiser and blend until smooth.
- Taste the soup and adjust the seasoning with salt and black pepper.
- Chill the soup in the fridge until you are ready to serve, then ladle into small bowls and garnish with Feta cubes.

281

SERVES 4

Baked Potatoes Stuffed with Sausage Meat

PREPARATION TIME 5 MINUTES

COOKING TIME 40 MINUTES

INGREDIENTS

4 medium baking potatoes
8 good quality pork sausages, skinned
1 tbsp wholegrain mustard
1 clove garlic, crushed

- Preheat the oven to 220⁰C (200⁰ fan), 430 F, gas 7.
- Prick the potatoes and cook them in a microwave on high for 5 minutes.
- Cut a slice off the top of the potatoes and scoop out the centres into a bowl.
- Mix it with the sausagemeat, mustard and garlic, then stuff it back into the potato shells.
- Turn the sliced-off sections cut side up and put them on top of the stuffing.
- Bake in the oven for 35 minutes or until golden brown and cooked through.

282

SERVES 4

Onion Bhajis

- Heat the oil in a deep fat fryer, according to the manufacturer's instructions, to a temperature of 180°C.
- Mix the flour with the lime zest, spices and a big pinch of salt.
- Make a well in the centre and break in the eggs, then incorporate all the flour from round the outside with a whisk.
- Stir the onions into the batter then use an ice cream scoop to portion the mixture into bhajis, dropping them straight into the hot oil, 4 at a time.
- Fry the bhajis for 1 – 2 minutes, turning halfway through, until they are crisp and golden brown.
- Transfer the bhajis to a kitchen paper lined bowl and continue with the rest of the batter.
- Sprinkle with a little sea salt to taste and serve immediately.

PREPARATION TIME 10 MINUTES

COOKING TIME 10 MINUTES

INGREDIENTS

110 g / 4 oz / ⅔ cup plain (all-purpose) flour
1 lime, zest finely grated
½ tsp cumin seeds, crushed
½ tsp coriander seeds, crushed
2 large eggs
3 red onions, halved and thinly sliced
2 - 3 litres / 3 ½ pints – 5 pints / 8-12 cups sunflower oil

Spicy Baby New Potatoes

283

SERVES 4

PREPARATION TIME 2 MINUTES

COOKING TIME 45 MINUTES

INGREDIENTS

800 g / 1 lb 12 oz / 4 ½ cups baby new potatoes
1 tsp mustard seeds
1 tsp coriander seeds

½ tsp ground cumin
½ tsp ground cinnamon
4 tbsp olive oil
coriander (cilantro) leaves, to garnish

- Preheat the oven to 200°C (180° fan), 390 F, gas 6.
- Boil the potatoes in salted water for 10 minutes then drain well and leave to steam dry for 2 minutes.
- Put the oil in a large roasting tin in the oven to heat for 2 minutes.
- Toss the potatoes with the spices and plenty of salt and pepper, then add them to the roasting tin and stir to coat in the oil.
- Roast the potatoes for 30 minutes or until golden brown then garnish with coriander leaves.

Red Curry Potatoes

284

SERVES 4

PREPARATION TIME 5 MINUTES

COOKING TIME 40 MINUTES

INGREDIENTS

800 g / 1 lb 12 oz / 4 ½ cups maris piper potatoes, peeled and cubed
2 tbsp Thai red curry paste
1 tsp mustard seeds

coriander (cilantro) leaves and strips of green chilli, to garnish

- Preheat the oven to 220°C (200° fan), 430 F, gas 7 and put a large roasting tin in to heat.
- Boil the potatoes in salted water for 8 minutes then drain well and leave to steam dry for 2 minutes.
- Mix the curry paste and mustard seeds together then brush it over the potatoes.
- Put the potatoes into the hot roasting tin and roast for 30 minutes or until golden and toasted at the edges, turning occasionally.
- Garnish with coriander leaves and green chilli just before serving.

285

SERVES 4

Aubergine and Courgettes with Walnuts

PREPARATION TIME 5 MINUTES

COOKING TIME 30 MINUTES

....

INGREDIENTS

4 tbsp olive oil
1 onion, finely chopped
1 aubergine (eggplant) (eggplant),
finely chopped
2 courgettes (zucchini), finely
chopped
1 clove garlic, crushed
100 g / 3 ½ oz / ¾ cup walnuts,
chopped
2 tbsp flat leaf parsley, chopped

- Heat the olive oil in a large sauté pan and fry the onion, aubergine and courgette with a pinch of salt for 25 minutes, stirring occasionally.
- When any liquid that comes out of the vegetables has evaporated and they start to turn golden, add the garlic and cook for 2 more minutes.
- Stir in the walnuts and parsley then season to taste with salt and pepper.

Sautéed Aubergine with Pine Nuts

286

- Replace the walnuts with toasted pine nuts.

287

SERVES 4

Courgettes Stuffed with Goats' Cheese

PREPARATION TIME 20 MINUTES

COOKING TIME 8 MINUTES

....

INGREDIENTS

4 courgettes (zucchini)
150 g / 5 ½ oz / 1 cup fresh goats'
cheese
1 tsp lemon zest, finely grated
2 tbsp chives, chopped

TO SERVE
4 large tomatoes, diced
2 tbsp olive oil
½ lemon, juiced
basil leaves, to garnish

- Cut the ends off the courgettes and remove the middles with an apple corer.
- Mix the goats' cheese with the lemon zest and chives and plenty of black pepper, then pack it into the cavities.
- Steam the courgettes for 8 minutes or until tender, then slice and serve on a bed of tomatoes.
- Drizzle over the oil and lemon and garnish with basil.

Courgettes Stuffed with Dolcelatte

288

- Replace the goat's cheese with an equal amount of Dolcelatte.

289

SERVES 4

Carrots with Cumin and Paprika Butter

- Cook the carrots in boiling salted water for 12 minutes or until tender. Drain well.
- Meanwhile, beat the butter with the spices and a pinch of salt until smooth.
- Toss the carrots with the spiced butter and divide between 4 warm bowls.

PREPARATION TIME 5 MINUTES

COOKING TIME 12 MINUTES

INGREDIENTS

450 g / 1 lb / 3 cups carrots, sliced
50 g / 1 ¾ oz / ¼ cup butter, softened
1 tsp ground cumin
½ tsp smoked paprika

Carrots with Coriander and Garlic Butter

290

- Substitute the cumin and paprika in the butter with 1 tsp of ground coriander and 1 tsp of crushed garlic.

291

SERVES 4

Jacket Potatoes with Chilli Con Carne

- Preheat the oven to 220°C (200° fan), 430 F, gas 7.
- Heat the oil in a large saucepan and fry the onion and pepper for 3 minutes. Add the garlic and Cayenne and cook for 2 minutes, then add the mince.
- Fry the mince until it starts to brown then add the chopped tomatoes, stock and kidney beans.
- Cook the chilli con carne for 30 minutes, stirring occasionally, until the mince is tender and the sauce has thickened a little.
- Meanwhile, prick the potatoes and microwave for 5 minutes. Transfer to the oven a bake for 25 minutes.
- Taste the chilli for seasoning and add salt and freshly ground black pepper as necessary.
- Cut the potatoes in half and spoon over the chilli then sprinkle with coriander.

PREPARATION TIME 5 MINUTES

COOKING TIME 40 MINUTES

INGREDIENTS

2 tbsp olive oil
1 red onion, chopped
1 red pepper, chopped
2 cloves garlic, crushed
½ tsp Cayenne pepper
450 g / 1 lb / 2 cups minced beef
400 g / 14 oz / 2 cups canned tomatoes, chopped
200 ml / 7 fl. oz / ¾ cup beef stock
400 g / 14 oz / 4 cups canned kidney beans, drained
4 baking potatoes
1 tbsp coriander (cilantro) leaves, chopped

Chilli Con Carne in a Roll

292

- Try serving the chilli con carne in hollowed out bread rolls for an even quicker dinner.

293

SERVES 4

Stuffed Courgettes

Crispy Stuffed Courgettes

294

- Top the sausagemeat mixture with a layer of fresh breadcrumbs and drizzle with olive oil before baking for a crispy topping.

Chorizo Stuffed Courgettes

295

- Replace the sausages with soft fresh cooking chorizo.

PREPARATION TIME 15 MINUTES

COOKING TIME 30 MINUTES

INGREDIENTS

4 courgettes (zucchini)
6 good quality pork sausages, skinned
2 tbsp crème fraiche
1 tsp lemon zest, finely grated
2 tbsp flat leaf parsley, chopped

- Preheat the oven to 220°C (200° fan), 430 F, gas 7.
- Cut the courgettes in half and use a melon baller to scoop out the middles.
- Mix the sausagemeat with the crème fraiche, lemon zest and parsley, then spoon it into the courgette cavities.
- Arrange the courgettes in a roasting tin and bake in the oven for 30 minutes or until golden brown and cooked through.

296

SERVES 4 Boiled Potatoes with Garlic Mayonnaise

- Boil the potatoes in salted water for 12 minutes or until tender then drain well and arrange on a warm serving plate.
- Mix the mayonnaise with the garlic and lemon juice and spoon the mixture over the potatoes.
- Sprinkle over the parsley and serve.

PREPARATION TIME 5 MINUTES

COOKING TIME 40 MINUTES

INGREDIENTS

800 g / 1 lb 12 oz / 4 ½ cup maris piper potatoes, peeled and cubed
4 tbsp mayonnaise
1 clove garlic, crushed
1 tbsp lemon juice
2 tbsp flat leaf parsley, chopped

Boiled Potatoes with Stilton Mayonnaise   297

- Omit the garlic and lemon juice and stir 75 g of crumbled Stilton into the mayonnaise.

298

SERVES 4 Tabbouleh

- Put the bulgur wheat in a bowl and pour over enough boiling water to just cover it. Cover the bowl tightly and leave to soak for 15 minutes.
- Tip the bulgur wheat into a sieve and run it under the cold tap to cool. Drain well.
- Stir the parsley, tomato and shallot into the bulgur and dress with the lemon juice and olive oil.
- Taste for seasoning and adjust with sea salt and black pepper.

PREPARATION TIME 20 MINUTES

INGREDIENTS

150 g / 5 ½ oz / ⅔ cup bulgur wheat
a small bunch flat leaf parsley, finely chopped
2 tomatoes, deseeded and finely chopped
2 shallots, finely chopped
1 lemon, juiced
2 tbsp extra virgin olive oil

Middle Eastern Tabbouleh   299

- For a more traditional Tabbouleh, halve the amount of bulgur wheat and increase the amount of finely chopped parsley to 100 g.

300

SERVES 4

Vegetable Soup

PREPARATION TIME 5 MINUTES

COOKING TIME 25 MINUTES

....

INGREDIENTS

2 tbsp olive oil
1 onion, finely chopped
2 cloves garlic, crushed
4 small new potatoes, quartered
100 g / 3 ½ oz / ¾ cup carrots, finely chopped
100 g / 3 ½ oz / ⅔ cup sweetcorn
100 g / 3 ½ oz / ⅔ cup fresh peas
600 ml / 1 pint vegetable stock
400 g / 14 oz / 2 ½ cup canned tomatoes, chopped

- Heat the oil in a saucepan and fry the onion for 5 minutes or until softened. Add the garlic and cook for 2 more minutes then stir in the vegetables.
- Pour in the vegetable stock and tomatoes and bring to the boil.
- Simmer for 15 minutes then ladle half of the soup into a liquidiser and blend until smooth.
- Return the blended soup to the pan, stir well and season with salt and pepper.

Chorizo and Vegetable Soup

301

- Add 150 g of chorizo in small cubes to the onions when you fry them.

302

SERVES 4

Deep Fried Mozzarella

PREPARATION TIME 15 MINUTES

COOKING TIME 4-5 MINUTES

....

INGREDIENTS

4 tbsp plain (all-purpose) flour
1 egg, beaten
75 g / 2 ½ oz / ½ cup panko breadcrumbs
4 mozzarella balls, sliced
2 - 3 litres / 3 ½ pints – 5 pints / 8-12 cups sunflower oil
rocket (arugula) leaves to serve

- Put the flour, egg and panko breadcrumbs in 3 separate bowls.
- Dip the mozzarella in the flour, then the egg, then the breadcrumbs, making sure it is well coated.
- Heat the oil in a deep fat fryer, according to the manufacturer's instructions, to a temperature of 180°C.
- Lower the mozzarella slices in the fryer basket and cook for 4 – 5 minutes or until crisp and golden brown.
- Line a large bowl with a thick layer of kitchen paper and when they are ready, tip them into the bowl to remove any excess oil.
- Sprinkle with a little sea salt to taste and serve immediately on a bed of rocket.

Deep-Fried Parmesan Mozzarella

303

- Add 2 tbsp finely grated Parmesan to the breadcrumbs before dipping the Mozzarella slices.

304

SERVES 4

Battered Prawns

Beer-Battered Prawns 305

- Replace one of the eggs with 50 ml of beer.

Battered Onion Rings 306

- Cut 2 peeled onions into thick rings and use instead of the prawns.

PREPARATION TIME 10 MINUTES

COOKING TIME 2-4 MINUTES

INGREDIENTS

110 g / 4 oz / ½ cup plain (all-purpose) flour
2 large eggs
24 raw king prawns (shrimps), peeled with tails left intact
2 - 3 litres / 3 ½ pints – 5 pints / 8-12 cups sunflower oil

- Heat the oil in a deep fat fryer, according to the manufacturer's instructions, to a temperature of 180°C.
- Mix the flour with a big pinch of salt and pepper.
- Make a well in the centre and break in the eggs, then incorporate all the flour from round the outside with a whisk.
- Hold the prawns by their tails and dip them into the batter then drop them straight into the hot oil.
- Fry for 1 – 2 minutes, turning halfway through, until they are crisp and golden brown.
- Transfer the prawns to a kitchen paper lined bowl to absorb the excess oil then serve immediately.

307

SERVES 4

Roasted Vegetable Tapenade

PREPARATION TIME 10 MINUTES

COOKING TIME 25 MINUTES

....

INGREDIENTS

1 courgette (zucchini), cubed
1 aubergine (eggplant) (eggplant), cubed
1 red pepper, cubed
1 yellow pepper, cubed
4 tbsp olive oil
50 g / 1 ¾ oz / ⅓ cup mixed olives, pitted
1 tbsp capers
toasted bread to serve

- Preheat the oven to 180°C (160° fan), 355 F, gas 4.
- Toss the vegetables with half of the oil and season with salt and pepper then roast for 25 minutes.
- Tip the vegetables into a food processor and add the olives, capers and the rest of the oil.
- Pulse until finely chopped and well mixed then spoon into a bowl.
- Serve with toasted bread to spoon it on to.

Pickled Vegetable Tapenade

308

- Replace the roasted vegetables with 100 g pickled beetroot slices and 100 g of sweet dill pickles.

309

SERVES 4

French Onion Soup

PREPARATION TIME 5 MINUTES

COOKING TIME 40 MINUTES

....

INGREDIENTS

2 tbsp olive oil
3 onions, sliced
2 cloves garlic, crushed
1 litre / 1 pint 16 fl. oz / 4 cups vegetable stock

FOR THE CROUTES
1 baguette, sliced
100 g / 3 ½ oz / 1 cup Gruyere, grated

- Heat the oil in a saucepan and fry the onions for 20 minutes. Add the garlic and cook for 2 more minutes then stir in the vegetable stock and bring to the boil.
- Simmer for 15 minutes then taste the soup and adjust the seasoning with salt and pepper.
- Meanwhile, preheat the grill to its highest setting.
- Toast the baguette slices on one side under the grill then turn them over and sprinkle with cheese.
- Grill the other side until the cheese is golden and bubbling.
- Ladle the soup into 4 warm bowls and float the croutes on top.

Beer and Onion Soup

310

- Replace 300 ml of the vegetable stock with 300 ml of beer and spread the baguette slices with grain mustard before topping with the cheese.

311
MAKES 20-24 Goats' Cheese Samosas

- Preheat the oven to 180°C (160° fan), 355 F, gas 4 and grease a large baking tray.
- Mash the goats' cheese with the garlic, lemon zest and parsley and season with salt and pepper.
- Cut the pile of filo sheets in half then take one halved sheet and brush it with melted butter.
- Arrange a heaped teaspoon of goat's cheese at one end then fold the corner across and triangle-fold it into a samosa shape.
- Transfer the samosa to the baking tray and repeat with the rest of the filo and goats' cheese.
- Bake the samosas for 12 – 15 minutes or until the filo is crisp and golden brown.
- Serve on a bed of spinach.

PREPARATION TIME 25 MINUTES

COOKING TIME 12-15 MINUTES

INGREDIENTS

200 g / 7 oz / 2 cups / 1 ¼ cup fresh goats' cheese
1 clove garlic, crushed
1 lemon, zest finely grated
2 tbsp flat leaf parsley, chopped
225 g / 8 oz filo pastry
100 g / 3 ½ oz / ½ cup butter, melted
baby leaf spinach, to serve

Goat's Cheese and Walnut Samosas
312

- Add 50 g of chopped walnuts to the goat's cheese mixture.

313
SERVES 4 Deep Fried Fish Balls

- Put the fish, spring onions, garlic, olives and spices in a food processor with a big pinch of salt and whizz to a sticky paste.
- Heat the oil in a deep fat fryer, according to the manufacturer's instructions, to a temperature of 180°C.
- Use an ice cream scoop to portion the mixture into balls and drop them straight into the hot oil.
- Fry the fish balls for 3 – 4 minutes, turning once, or until they are golden brown.
- Line a large bowl with a thick layer of kitchen paper and when they are ready, tip them into the bowl to remove any excess oil.
- Sprinkle with a little sea salt to taste and serve immediately on a bed of lettuce.

PREPARATION TIME 15 MINUTES

COOKING TIME 3-4 MINUTES

INGREDIENTS

400 g / 14 oz / 2 cups white fish fillets
4 spring onions (scallions), chopped
1 clove garlic, crushed
50 g / 1 ¾ oz / ⅓ cup black olives, pitted
1 tsp ground cumin
½ tsp ground coriander
½ tsp ground cinnamon
2 - 3 litres / 3 ½ pints – 5 pints / 8-12 cups sunflower oil
lettuce leaves, to serve

Thai Fish Balls
314

- Replace the olives and spices with 1 tbsp of Thai red curry paste.

315

SERVES 4

Stuffed Vine Tomatoes

Stuffed Celery Sticks   316

- Cut 4 celery sticks into short lengths and fill the cavities with the stuffing mixtures.

Stuffed Avocados   317

- Cut 4 avocados in half and fill 4 halves with each stuffing. Serve each person with one of each kind.

PREPARATION TIME 15 MINUTES

INGREDIENTS

4 tomato vines
200 g / 7 oz / 2 cups / 1 cup cream cheese
4 tbsp chives, chopped
75 g / 2 ½ oz / ½ cup smoked salmon, chopped
75 g / 2 ½ oz / ½ cup cooked ham, chopped

- Cut the tops off the tomatoes and scoop out and discard the seeds.
- Mix the cream cheese with the chives and season with salt and pepper, then divide it into 2 separate bowls.
- Add the salmon to one and the ham to the other then use the mixture to stuff the tomatoes.
- Transfer to a serving plate and serve immediately.

318

SERVES 4

Potato Wedges and Sprouts

- Preheat the oven to 220°C (200° fan), 430 F, gas 7.
- Put the oil in a large roasting tin and heat in the oven for 5 minutes.
- Carefully tip the potato wedges into the pan and turn to coat in the oil, then sprinkle with salt and pepper and bake for 15 minutes.
- Meanwhile, wrap the sprouts in bacon and secure with cocktails sticks.
- When the 15 minutes are up, add the sprouts to the pan and stir to coat in the oil.
- Roast for another 25 minutes or until the sprouts and potatoes are cooked through.

PREPARATION TIME 5 MINUTES

COOKING TIME 40 MINUTES

INGREDIENTS

4 tbsp olive oil
800 g / 1 lb 12 oz / 4 ½ cup maris piper potatoes, cut into wedges
400 g / 14 oz / 4 cups Brussels sprouts, trimmed
200 g / 7 oz / 2 cups streaky bacon

Sprouts and Chestnuts Wrapped in Bacon

319

- Omit potatoes and halve the amount of sprouts. Use left over bacon to wrap 150 g of cooked, peeled chestnuts and roast with sprouts for 15 minutes.

320

SERVES 4

Honey and Spice Roasted Parsnips

- Preheat the oven to 180°C (160° fan), 355 F, gas 4.
- Rub the vegetables with oil sprinkle with the spices and salt then roast for 35 minutes.
- Drizzle over the honey and return to the oven for 5 minutes to glaze.

PREPARATION TIME 5 MINUTES

COOKING TIME 40 MINUTES

INGREDIENTS

450 g / 1 lb / 3 cups parsnips, halved or quartered if large
2 tbsp olive oil
2 cinnamon sticks
3 star anise
1 tsp ground cumin
2 tbsp runny honey

Honey and Spice Roasted Carrots

321

- Replace the parsnips with an equal weight of carrots and reduce the cooking time to 30 minutes.

322

SERVES 4

Roasted Carrots and Parsnips

PREPARATION TIME 5 MINUTES

COOKING TIME 35 MINUTES

....

INGREDIENTS

6 small carrots, quartered
lengthways
6 small parsnips, quartered
lengthways
2 tbsp olive oil
1 tbsp basil, chopped

- Preheat the oven to 180°C (160° fan), 355 F, gas 4.
- Rub the vegetables with oil and season with salt and pepper then roast for 35 minutes.
- Transfer the vegetables to a warm serving dish and sprinkle with chopped basil.

Roasted Beetroot
and Sweet Potato

323

- Substitute the carrots and parsnips with 6 quartered baby beetroot and a large sweet potato, cut into wedges.

324

SERVES 4

Matchstick Parsnips and Carrots

PREPARATION TIME 15 MINUTES

COOKING TIME 2-3 MINUTES

....

INGREDIENTS

2 carrots
2 parsnips
2 - 3 litres / 3 ½ pints – 5 pints / 8-12 cups sunflower oil

- Cut the carrots and parsnips into a very fine julienne with a mandolin or sharp knife.
- Heat the oil in a deep fat fryer, according to the manufacturer's instructions, to a temperature of 180°C.
- Lower the vegetable matchsticks in the fryer basket and cook for 2 – 3 minutes or until crisp and golden brown.
- Line a large bowl with a thick layer of kitchen paper and when they are ready, tip them into the bowl to remove any excess oil.
- Sprinkle with a little sea salt to taste and serve immediately.

Matchstick Potatoes

325

- Replace the carrots and parsnips with 300 g of charlotte potatoes. Dry them off well with kitchen paper after cutting.

326

MAKES 20

Goats' Cheese and Chive Canapés

Goat's Cheese and Apricot Canapés

327

- Replace the chives with 50 g of very finely chopped dried apricots.

Goat's Cheese and Tarragon Canapés

328

- Replace the chives with 4 tbsp of finely chopped French tarragon.

PREPARATION TIME 10 MINUTES

INGREDIENTS

250 g / 9 oz / 1 ¼ cup soft goats' cheese
4 tbsp chives, finely chopped

- Divide the goat's cheese into 20 pieces and roll into balls with your hands.
- Roll the balls in the chopped chives to coat in an even layer then chill in the fridge until needed.

329

SERVES 4

Piri-Piri Prawn Skewers

PREPARATION TIME 35 MINUTES

COOKING TIME 4 MINUTES

··

INGREDIENTS

3 cloves garlic, crushed
2 red chillies, finely chopped
1 tbsp flat leaf parsley, finely chopped
½ tsp smoked paprika
2 tbsp olive oil
450 g / 1 lb / 1 ¾ cup prawns (shrimps), peeled with tails intact
2 red peppers, cut into chunks
lemon wedges and crusty bread, to serve

- Mix the garlic, chilli, parsley, paprika and oil together with a pinch of salt. Put the prawns and peppers in a large freezer bag, add the piri piri marinade and massage it in. Leave to marinade for 30 minutes.
- Meanwhile, soak 12 wooden skewers in cold water for 20 minutes.
- Preheat the grill to its highest setting.
- Thread the prawns and peppers onto the skewers and grill for 2 minutes on each side or until the prawns have turned opaque.
- Serve immediately with lemon wedges and crusty bread.

Piri-Piri Chicken Skewers

330

- Replace the prawns with the same weight of skinless chicken breasts, cut into small chunks.

331

SERVES 4

Potato Wedges

PREPARATION TIME 5 MINUTES

COOKING TIME 35-40 MINUTES

··

INGREDIENTS

4 tbsp olive oil
800 g / 1 lb 12 oz / 4 ½ cup maris piper potatoes, cut into wedges

- Preheat the oven to 220°C (200° fan), 430 F, gas 7.
- Put the oil in a large roasting tin and heat in the oven for 5 minutes.
- Carefully tip the potato wedges into the pan and turn to coat in the oil, then season well with salt and black pepper.
- Bake the wedges for 35 – 40 minutes, turning them every 15 minutes.

Spicy Potato Wedges

332

- Dust the potatoes with 1 tbsp of curry powder before roasting.

333

SERVES 4 # Homemade Crisps

- Cut the potatoes into very thin slices with a mandolin or sharp knife.
- Put the slices in a bowl of cold water and leave them to soak for 25 minutes to remove some of the starch.
- Drain the potatoes and dry them completely.
- Heat the oil in a deep fat fryer, according to the manufacturer's instructions, to a temperature of 130°C.
- Lower the potatoes in the fryer basket and fry for 5 minutes so they cook through but don't brown.
- Pull up the fryer basket and increase the temperature to 190°C. Cook the crisps at the hotter temperature for 1 - 2 minutes or until crisp and golden brown.
- Line a large bowl with a thick layer of kitchen paper and when the crisps are ready, tip them into the bowl to remove any excess oil.
- Leave to cool then sprinkle with sea salt flakes and garnish with rosemary.

PREPARATION TIME 35 MINUTES

COOKING TIME 7 MINUTES

INGREDIENTS

4 large floury potatoes (eg. Maris Piper or King Edwards)
2 - 3 litres / 3 ½ pints – 5 pints / 8-12 cups sunflower oil

Salt and Vinegar Crisps 334

- Glaze the potatoes with vinegar before baking them for a classic tasting crisp.

335

SERVES 4 # Gorgonzola and Tomato Toasts

- Preheat the grill to its highest setting.
- Toast the slices of sourdough on one side under the grill.
- Turn them over and top each one with a slice of Gorgonzola, a tomato and a drizzle of olive oil.
- Grill for 3 more minutes or until the tomato is soft and the bread is toasted at the edges.
- Serve 2 toasts per person.

PREPARATION TIME 5 MINUTES

COOKING TIME 5 MINUTES

INGREDIENTS

8 slices sourdough bread
8 slices Gorgonzola
8 cherry tomatoes
olive oil, to drizzle

Mascarpone and Tomato Toasts 336

- Substitute the Gorgonzola with 150 g of Mascarpone and sprinkle the tops with a little smoked paprika before grilling.

337

SERVES 4

Potatoes Stuffed with Bacon and Cheese

Three Cheese Potatoes

338

- Omit the bacon and crème fraiche stuffing. Stir 100 g of Roquefort into 150 g of Mascarpone and spoon it into the potatoes. Top with the Raclette and finish as before.

Potatoes Stuffed with Tuna and Cheese

339

- Replace the bacon with 150 g of canned tuna.

PREPARATION TIME 10 MINUTES

COOKING TIME 25 MINUTES

INGREDIENTS

4 medium baking potatoes
150 g / 5 ½ oz / ⅔ cup streaky bacon, chopped
1 tbsp olive oil
2 tbsp crème fraiche
2 tbsp chives, chopped
4 slices Raclette cheese

- Preheat the oven to 220°C (200° fan), 430 F, gas 7.
- Prick the potatoes and cook them in a microwave on high for 5 minutes.
- Meanwhile, fry the bacon in the oil for 4 minutes then stir in the crème fraiche and chives.
- Cut a slice off the top of the potatoes and scoop out the centres with a teaspoon.
- Mix 4 tablespoon of the scooped out potato with the bacon mixture, then stuff it back into the potato shells.
- Lay a slice of Raclette over each potato then bake in the oven for 20 minutes or until golden brown.

340
SERVES 4

Prawn Cocktail in Courgette Cups

- Use a sharp paring knife to cut the tops off the courgettes in a zigzag pattern. Scoop out the centres with a teaspoon and discard.
- Mix the mayonnaise with the ketchup, paprika and lemon juice then stir in the prawns.
- Taste for seasoning and add salt and pepper as necessary.
- Spoon the prawn cocktail into the courgette cups and put the lids back on.
- Sprinkle with chopped oregano.

PREPARATION TIME 10 MINUTES

INGREDIENTS

4 round courgettes (zucchini)
200 g / 7 oz / 2 cups / ⅔ cup mayonnaise
2 tbsp tomato ketchup
½ tsp smoked paprika
1 tbsp lemon juice
200 g / 7 oz / 2 cups / ¾ cup cooked prawns (shrimps), peeled
2 tbsp oregano, chopped

Tuna Mayonnaise in Courgette Cups

341

- Omit the tomato ketchup and replace the prawns with canned tuna.

342
SERVES 6

Gazpacho Soup

- Put all of the ingredients in a liquidiser with a big pinch of salt and freshly ground black pepper and blend until smooth.
- Pass the soup through a sieve, then taste for seasoning and add more salt and pepper if necessary.
- Ladle the soup into bowls and garnish with chive flowers. Serve with small bowls of cubed vegetables that can be added to the soup like croutons.

PREPARATION TIME 10 MINUTES

INGREDIENTS

1 cucumber, peeled and chopped
4 large, ripe tomatoes, chopped
1 red pepper, chopped
½ clove of garlic, crushed
2 spring onions (scallions), finely chopped
1 tbsp sherry vinegar
100 ml / 3 ½ fl. oz / ½ cup extra virgin olive oil

TO SERVE
small cubes of onion, peppers, tomato and cucumber
chive flowers, to garnish

Spicy Gazpacho Soup

343

- Add 1 finely chopped green pepper and a few drops of Tabasco sauce to the vegetables before blending.

344

SERVES 4

Mixed Vegetable Tortilla

PREPARATION TIME 10 MINUTES

COOKING TIME 20 MINUTES

....

INGREDIENTS

4 tbsp olive oil
1 red onion, thinly sliced
1 red pepper, finely chopped
3 boiled potatoes, cooled and cubed
75 g / 2 ½ oz / ½ cup frozen peas, defrosted
6 eggs

- Heat half the oil in a non-stick frying pan and fry the onion and peppers for 5 minutes.
- Meanwhile, gently beat the eggs in a jug to break up the yolks. When the onions are ready, stir them into the eggs with the potatoes and peas and season with salt and pepper.
- Heat the rest of the oil in the frying pan then pour in the egg mixture.
- Cook over a gentle heat for 6 – 8 minutes or until the egg has set round the outside, but the centre is still a bit runny.
- Turn it out onto a plate, then slide it back into the pan and cook the other side for 4 – 6 minutes.
- Leave to cool for 5 minutes then cut into wedges and serve.

Vegetable and Anchovy Tortilla   345

- Finely chop 6 anchovy fillets in oil and add them to the vegetables. Leave out the salt when seasoning to balance the salty anchovies.

346

SERVES 4

Tortilla Espanol

PREPARATION TIME 10 MINUTES

COOKING TIME 20 MINUTES

....

INGREDIENTS

4 tbsp olive oil
1 onion, thinly sliced
4 boiled potatoes, cooled and cubed
6 eggs

- Heat half the oil in a non-stick frying pan and fry the onion with a pinch of salt and pepper for 5 minutes.
- Meanwhile, gently beat the eggs in a jug to break up the yolks. When the onions are ready, stir them into the eggs with the potatoes and season with salt and pepper.
- Heat the rest of the oil in the frying pan then pour in the egg mixture.
- Cook over a gentle heat for 6 – 8 minutes or until the egg has set round the outside, but the centre is still a bit runny.
- Turn it out onto a plate, then slide it back into the pan and cook the other side for 4 – 6 minutes.
- Leave to cool for 5 minutes then cut into wedges and serve.

Potato and Chorizo Tortilla   347

- Slice 150 g of chorizo and add it to the onions when you fry them.

348

SERVES 4

Baked New Potatoes

Baked Jerusalem Artichokes

349

- Replace the potatoes with an equal quantity of Jerusalem artichokes.

Baked New Potatoes with Garlic

350

- Break a bulb of garlic into individual cloves and add them to the foil parcel.

PREPARATION TIME 5 MINUTES

COOKING TIME 40 MINUTES

INGREDIENTS

8 medium new potatoes
2 tbsp olive oil
2 sprigs rosemary

- Preheat the oven to 220°C (200° fan), 430 F, gas 7.
- Prick the potatoes and cook them in a microwave on high for 5 minutes.
- Put the potatoes in the centre of a large sheet of foil, drizzle with olive oil and sprinkle with sea salt flakes.
- Add the rosemary sprigs, then fold up the foil and scrunch to seal.
- Bake the potato parcel in the oven for 35 minutes or until cooked through.

351

SERVES 4

Patatas Bravas

PREPARATION TIME 5 MINUTES

COOKING TIME 25 MINUTES

··

INGREDIENTS

4 large floury potatoes (eg. Maris
Piper or King Edwards)
2 - 3 litres / 3 ½ pints – 5 pints / 8-12
cups sunflower oil

FOR THE BRAVAS SAUCE
4 tbsp mayonnaise
1 large ripe tomato
1 tsp smoked paprika
2 tbsp olive oil

FOR THE GARLIC MAYONNAISE
1 clove garlic, crushed
2 tsp lemon juice
4 tbsp mayonnaise

- Peel the potatoes and cut them into large chunks.
- Heat the oil in a deep fat fryer, according to the manufacturer's instructions, to a temperature of 130°C.
- Lower the potatoes in the fryer basket and cook for 15 minutes so that they cook all the way through but don't brown. You may need to do this in batches so that the fryer isn't overcrowded.
- While the potatoes are cooking, put the ingredients for the bravas sauce in a liquidiser and blend until smooth.
- When the 15 minutes are up, pull up the fryer basket then increase the fryer temperature to 190°C.
- When the oil has come up to temperature, lower the fryer basket and cook the potatoes for 4 – 5 minutes or until crisp and golden brown.
- Line a large bowl with a thick layer of kitchen paper and when the potatoes are ready, tip them into the bowl to remove any excess oil.
- Transfer the potatoes to a serving bowl and drizzle over the bravas sauce.
- Stir the garlic and lemon juice into the mayonnaise and dollop it on top.

352

SERVES 4-6

Creamy Mushroom Soup with Pesto

PREPARATION TIME 10 MINUTES

COOKING TIME 30 MINUTES

··

INGREDIENTS

2 tbsp olive oil
1 onion, finely chopped
400 g / 14 oz / 4 cups mushrooms
2 cloves garlic, crushed
1 tbsp fresh thyme leaves
1 litre / 1 pint 16 fl. oz / 4 cups
vegetable stock
4 tbsp crème fraiche
2 tbsp pesto

- Heat the oil in a saucepan and fry the onion for 5 minutes or until softened.
- Add the mushrooms and garlic and cook for 2 more minutes, then pour in the vegetable stock and bring to the boil.
- Simmer for 20 minutes then stir in the crème fraiche and blend until smooth with an emersion blender.
- Try the soup and adjust the seasoning with salt and pepper.
- Ladle the soup into warm bowls and stir a spoonful of pesto into the top of each one.

353

SERVES 4

Leek, Potato and Parsley Soup

- Heat the oil and butter in a saucepan and fry the leeks for 8 minutes or until softened.
- Remove a spoonful of the leeks from the pan and reserve for a garnish.
- Add the garlic and potatoes to the pan and cook for 2 more minutes, then stir in the vegetable stock and bring to the boil.
- Simmer for 15 minutes then stir in the crème fraiche and parsley.
- Blend the soup until smooth with a liquidiser or emersion blender.
- Try the soup and adjust the seasoning with salt and pepper.
- Ladle the soup into 4 warm bowls and top each one with a few strands of fried leek.

PREPARATION TIME 5 MINUTES

COOKING TIME 30 MINUTES

INGREDIENTS

2 tbsp olive oil
2 tbsp butter
3 leeks, julienned
2 cloves garlic, crushed
2 maris piper potatoes, peeled and cubed
1 litre / 1 pint 16 fl. oz / 4 cups vegetable stock
2 tbsp crème fraiche
a small bunch of parsley, chopped

354

SERVES 4

Sweet Potato and Prawn Soup

PREPARATION TIME 5 MINUTES

COOKING TIME 40 MINUTES

INGREDIENTS

2 tbsp olive oil
1 onion, finely chopped
2 cloves garlic, crushed
1 red chilli, finely chopped

400 g / 14 oz / 2 ¼ cups sweet potato, peeled and chopped
1 litre / 1 pint 16 fl. oz / 4 cups vegetable stock
100 g / 3 ½ oz / ½ cup cooked prawns (shrimps), peeled
2 spring onions (scallions), chopped
Cayenne pepper, for sprinkling

- Heat the oil in a saucepan and fry the onion for 5 minutes.
- Add the garlic and chilli and cook for 2 more minutes then add the sweet potato and vegetable stock and bring to the boil.
- Simmer for 25 minutes then blend until smooth with an emersion blender.
- Try the soup and adjust the seasoning with salt and pepper, then ladle into warm bowls.
- Top with the prawns, spring onions and a sprinkle of Cayenne pepper.

355

SERVES 4

Tomato, Onion and Egg Soup

PREPARATION TIME 5 MINUTES

COOKING TIME 40 MINUTES

INGREDIENTS

2 tbsp olive oil
3 onions, sliced
2 cloves garlic, crushed
500 ml / 17 ½ fl. oz / 2 cups vegetable stock
500 ml / 17 ½ fl. oz / 2 cups tomato passata
4 very fresh eggs
1 tbsp flat leaf parsley, finely chopped

- Heat the oil in a saucepan and fry the onions for 20 minutes. Add the garlic and cook for 2 more minutes then stir in the vegetable stock and passata and bring to the boil.
- Simmer for 15 minutes then taste the soup and adjust the seasoning with salt and pepper.
- Break the eggs into the soup and poach for 4 minutes.
- Ladle the soup into 4 warm bowls and top each one with a poached egg. Garnish with chopped parsley.

MAINS

356

SERVES 2

Griddled Salmon with Summer Vegetables

PREPARATION TIME 4 MINUTES

COOKING TIME 8-10 MINUTES

....

INGREDIENTS

75 g / 2 ½ oz / ½ cup French beans
75 g / 2 ½ oz / ½ cup fresh peas
1 courgette (zucchini)
2 portions salmon fillet, skinned
3 tbsp olive oil
75 g / 2 ½ oz / ¾ cup mange tout
1 tbsp garden mint, chopped
1 tbsp flat leaf parsley, chopped
½ lemon, juiced

- Blanch the French beans and peas for 4 minutes then drain and refresh in cold water.
- Use a vegetable peeler to shave the courgette into long ribbons.
- Heat a griddle pan until smoking hot on the stove.
- Brush the salmon fillets with 1 tablespoon of the oil and season with salt and pepper.
- Griddle the salmon for 2 minutes on each side.
- Meanwhile, heat the rest of the oil in a large sauté pan and add the beans, peas, courgette ribbons and mange tout.
- Stir fry the vegetables for 4 minutes then sprinkle over the herbs and a squeeze of lemon juice.
- Spoon the vegetables into a warm serving dish. Turn the salmon fillets in any lemony juices left in the sauté pan before arranging them on top of the vegetables.

Griddled Sword Fish with Summer Vegetables

357

- Replace the salmon with sword fish steaks.

358

SERVES 2

Sesame-Crusted Salmon with Soy Carrots

PREPARATION TIME 5 MINUTES

COOKING TIME 8 -10 MINUTES

....

INGREDIENTS

1 egg white, beaten
1 tbsp cornflour
2 portions salmon fillet, skinned
50 g / 1 ¾ oz / ¼ cup sesame seeds
4 tbsp olive oil
1 clove garlic, crushed
2 large carrots, julienned
2 tbsp soy sauce

- Mix the egg white with the cornflour and brush a thin layer onto the skinned side of the salmon. Dip the salmon in the sesame seeds, pressing down firmly so they stick in an even layer.
- Heat half the oil in a large frying pan and cook the salmon, sesame side down, for 4 minutes.
- Meanwhile, heat the rest of the oil in a sauté pan and fry the garlic and carrots for 3 minutes. Add the soy sauce and 2 tablespoons of water then put a lid on the pan and cook for 2 more minutes.
- Turn the salmon over, turn off the heat and let the other side cook in the residual heat of the pan for 2 minutes.
- Spoon the carrots on to 2 warm dinner plates and top with the salmon fillets.

Sesame-Crusted Sea Bass

359

- Replace the salmon with 2 portions cut from a large sea bass fillet.

360

SERVES 4

Tuna Tortilla Wraps

- Fry the onion and chilli in the oil for 5 minutes or until starting to caramelise then add the tuna, sweetcorn, kidney beans and coriander. Cook for 3 minutes or until piping hot.
- Divide the tuna mixture between the tortillas and top with lettuce and tomato.

PREPARATION TIME 2 MINUTES

COOKING TIME 8 MINUTES

INGREDIENTS

1 onion, finely chopped
1 red chilli, finely chopped
2 tbsp olive oil
200 g / 7 oz / 2 cups / ¾ cup canned tuna, drained
100 g / 3 ½ oz / ½ cup canned sweetcorn, drained
100 g / 3 ½ oz / 1 cup canned kidney beans, drained
2 tbsp coriander leaves, chopped

TO SERVE
4 flour tortillas
¼ iceberg lettuce, shredded
2 tomatoes, diced

Tuna Wraps with Guacamole   361

- Cube an avocado and put it in a food processor with 2 spring onions, 1 chopped red chilli and the juice of a lime and blend. Spoon on top of the tuna mixture instead of the salad.

362

SERVES 2

Tagliatelle with Pear and Roquefort

- Cook the tagliatelle in boiling salted water according to the packet instructions or until al dente.
- While the pasta is cooking, use a vegetable peeler to shave the pears into thin slices.
- When the pasta is ready, drain it well and toss with the olive oil then arrange it on 2 hot serving plates with the pear, Roquefort, walnuts and peppercorns.

PREPARATION TIME 2 MINUTES

COOKING TIME 12 MINUTES

INGREDIENTS

200 g / 7 oz / 2 cups / 2 cups tagliatelle
1 ripe pear, quartered and cored
2 tbsp olive oil
100 g / 3 ½ oz / 1 cup Roquefort, cubed
1 tbsp walnuts, chopped
1 tsp pink peppercorns, crushed

Pear and Roquefort Salad   363

- Omit the tagliatelle and use the pear, Roquefort and walnuts to dress a spinach and rocket salad.

364

SERVES 2

Cod with Balsamic Onions

Steamed Turbot with Balsamic Onions

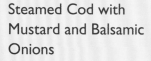
365

- Replace the cod with 2 thick turbot steaks.

Steamed Cod with Mustard and Balsamic Onions

366

- Stir 2 tsp of Dijon mustard into the pan when you add the balsamic vinegar.

PREPARATION TIME 4 MINUTES

COOKING TIME 18 MINUTES

....

INGREDIENTS

150 g / 5 ½ oz / ⅔ cup bulgur wheat
1 large onion, quartered and finely sliced
4 tbsp olive oil
2 tbsp balsamic vinegar
2 large cod steaks

- Put the bulgur wheat in a bowl and pour over enough boiling water to just cover it. Cover the bowl tightly and leave to soak for 15 minutes.
- Fry the onion in half the oil for 10 minutes or until starting to caramelise then stir in the balsamic vinegar.
- Arrange the cod steaks in a shallow bowl and pour the balsamic onion mixture over the top.
- Cover the bowl with clingfilm and transfer it to a steamer. Steam for 8 minutes or until the cod is just cooked in the centre.
- Stir the rest of the oil into the bulgur wheat and season with salt and pepper. Split it between 2 warm plates and top with the cod and balsamic onions.

367

SERVES 2 # Gammon with Pineapple and Chips

- Preheat the oven to 200°C (180° fan), 390 F, gas 6.
- Spread the chips out on a baking tray and cook for 10 minutes or according to the packet instructions.
- Meanwhile, heat the oil in a large frying pan and fry the gammon steaks for 3 minutes on each side.
- While the gammon is cooking, boil the peas for 4 minutes then drain.
- Move the gammon to the side of the frying pan and add the pineapple slices to heat through.
- Serve the gammon with the pineapple on top and the chips and peas on the side.
- Spoon over any of the juices that have come out of the gammon and pineapple.

PREPARATION TIME 2 MINUTES

COOKING TIME 10 -15 MINUTES

INGREDIENTS

200 g / 7 oz / 2 cups / 1 ½ cup oven chips
2 tbsp olive oil
2 large gammon steaks
2 pineapple rings
150 g / 5 ½ oz / 1 cup frozen peas

Gammon, Egg and Chips

368

- Omit the pineapple rings and top the gammon steaks with 2 fried eggs.

369

SERVES 4 # Lentils with Chorizo

- Cook the lentils in simmering, unsalted water for 30 minutes or until tender, then drain.
- Meanwhile, fry the onion in the oil for 5 minutes then add the chorizo, garlic and thyme and cook for 2 more minutes.
- Add the tomato and balsamic and cook over a low heat for 10 minutes.
- Stir the lentils into the chorizo mixture and season to taste with salt and black pepper.

PREPARATION TIME 2 MINUTES

COOKING TIME 30 MINUTES

INGREDIENTS

400 g / 14 oz / 2 cups puy lentils
1 red onion, halved and sliced
4 tbsp olive oil
150 g / 5 ½ oz / 1 cup chorizo, sliced
2 cloves garlic, crushed
2 tbsp fresh thyme leaves
1 tomato, chopped
1 tbsp balsamic vinegar

Lentils with Lardons

370

- Substitute the chorizo with an equal weight of lardons.

371

SERVES 4

Pork and Broccoli with Mustard Sauce

PREPARATION TIME 2 MINUTES

COOKING TIME 20 MINUTES

INGREDIENTS

2 tbsp olive oil
1 large onion, halved and sliced
2 garlic cloves, crushed
450 g / 1 lb / 3 cups pork fillet, thinly sliced
2 tsp Dijon mustard
1 tsp grain mustard
100 ml / 3 ½ fl. oz / ½ cup white wine
1 small head broccoli, broken into florets
400 ml / 14 fl. oz / 1 ⅔ cup double cream
½ lemon, juiced

- Heat the oil in a large sauté pan and fry the onion for 5 minutes. Add the garlic and cook for 2 more minutes then add the pork to the pan.
- Stir-fry the pork for 2 minutes until it starts to colour, then stir in the mustards and the wine.
- When the sauce starts to bubble, add the broccoli and stir to coat in the juices.
- Pour in the double cream and bring to a gentle simmer, then put the lid on and cook for 4 minutes.
- Stir the lemon juice into the sauce and season with salt and pepper just before serving.

Pork and Broccoli with Ginger Sauce

372

- Omit the mustards and add 1 tbsp of thinly sliced root ginger to the onions when you fry them.

373

SERVES 4

Guacamole Tacos

PREPARATION TIME 4 MINUTES

INGREDIENTS

4 ripe avocados
1 red onion, finely chopped
1 red chilli, finely chopped
3 medium tomatoes, diced
2 tbsp coriander leaves, chopped
2 limes, juiced

TO SERVE
8 corn tacos

- Mash the avocados with a fork then stir in the rest of the guacamole ingredients. Season to taste with salt and white pepper.
- Divide the guacamole between 8 tacos and serve 2 tacos per person.

Guacamole and Chorizo Tacos

374

- Fry 150 g of sliced chorizo in 2 tbsp of olive oil then spoon it on top of the guacamole.

375

SERVES 4

Beef and Parsley Burgers

Beef and Basil Burgers

376

- Replace the parsley with basil and replace the mustard with 2 tsp of pesto.

Boar and Parsley Burgers

377

- Replace the minced beef with an equal weight of minced wild boar.

PREPARATION TIME 10 MINUTES

COOKING TIME 10-12 MINUTES

INGREDIENTS

450 g / 1 lb / 2 cups minced beef
2 salad onions, finely chopped
4 tbsp flat leaf parsley, chopped
1 tbsp baby capers
1 tsp Dijon mustard
2 tbsp olive oil

TO SERVE
baby salad leaves
4 salad onions, halved
4 sprigs flat leaf parsley

- Put the mince in a bowl with the onion, parsley, capers and mustard, and knead with your hands until well mixed and starting to get sticky.
- Divide the mixture into 4 and shape it into burgers, squeezing the patties firmly with your hands.
- Heat the oil in a large frying pan and cook the burgers for 10 – 12 minutes, turning every 2 minutes.
- Serve the burgers on a bed of salad leaves, garnished with salad onions and parsley.

378

SERVES 2

Duck Breast with Raspberry Sauce

PREPARATION TIME 2 MINUTES

COOKING TIME 18 - 20 MINUTES

....

INGREDIENTS

1 large duck breast, skin pierced
1 tbsp raspberry vinegar
3 tbsp red wine
1 tsp raspberry jam
a handful of fresh raspberries
1 tbsp chives, chopped

- Preheat the oven to 200°C (180° fan), 390 F, gas 6.
- Put the duck breast, skin side down, in a cold oven-proof frying pan then put the pan on the hob and turn the heat up high.
- Cook the duck without disturbing for 8 minutes.
- When the skin side is golden brown, turn the duck over and transfer the pan to the oven to cook for 6 minutes.
- Leave the duck to rest on a warm plate, covered with a double layer of foil while you make the sauce.
- Pour off all but 1 tbsp of the duck fat into a ramekin, then put the pan back on the heat and add the vinegar and wine. Reduce the liquid by half then stir in the jam and raspberries.
- Slice the duck and divide it between 2 plates then spoon over the sauce and sprinkle with chives.
- Serve with mashed or boiled potatoes.

Duck Breast with Cherry Sauce 379

- Replace the raspberry jam with cherry jam and substitute the raspberries with fresh cherries that have been stoned and halved.

380

SERVES 4

Vegetable Fajitas

PREPARATION TIME 5 MINUTES

COOKING TIME 10 MINUTES

....

INGREDIENTS

3 tbsp olive oil
1 red pepper, chopped
1 green pepper, chopped
1 yellow pepper, chopped
½ aubergine (eggplant), cubed
100 g / 3 ½ oz / 1 ¼ cup button mushrooms, thickly sliced
2 tbsp fajita seasoning mix
8 soft flour tortillas

- Heat the oil in a large sauté pan and stir-fry the vegetables for 8 minutes or until starting to soften.
- Sprinkle over the seasoning mix and cook for 2 more minutes then divide the mixture between the tortillas, roll up and serve.

Vegetable and Kidney Bean Fajitas 381

- Add 200 g of canned kidney beans to the pan when you add the seasoning mix.

Lamb Chops with Garlic and Rosemary

382

SERVES 2

- Preheat the oven to 200°C (180° fan), 390 F, gas 6.
- Massage the lamb, garlic and rosemary with the olive oil and arrange in a roasting tin.
- Season well with salt and pepper then bake for 25 minutes, turning the lamb chops over half way through.
- Split the lamb and garlic between 2 plates and garnish with a slice of lemon.

PREPARATION TIME 5 MINUTES

COOKING TIME 25 MINUTES

INGREDIENTS

6 lamb chops
1 bulb of garlic, separated into cloves
a few sprigs rosemary
2 tbsp olive oil
2 slices lemon

Pork Chops with Garlic and Sage

383

- Substitute the lamb with pork chops and use fresh sage leaves instead of the rosemary.

Macaroni with Fresh Tomato Sauce

384

SERVES 2

- Cook the macaroni in boiling salted water according to the packet instructions or until al dente.
- While the pasta is cooking, score a cross in the top of each tomato and add them to the pasta water. When the skin of the tomatoes starts to curl up, remove them with a slotted spoon and dunk in a bowl of cold water.
- Peel off and discard the skins then chop the tomato flesh into small cubes.
- Mix the tomato in a bowl with the basil and olive oil and season well with salt and freshly ground black pepper.
- Drain the pasta and return it to the saucepan, then stir in the tomato dressing. Put the pan back over the heat for 1 minute to warm through before serving.

PREPARATION TIME 5 MINUTES

COOKING TIME 12 MINUTES

INGREDIENTS

200 g / 7 oz / 2 cups / 2 cups
macaroni pasta
2 medium tomatoes
2 tbsp fresh basil leaves, shredded
6 tbsp extra virgin olive oil

Macaroni with Tomato and Tuna Sauce

385

- Add 100 g of canned tuna to the tomatoes before dressing the pasta.

386

SERVES 2

Poached Egg and Bacon Rolls

Poached Egg and Sausage Baps

387

- Fry 4 pork sausages over a low heat for 15 minutes, turning occasionally, and use in place of the bacon.

BLT Baps

388

- Omit the poached eggs for a classic bacon, lettuce and tomato bap.

PREPARATION TIME 4 MINUTES

COOKING TIME 4 MINUTES

INGREDIENTS

4 thick rashers streaky bacon
2 very fresh eggs
2 sesame rolls
2 lettuce leaves
1 large tomato, sliced

- Preheat the grill to its highest setting and bring a wide saucepan of water to a gentle simmer.
- Grill the bacon for 2 minutes on each side or until crisp and golden brown.
- Meanwhile, crack each egg into a cup and pour them smoothly into the water, one at a time.
- Simmer gently for 3 minutes.
- Cut the rolls in half and add a lettuce leaf and a thick slice of tomato to the bottom halves.
- Top the tomato with the bacon. Use a slotted spoon to take the eggs out of the water and blot the underneath on a piece of kitchen paper before laying them on top of the bacon.
- Put the lids on the rolls and hold everything together with a wooden skewer.
- Serve with roasted new potatoes and extra salad.

389

SERVES 2

Cheese and Red Onion Burgers

- Preheat the grill to its highest setting.
- Put the burgers and onion slices on a grill tray and brush with olive oil. Grill for 4 minutes on each side or until the burgers are cooked to your liking and the onions are caramelised at the edges.
- Cut the baps in half and add a lettuce leaf and the tomato slices to the bottom halves.
- Top the tomato with the burgers and lay the cheese on top, followed by the onions.
- Put the lids on the baps and serve.

PREPARATION TIME 2 MINUTES

COOKING TIME 8 MINUTES

INGREDIENTS

2 beef burgers
1 red onion, peeled and sliced
2 tbsp olive oil
2 white baps
2 lettuce leaves
1 large tomato, sliced
4 slices mild Cheddar

Stilton and Red Onion Burgers   390

- Replace the cheddar with crumbled Stilton.

391

SERVES 4

Farfalle with Pepper and Basil Sauce

- Cook the farfalle in boiling salted water according to the packet instructions or until al dente.
- While the pasta is cooking, heat the olive oil in a large frying pan and cook the garlic and peppers for 8 minutes, stirring occasionally.
- Scrape the mixture into a food processor and blend to a smooth puree, then return it to the frying pan.
- Drain the pasta and stir it into the pepper puree. Add the basil leaves and put the pan back over the heat for 1 minute to warm through before serving.

PREPARATION TIME 2 MINUTES

COOKING TIME 12 MINUTES

INGREDIENTS

400 g / 14 oz / 2 cups farfalle pasta
4 tbsp olive oil
4 cloves garlic, crushed
2 orange peppers, finely chopped
a small bunch of basil, leaves only

Farfalle with Chilli Pepper Sauce   392

- Replace the orange peppers with red peppers and add 2 finely chopped red chillies to the frying pan.

Gruyere and Mushroom Cannelloni

SERVES 4

PREPARATION TIME 10 MINUTES

COOKING TIME 35 MINUTES

INGREDIENTS

50 g / 1 ¾ oz / ¼ cup butter
2 shallots, chopped
2 cloves garlic, crushed
200 g / 7 oz / 2 cups / 2 cups button mushrooms, chopped
12 sheets ready-made fresh pasta
2 tbsp plain (all purpose) flour
600 ml / 1 pint / 2 ½ cup milk
200 g / 7 oz / 2 cups / 2 cups Gruyere, grated

- Preheat the oven to 200°C (180° fan), 390 F, gas 6.
- Melt half the butter in a frying pan and fry the shallots and garlic for 5 minutes. Add the mushrooms with a pinch of salt and cook for another 5 minutes.
- Meanwhile, melt the rest of the butter in a small saucepan. Stir in the flour then gradually incorporate the milk, stirring continuously.
- When iy starts to bubble, stir in half the cheese and a grind of black pepper then take the pan off the heat.
- Add half the cheese sauce to the mushrooms and stir.
- Split the mushroom filling between the pasta sheets, then roll the up and pack them into a baking dish in a double layer.
- Pour over the rest of the sauce and sprinkle with the other half of the cheese.
- Bake the cannelloni for 20 minutes.

Gorgonzola and Lardon Cannelloni

394

- Replace the Gruyere with cubed Gorgonzola and fry 150 g lardons instead of the mushrooms.

Ricotta and Olive Pizza

SERVES 2

PREPARATION TIME 2 MINUTES

COOKING TIME 12 MINUTES

INGREDIENTS

1 large pizza base
3 tbsp tomato passata
100 g / 3 ½ oz / 1 cup salted ricotta
50 g / 1 ¾ oz / ⅔ cup mixed olives, pitted and sliced
2 tbsp caperberries
6 cherry tomatoes, halved
a handful rocket leaves

- Preheat the oven to 220°C (200° fan), 430 F, gas 7 and put a baking tray in to heat
- Spread the pizza base thinly with passata and crumble over the ricotta.
- Scatter over the olives and caperberries then arrange the tomato halves, cut side up.
- Give the top a good grind of black pepper then bake for 10 minutes or until the toppings are bubbling.
- Scatter over the rocket leaves and serve immediately.

Ricotta, Olive and Anchovy Pizza

396

- Omit the tomatoes and add 4 chopped anchovy fillets instead.

Pepperoni and Green Pepper Pizza

397

SERVES 2

Pepperoni and Artichoke Pizza

398

- Replace the peppers with half a jar of preserved artichokes in oil.

Green Pepper and Sweetcorn Pizza

399

- Omit the pepperoni and use 200 g of canned sweetcorn instead.

PREPARATION TIME 2 MINUTES

COOKING TIME 12 MINUTES

INGREDIENTS

1 large pizza base
3 tbsp passata sauce
100 g / 3 ½ oz / 1 cup mozzarella, sliced
100 g / 3 ½ oz / ⅔ cup pepperoni, sliced
½ green pepper, sliced
a few sprigs mint

- Preheat the oven to 220°C (200° fan), 430 F, gas 7 and put a baking tray in to heat
- Spread the pizza base thinly with passata and arrange the mozzarella slices on top.
- Scatter over the pepperoni and green pepper and sprinkle with black pepper.
- Bake the pizza for 10 minutes or until the toppings are bubbling.
- Garnish with mint and serve immediately.

400

SERVES 2

Spiced Tomato Flatbreads

PREPARATION TIME 4 MINUTES

COOKING TIME 20 MINUTES

....

INGREDIENTS

½ tsp mustard seeds
½ tsp cumin seeds
½ tsp coriander seeds
½ tsp chilli flakes
3 tbsp olive oil
1 onion, thinly sliced
1 clove garlic, crushed
3 tomatoes, cut into wedges
2 flatbreads
2 tbsp coriander leaves, chopped
50 g / 1 ¾ oz / ½ cup Emmental, grated

- Preheat the oven to 220°C (200° fan), 430 F, gas 7 and put a baking tray in to heat.
- Grind the spices with a pestle and mortar to a rough powder.
- Heat the oil in a frying pan and fry the onion and spices for 10 minutes or until starting to caramelise.
- Add the garlic and tomatoes to the pan and cook for 2 minutes to heat through.
- Stir in the coriander leaves then divide the mixture between the flatbreads and sprinkle over the cheese.
- Bake for 8 minutes to toast the tops and warm through the bread.

Mattar Paneer Flatbreads   401

- Add 150 g of defrosted frozen peas to the onions when you add the tomatoes and replace the Emmental with 100 g of cubed Paneer or Halloumi cheese.

402

SERVES 2

Pancetta and Sundried Tomato Pizza

PREPARATION TIME 2 MINUTES

COOKING TIME 12 MINUTES

....

INGREDIENTS

1 large pizza base
3 tbsp crème fraiche
100 g / 3 ½ oz / 1 cup mozzarella, sliced
50 g / 1 ¾ oz / ⅓ cup pancetta, thinly sliced
3 tbsp sundried tomatoes in oil, drained
2 tbsp black olives, pitted and sliced
1 tbsp fresh thyme leaves

- Preheat the oven to 220°C (200° fan), 430 F, gas 7 and put a baking tray in to heat
- Spread the pizza base thinly with creme fraiche° and arrange the mozzarella on top.
- Lay the pancetta slices on top and scatter over the olives and thyme.
- Give the top a good grind of black pepper then bake for 10 minutes or until the toppings are bubbling.

Fennel Sausage and Caper Pizza   403

- Omit the pancetta. Skin 2 fennel sausages and dot the meat over the pizza. Replace the olives with 1 tbsp of capers.

404

SERVES 2 # Prosciutto and Caper Pizza

- Preheat the oven to 220°C (200° fan), 430 F, gas 7 and put a baking tray in to heat
- Spread the pizza base thinly with passata and arrange the mozzarella slices on top.
- Lay the prosciutto slices on top and scatter with the capers and olives, then grind over some black pepper.
- Bake the pizza for 10 minutes or until the toppings are bubbling.
- Garnish with rocket and serve immediately.

PREPARATION TIME 2 MINUTES

COOKING TIME 12 MINUTES

INGREDIENTS

1 large pizza base
3 tbsp passata sauce
100 g / 3 ½ oz / 1 cup mozzarella, sliced
100 g / 3 ½ oz / ⅔ cup prosciutto slices
2 tbsp baby capers
a handful rocket leaves
8 black olives, pitted

Prosciutto and Gorgonzola Pizza   405

- Omit the capers and olives and sprinkle over 100 g of cubed Gorgonzola.

406

SERVES 2 # Tagliatelle with Savoy Cabbage and Ham

- Cook the tagliatelle in boiling salted water according to the packet instructions or until al dente.
- 4 minutes before the end of cooking time, add the cabbage to the pan.
- Meanwhile, melt the butter in a frying pan and cook the caraway seeds for 1 minute. Stir in the mustard and cream and ham.
- Drain the pasta and cabbage and stir them into the cream. Cook for 2 minutes for the flavours to mingle then serve.

PREPARATION TIME 2 MINUTES

COOKING TIME 14 MINUTES

INGREDIENTS

200 g / 7 oz / 2 cups / 2 cups tagliatelle
200 g / 7 oz / 2 cups / 2 cups Savoy cabbage, sliced
1 tbsp butter
1 tsp caraway seeds
1 tsp Dijon mustard
200 ml / 7 fl. oz / ¾ cup double cream
100 g / 3 ½ oz / ⅔ cup cooked ham, in strips

Tagliatelle with Cabbage and Walnuts   407

- Replace the ham with 75 g of roughly chopped walnuts.

408

SERVES 2

Tagliatelle with Broccoli and Parmesan

Tagliatelle with Broccoli, Chilli and Anchovy

409

- Add a finely chopped red chilli and 4 chopped anchovy fillets in oil when you fry the garlic.

Tagliatelle with Broccoli and Stilton

410

- Replace the Parmesan with 100 g of cubed Stilton.

PREPARATION TIME 2 MINUTES

COOKING TIME 12 MINUTES

INGREDIENTS

200 g / 7 oz / 2 cups / 2 cups tagliatelle
200 g / 7 oz / 2 cups / 1 ¼ cup broccoli, broken into small florets
4 tbsp olive oil
3 cloves garlic, crushed
75 g / 2 ½ oz / ¾ cup Parmesan, finely grated

- Cook the tagliatelle in boiling salted water according to the packet instructions or until al dente.
- Meanwhile, blanch the broccoli in boiling salted water for 3 – 4 minutes or until just tender. Drain well.
- Heat the oil in a sauté pan and fry the garlic for 2 minutes. Add the drained broccoli and cook, stirring occasionally, for 3 minutes so it can take on the flavour from the oil. Season to taste with salt and pepper.
- Reserve a couple of ladles of pasta water and drain the rest.
- Stir the pasta into the broccoli pan with 3 tablespoons of the pasta water and shake to emulsify with the oil. If it looks a bit dry, add some more pasta water.
- Divide between 2 warm bowls and top with plenty of Parmesan.

411

SERVES 2 # Linguini with Fresh Tomato Sauce

- Cook the linguini in boiling salted water according to the packet instructions or until al dente.
- While the pasta is cooking, score a cross in the top of each tomato and add them to the pasta water. When the skin of the tomatoes starts to curl up, remove them with a slotted spoon and dunk in a bowl of cold water.
- Peel off and discard the skins then chop the tomato flesh into small cubes.
- Mix the tomato in a bowl with the basil and olive oil and season well with salt and freshly ground black pepper.
- Drain the pasta and return it to the saucepan, then stir in the tomato dressing. Put the pan back over the heat for 1 minute to warm through.
- Divide the pasta between 2 bowls and sprinkle with Pecorino.

PREPARATION TIME 2 MINUTES

COOKING TIME 12 MINUTES

INGREDIENTS

200 g / 7 oz / 2 cups / 2 cups linguini
2 medium tomatoes
2 tbsp fresh basil leaves, shredded
6 tbsp extra virgin olive oil
50 g / 1 ¾ oz / ½ cup Pecorino, grated

Linguini with Fresh Tomatoes and Olives

412

- Add 75 g of chopped, pitted kalamata olives and a finely chopped raw shallot to the tomatoes before dressing the pasta.

413

SERVES 4 # Stilton and Prosciutto Crustless Quiche

- Preheat the oven to 180°C (160° fan), 355 F, gas 4.
- Lightly beat the eggs and mix them with the prosciutto, cheese and basil then season well with black pepper.
- Pour the mixture into a small baking dish and bake in the oven for 20 – 25 minutes or until just set in the centre.
- Serve warm or at room temperature.

PREPARATION TIME 2 MINUTES

COOKING TIME 15-20 MINUTES

INGREDIENTS

6 free-range eggs
100 g / 3 ½ oz / ⅔ cup prosciutto slices, chopped
100 g / 3 ½ oz / 1 cup Stilton, cubed
3 tbsp basil, finely shredded

Mozzarella and Prosciutto Crustless Quiche

 414

- Replace the Stilton with 150 g cubed Mozzarella and serve warm.

415

SERVES 4

Smoked Haddock and Prawn Pie

PREPARATION TIME 10 MINUTES

COOKING TIME 35 MINUTES

INGREDIENTS

450 g / 1 lb / 2 ½ cup potatoes, peeled and cubed
600 ml / 1 pint / 2 ½ cup whole milk
450 g / 1 lb / 2 ¼ cups smoked haddock
3 tbsp butter
1 tbsp plain flour
1 tsp wholegrain mustard
150 g / 5 ½ oz / ½ cup cooked king prawns, shelled
1 tbsp chives, chopped

- Cook the potatoes in boiling salted water for 15 minutes. Drain well. Meanwhile, bring the milk to a simmer then pour it over the smoked haddock. Cover the dish with film and leave to steep for 10 minutes.
- Drain and reserve the milk and flake the haddock, discarding any skin and bones. When the potatoes are ready, mash them until smooth with 1 tablespoon of the butter and a little of the haddock milk.
- Heat 1 tablespoon of butter in a saucepan and stir in the flour. Gradually incorporate the rest of the haddock milk. Stir until it starts to bubble then stir in the mustard, prawns, chives and flaked haddock.
- Preheat the grill to its highest setting. Pour the haddock mixture into a baking dish and top with the mashed potato.
- Dot the final tablespoon of butter over the top and grill for 5 minutes or until the top is golden and bubbling.

Smoked Haddock and Chorizo Pie

416

- Replace the prawns with 100 g of sliced chorizo.

417

SERVES 2

Penne with Cherry Tomatoes and Basil

PREPARATION TIME 2 MINUTES

COOKING TIME 12 MINUTES

INGREDIENTS

200 g / 7 oz / 2 cups / 2 cups penne
4 tbsp olive oil
½ tsp chilli flakes
2 cloves of garlic, crushed
100 g / 3 ½ oz / ¾ cup cherry tomatoes
28 g / 1 oz / ¼ cup Parmesan
2 tbsp fresh basil leaves, shredded

- Cook the penne in boiling salted water according to the packet instructions or until al dente.
- While the pasta is cooking, heat the oil in a frying pan and fry the chilli flakes and garlic for 2 minutes. Squeeze each tomato over the pan to burst it then stir into the oil.
- Cook for 4 minutes or until just starting to soften.
- Drain the pasta and stir it into the tomato sauce then divide between 2 warm bowls.
- Use a vegetable peeler to shave over some Parmesan then sprinkle with basil.

Penne Puttanesca

418

- Add 4 chopped anchovy fillets in oil and 8 chopped, pitted black olives to the frying garlic. Replace the basil with plenty of chopped flat leaf parsley.

419

SERVES 2

Penne with Tomato Sauce

Penne with Tomato and Bacon Sauce

420

- Fry 2 chopped rashers of streaky bacon with the garlic.

Penne with Creamy Tomato Sauce

421

- Stir 100 g of Mascarpone into the sauce at the end.

PREPARATION TIME 2 MINUTES

COOKING TIME 12 MINUTES

INGREDIENTS

200 g / 7 oz / 2 cups / 2 cups penne
4 tbsp olive oil
2 cloves of garlic, crushed
100 g / 3 ½ oz / ½ cup canned tomatoes, chopped
28 g / 1 oz / ¼ cup Parmesan
a few sprigs basil

- Cook the penne in boiling salted water according to the packet instructions or until al dente.
- While the pasta is cooking, heat the oil in a frying pan and fry the garlic for 2 minutes.
- Add the canned tomatoes and simmer for 5 minutes.
- Taste for seasoning, adding plenty of freshly ground black pepper.
- Drain the pasta and stir it into the tomato sauce then divide between 2 warm bowls.
- Use a vegetable peeler to shave over some Parmesan then sprinkle with basil.

422

SERVES 4

Rigatoni, Chicken and Apple Salad

PREPARATION TIME 5 MINUTES

COOKING TIME 12 MINUTES

INGREDIENTS

200 g / 7 oz / 2 cups / 2 cups rigatoni pasta
3 tbsp mayonnaise
3 tbsp double cream
1 tbsp lemon juice
2 tbsp French tarragon, leaves only
200 g / 7 oz / 2 cups / 1 ¾ cup pre-cooked chicken breast, sliced
1 apple, cored and thinly sliced
1 head chicory, separated into leaves

- Cook the rigatoni in boiling salted water according to the packet instructions or until al dente.
- Drain well then plunge into iced water to cool for 5 minutes. Drain well.
- Meanwhile, mix the mayonnaise, cream and lemon juice together and stir in the tarragon. Season to taste with salt and pepper.
- Toss the rigatoni, chicken, apple and chicory with the dressing and divide between 4 serving bowls.

423

SERVES 4

Penne with Smoked Salmon

PREPARATION TIME 2 MINUTES

COOKING TIME 25 MINUTES

INGREDIENTS

400 g / 14 oz / 4 cups penne
2 tbsp butter
200 g / 7 oz / 2 cups / 2 ¼ cups chestnut mushrooms, sliced
300 ml / 10 ½ oz / 1 ½ cup double cream
150 g / 5 ½ oz / 1 cup smoked salmon, chopped
2 tbsp Greek basil leaves
150 g / 5 ½ oz / 1 ½ cup Morbier cheese, cubed

- Preheat the oven to 220°C (200° fan), 430 F, gas 7.
- Cook the penne in boiling salted water according to the packet instructions or until al dente. Drain well.
- Meanwhile, melt the butter in a frying pan and cook the mushrooms with a pinch of salt for 10 minutes or until any liquid that comes out of them has evaporated and they start to brown.
- Add the double cream and bring to the boil then stir in the drained pasta, smoked salmon, basil and Morbier.
- Spoon it into a baking dish and level the top then bake for 10 minutes or until the top is bubbling.

Chicken Noodle Curry

424

SERVES 2

- Coat the chicken pieces with the curry paste and leave to marinate for 10 minutes.
- Meanwhile, cover the noodles in boiling water and leave to soften for 5 minutes. Drain well.
- Heat the oil in a wok and stir-fry the marinated chicken for 5 minutes or until cooked through.
- Add the coconut milk and bring to a simmer, then add the noodles and cook for 2 minutes or until tender.
- Garnish with coriander and serve.

PREPARATION TIME 10 MINUTES

COOKING TIME 10 MINUTES

INGREDIENTS

2 skinless chicken breasts, sliced
2 tbsp Thai yellow curry paste
150 g / 5 ½ oz / 2 cups fine rice noodles
2 tbsp vegetable oil
200 ml / 7 fl. oz / ¾ cup coconut milk
2 tbsp coriander leaves, chopped

Mushroom and Ham Cannelloni

425

SERVES 4

PREPARATION TIME 10 MINUTES

COOKING TIME 35 MINUTES

INGREDIENTS

50 g / 1 ¾ oz / ¼ cup butter
2 shallots, chopped
2 cloves garlic, crushed
200 g / 7 oz / 2 cups / 2 ¼ cups button mushrooms, chopped
12 sheets ready-made fresh pasta
2 tbsp plain flour
600 ml / 1 pint / 2 ½ cup milk
200 g / 7 oz / 2 cups / 2 cups Emmental, grated
150 g / 5 ½ oz / 1 cup cooked ham, in small cubes
1 tbsp basil leaves, chopped

- Preheat the oven to 200°C (180° fan), 390 F, gas 6.
- Melt half the butter in a frying pan and fry the shallots and garlic for 5 minutes. Add the mushrooms with a pinch of salt and cook for another 5 minutes.
- Meanwhile, melt the rest of the butter in a small saucepan. Stir in the flour then gradually incorporate the milk, stirring continuously to avoid any lumps forming.
- When the mixture starts to bubble, stir in half the cheese, the ham, basil and a grind of black pepper then take the pan off the heat.
- Add half of the sauce to the mushroom mixture and stir.
- Split the mushroom filling between the pasta sheets, then roll them up and pack them into 4 individual baking dishes.
- Pour over the rest of the sauce and sprinkle with the other half of the cheese.
- Bake the cannelloni for 20 minutes or until golden brown.

Rigatoni with King Prawns

426

SERVES 4

PREPARATION TIME 2 MINUTES

COOKING TIME 12 MINUTES

INGREDIENTS

400 g / 14 oz / 4 cups rigatoni
4 tbsp olive oil
2 shallots, finely chopped
2 cloves of garlic, crushed
200 g / 7 oz / 2 cups / 1 cup canned tomatoes, chopped
1 leek, trimmed, halved and thinly sliced
3 tbsp crème fraiche
300 g / 10 ½ oz / 1 ½ cup raw king prawns, peeled
flat leaf parsley to garnish

- Cook the rigatoni in boiling salted water according to the packet instructions or until al dente.
- While the pasta is cooking, heat half the oil in a frying pan and fry the shallots and garlic for 2 minutes. Add the canned tomatoes and bring to a simmer.
- Meanwhile, fry the leeks with a pinch of salt in the other half of the oil for 6 minutes or until very soft.
- Stir the crème fraiche into the tomato sauce and season to taste with salt and pepper.
- When the pasta is almost ready, add the prawns to the leeks and stir fry for 2 minutes or until they just turn opaque.
- Drain the pasta and divide it between 4 warm bowls.
- Spoon the tomato sauce over the pasta then top with the prawns and a few sprigs of parsley.

427

SERVES 2

Mediterranean Lumache

PREPARATION TIME 2 MINUTES

COOKING TIME 12 MINUTES

....

INGREDIENTS

200 g / 7 oz / 2 cups / 2 cups lumache
pasta
4 tbsp olive oil
½ tsp chilli flakes
2 cloves of garlic, crushed
100 g / 3 ½ oz / 1 ¼ cup button
mushrooms, sliced
100 g / 3 ½ oz / ¾ cup cherry
tomatoes, halved
75 g / 2 ½ oz / ½ cup mixed olives,
pitted and halved

- Cook the lumache in boiling salted water according to the packet instructions or until al dente.
- While the pasta is cooking, heat the oil in a frying pan and fry the chilli flakes and garlic for 2 minutes. Add the mushrooms and fry over a high heat until starting to colour.
- Add the cherry tomato halves to the pan, cut side down, and cook until starting to soften, then add the olives and season with salt and pepper.
- Drain the pasta and toss it with the sauce, adding a few tablespoons of the cooking water if it looks dry.

Mediterranean Sausage Lumache

428

- Omit the mushrooms and fry 4 skinless sausages in small pieces with the garlic and chilli instead.

429

SERVES 4

Pasta and Vegetable Broth

PREPARATION TIME 2 MINUTES

COOKING TIME 25 MINUTES

....

INGREDIENTS

6 tbsp extra virgin olive oil
1 onion, quartered and finely sliced
½ red pepper, diced
½ green pepper, diced
2 cloves of garlic, crushed
1.5 litres / 2 pints 12 fl. oz / 8 cup
vegetable stock
100 g / 3 ½ oz / 1 cup dried spaghetti,
broken into short lengths
2 tbsp flat leaf parsley, chopped

- Heat 4 tbsp of the oil in a large saucepan and fry the onion and peppers for 10 minutes or until soft and sweet.
- Add the garlic and cook for 2 more minutes then pour in the stock and bring to the boil.
- Add the spaghetti and simmer for 12 minutes then taste for seasoning, stir in the parsley and the final 2 tablespoons of oil and serve.

Alphabet Soup

430

- Replace the spaghetti with an equal weight of alfabeto pasta letters.

431

SERVES 2

Macaroni with White Wine and Clams

- Cook the macaroni in boiling salted water according to the packet instructions or until only just al dente.
- While the pasta is cooking, heat the oil in a large sauté pan and fry the garlic and half of the parsley for 1 minute.
- Pour in the wine and bring to the boil for 2 minutes.
- Add the clams to the pan and put on the lid, allowing them to steam for 5 minutes or until they have all opened.
- Remove the clams from the pan with a slotted spoon and reserve.
- Drain the macaroni and tip it into the sauté pan with the rest of the parsley. Cook for 2 more minutes so that it absorbs the some of the flavour of the wine and clams.
- Divide the pasta between 2 warm bowls and top with the clams.

PREPARATION TIME 5 MINUTES

COOKING TIME 14 MINUTES

INGREDIENTS

200 g / 7 oz / 2 cups macaroni
3 tbsp olive oil
3 cloves of garlic, crushed
4 tbsp flat leaf parsley, finely chopped
250 ml / 9 fl. oz / 1 cup dry white wine
250 g / 9 oz / 1 ¼ cup live clams, scrubbed

Spaghetti alle Vongole   432

- Replace the macaroni with spaghetti. Add ½ tsp of chilli flakes to the garlic and squeeze in 6 ripe cherry tomatoes with your fingers before adding the wine.

433

SERVES 2

Maccheroncini with Spring Vegetables

- Cook the maccheroncini in boiling salted water according to the packet instructions or until al dente.
- Meanwhile, blanch the carrots, runner beans and peas in boiling salted water for 3 minutes or until just tender. Drain well.
- Heat the oil in a sauté pan and fry the shallot for 2 minutes without colouring. Add the radishes, drained vegetables and the mint and season to taste with salt and white pepper.
- Reserve a couple of ladles of pasta water and drain the rest.
- Stir the pasta into the vegetable pan with 3 tablespoons of the pasta water and shake to emulsify with the oil. If it looks a bit dry, add some more pasta water.
- Divide between 2 warm bowls and serve immediately.

PREPARATION TIME 2 MINUTES

COOKING TIME 12 MINUTES

INGREDIENTS

200 g / 7 oz / 2 cups maccheroncini pasta
1 small carrot, thinly sliced
1 runner bean, thinly sliced on the diagonal
50 g / 2 ½ oz / ⅓ cup fresh peas
4 tbsp olive oil
1 shallot, finely chopped
3 radishes, thinly sliced
2 tbsp garden mint, finely chopped

Creamy Maccheroncini with Vegetables   434

- Add 100 ml of double cream and the grated zest of a lemon to the vegetables before adding the pasta.

435

SERVES 2

Mafaldine with Cherry Tomatoes

Mafaldine with Roasted Peach

436

- Cut 3 stoned peaches into large chunks and roast in place of the tomatoes. Replace the goat's cheese with Gorgonzola.

Roasted Tomato Sauce for Pasta

437

- Roast the tomatoes as above then tip them into a food processor with a small bunch of oregano and 4 tbsp olive oil and blend to a smooth sauce.

PREPARATION TIME 2 MINUTES

COOKING TIME 12 MINUTES

INGREDIENTS

100 g / 3 ½ oz / ¾ cup yellow cherry tomatoes
50 g / 1 ¾ oz / ⅓ cup red cherry tomatoes
75 g / 2 ½ oz / ½ cup baby plum tomatoes
4 tbsp olive oil
4 tbsp basil leaves
200 g / 7 oz / 2 cups mafaldine pasta
150 g / 5 ½ oz / ¾ cup fresh goats' cheese with herbs

- Preheat the oven to 220°C (200° fan), 430 F, gas 7.
- Rub the tomatoes with half of the oil and sprinkle with half of the basil. Season well with salt and pepper then roast for 20 minutes, stirring halfway through.
- At the halfway stage, cook the mafaldine in boiling salted water according to the packet instructions or until al dente.
- Drain the pasta, reserving 3 tbsp of the cooking water, then put the pasta back in the pan with the remaining olive oil and reserved cooking water.
- Shake to emulsify and tip the pasta into a warm serving bowl.
- Spoon the roasted tomatoes on top and crumble over the cheese then sprinkle with the remaining basil leaves.

438
SERVES 8

Mushroom Meatloaf

- Preheat the oven to 200°C (180° fan), 390 F, gas 6 and line a loaf tin with greaseproof paper.
- Heat the oil in a large sauté pan and fry the onion, mushrooms and garlic together for 5 minutes or until softened.
- Scrape the mixture into a large mixing bowl and add the rest of the ingredients then squidge it all together with your hands until it is really well mixed.
- Pack the meat into the prepared loaf tin and bake for 35 – 40 minutes or until the top is golden and the centre is cooked.

PREPARATION TIME 5 MINUTES

COOKING TIME 45 MINUTES

INGREDIENTS

2 tbsp olive oil
1 onion, finely chopped
200 g / 7 oz / 2 ¾ cups button mushrooms, sliced
1 clove garlic, crushed
400 g / 14 oz / 1 ¾ cup pork sausage meat
400 g / 14 oz / 1 ¾ cup minced veal
2 large eggs, beaten
2 tsp rosemary, finely chopped
1 tbsp thyme leaves
150 g / 5 ½ oz / 1 cup fresh white breadcrumbs

Saltimbocca Meatloaf 439

- Omit the mushrooms and replace the thyme and rosemary with 1 tbsp of chopped sage leaves. Line the loaf tin with thin slices of prosciutto before adding the mince mixture.

440
SERVES 6

Sausage Meat Stuffing Loaf

- Preheat the oven to 200°C (180° fan), 390 F, gas 6 and line a baking tray with greaseproof paper.
- Heat the oil in a large sauté pan and fry the onion, carrot, celery, garlic and sage together for 5 minutes.
- Spoon half of the mixture into a large mixing bowl and keep the rest in the pan.
- Add the sausagemeat and breadcrumbs to the mixing bowl and squidge it all together until well mixed.
- Shape the stuffing into a mound on the baking tray and bake for 35 – 40 minutes.
- Meanwhile, add the canned tomatoes to the rest of the vegetables and simmer for 20 minutes, adding a drop of water if it looks dry. Season with salt and pepper.
- When the stuffing loaf is ready, transfer it to a warm serving plate and spoon the sauce over the top. Garnish with basil.

PREPARATION TIME 5 MINUTES

COOKING TIME 45 MINUTES

INGREDIENTS

2 tbsp olive oil
1 onion, finely chopped
1 carrot, finely chopped
1 celery stick, finely chopped
1 clove garlic, crushed
2 tbsp sage leaves, finely chopped
450 g / 1 lb / 1 ¾ cup pork sausagemeat
100 g / 3 ½ oz / ⅔ cup fresh white breadcrumbs
300 g / 10 ½ oz / 1 ½ cup canned tomatoes, chopped
a few basil leaves to garnish

Vegetarian Meatloaf 441

- For a simple vegetarian version of this dish, omit the sausagemeat and use your favourite uncooked veggie burgers, defrosted if frozen.

442

SERVES 2

Spaghetti with Onion and Chicory

PREPARATION TIME 35 MINUTES

COOKING TIME 12 MINUTES

INGREDIENTS

1 red onion, halved and sliced
60 ml / 2 fl. oz / ¼ cup red wine vinegar
½ tsp salt
2 tsp caster (superfine) sugar
200 g / 7 oz / 2 cups spaghetti
2 tbsp extra virgin olive oil
1 head red chicory, chopped
2 tbsp fresh basil leaves, chopped

- Put the onion in a bowl with the vinegar, salt and sugar and leave to macerate for 30 minutes.
- Meanwhile, cook the spaghetti in boiling salted water according to the packet instructions or until al dente.
- When the pasta is ready, drain it well and tip it back into the saucepan.
- Add the marinated onions and the olive oil and stir to coat.
- Add the chicory and basil then divide it between 2 warm serving plates and sprinkle with plenty of freshly ground black pepper.

Spaghetti with Marinated Onions and Goat's Cheese

443

- Add 100 g of cubed goat's cheese to the spaghetti just before serving.

444

SERVES 4

Chicken and Vegetable Couscous

PREPARATION TIME 5 MINUTES

COOKING TIME 35 MINUTES

INGREDIENTS

4 tbsp olive oil
1 onion, sliced
1 red chilli, sliced
8 chicken thighs
2 carrots, cut into chunks
2 courgettes (zucchini), cut into chunks
6 baby turnips, quartered
200 g / 7 oz / 1 ¼ cups canned chickpeas, drained
¼ small white cabbage, cut into wedges
300 g / 10 ½ oz / 1 ¾ cup couscous
a few sprigs fresh coriander

- Heat the oil in a large saucepan and fry the onion and chilli for 4 minutes to soften.
- Add the chicken, carrots, courgettes and turnips to the pan with 1 litre of cold water and bring to a gentle simmer. Simmer for 20 minutes.
- Add the chickpeas and cabbage slices and simmer for a further 10 minutes.
- Put the couscous in a large serving bowl and pour over 300 ml of the boiling chicken stock.
- Cover the bowl with clingfilm and let it stand for 5 minutes then fluff up the grains with a fork.
- Divide the couscous between 4 warm plates and top with the chicken and vegetables.
- Garnish with fresh coriander before serving.

Pheasant and Vegetable Couscous

445

- During pheasant season, try replacing the chicken with a whole pheasant, to be carved after cooking.

446

SERVES 4

Lamb and Vegetable Couscous

Lamb and Apricot Couscous

447

- Stir the dried fruit mixture into the lamb and vegetables, 5 minutes before the end of cooking time, and add 100 g of dried apricots.

Meatball Couscous

448

- Put the lamb, spices, onion and fruit in a food processor and pulse. Form into meatballs and fry until golden before adding the vegetables and water and cooking as before.

PREPARATION TIME 5 MINUTES

COOKING TIME 35 MINUTES

....

INGREDIENTS

2 lamb neck fillets, cut into chunks
2 carrots, chopped
2 courgettes (zucchini), chopped
1 parsnip, chopped
1 onion, finely chopped
1 tsp ras al hanout spice mix
4 tbsp olive oil
2 cloves of garlic, chopped
50 g / 1 ¾ oz / ¼ cup raisins
50 g / 1 ¾ oz / ¼ cup dates, stoned and chopped
300 g / 10 ½ oz / 4 ½ cup couscous

- Put the lamb, carrots, courgettes and parsnip in a saucepan with 1 litre of cold water and bring to a gentle simmer. Simmer for 30 minutes.

- Meanwhile, fry the onion and ras al hanout in the oil for 10 minutes or until starting to caramelise. Add the garlic, raisins and dates and cook for 2 more minutes.

- Put the couscous in a large serving bowl and pour over 300 ml of the boiling lamb stock. Cover the bowl with clingfilm and let it stand for 5 minutes then fluff up the grains with a fork.

- Spoon the onion and raisin mixture round the outside of the bowl and top with the lamb and vegetables.

- Serve any leftover lamb stock in a jug on the side.

449

SERVES 4

Spicy Potatoes

PREPARATION TIME 5 MINUTES

COOKING TIME 40 MINUTES

INGREDIENTS

800 g / 1 lb 12 oz / 4 ½ cup maris
piper potatoes, peeled and cubed
4 tbsp olive oil
1 tbsp curry powder
Basmati rice, to serve

- Preheat the oven to 220°C (200° fan), 430 F, gas 7 and put a large roasting tin in to heat.
- Boil the potatoes in salted water for 8 minutes then drain well and leave to steam dry for 2 minutes.
- Mix the oil and curry powder together with a big pinch of salt then spoon it over the potatoes, turning to coat.
- Put the potatoes into the hot roasting tin and roast for 30 minutes or until golden and toasted at the edges, turning occasionally.
- Serve with basmati rice.

Spicy Root Vegetables

 450

- Use a combination of parsnips, carrots, Jerusalem artichokes and potatoes and cook as above.

 451

SERVES 4

Lentil Burgers

PREPARATION TIME 30 MINUTES

COOKING TIME 30 MINUTES

INGREDIENTS

250 g / 9 oz / 1 ¼ cup red lentils
2 onions, finely chopped
1 red chilli, finely chopped
4 tbsp olive oil
2 cloves garlic, crushed
2 tsp ground cumin
1 tsp ground turmeric
a small bunch coriander, chopped
100 g / 3 ½ oz / 1 ¼ cup chickpea
flour

TO SERVE

4 sesame rolls
1 large tomato, sliced
a handful spinach leaves
4 tbsp mango chutney
4 tbsp beansprouts

- Cook the lentils in boiling water for 20 minutes or until tender, then drain well.
- While the lentils are cooking, fry the onion and chilli in half the oil for 5 minutes then add the garlic and spices and cook for 2 more minutes. Season with salt and pepper.
- Put the lentils in a food processor with the chickpea flour and spiced onion mixture and pulse.
- Shape the mixture into 4 burgers, then chill in the fridge for 30 minutes or until firm.
- Heat the rest of the oil in a large frying pan and fry the burgers for 4 minutes on each side.
- To build the burgers, lay a slice of tomato on the roll bottoms and top with some spinach leaves. Position the burgers on top and spoon over some mango chutney then sprinkle with beansprouts before putting on the lids.

Lentil Meatballs

452

- Follow the burger recipe above and shape the mixture into small meatballs. Fry on all sides until golden and cooked through then serve in a warm pita bread or with pasta in

453
SERVES 2

Mushroom and Red Onion Pizza

- Preheat the oven to 220⁰C (200⁰ fan), 430 F, gas 7 and put a baking tray in to heat
- Spread the pizza base thinly with crème fraiche and arrange the mozzarella on top.
- Arrange the mushrooms and red onion on top.
- Sprinkle with freshly ground black pepper then bake for 10 minutes or until the toppings are bubbling.

PREPARATION TIME 2 MINUTES

COOKING TIME 10 MINUTES

INGREDIENTS

1 large pizza base
3 tbsp crème fraiche
100 g / 3 ½ oz / 1 cup mozzarella, sliced
50 g / 1 ¾ oz / ¾ cup mushrooms, sliced
½ red onion, thinly sliced

Mushroom and Spring Onion Pizza
454

- Replace the red onion with a shredded bunch of spring onions.

455
SERVES 2

Scallops and Potatoes

- Boil the potatoes in salted water for 12 minutes or until tender in the middle, then drain well.
- Heat the oil in a large frying pan and sear the scallops for 2 minutes on each side. Season well with salt and pepper.
- Divide the potatoes between 2 warm plates and arrange the scallops on top.
- Sprinkle over the chives and add a lemon wedge to each plate.

PREPARATION TIME 5 MINUTES

COOKING TIME 12 MINUTES

INGREDIENTS

300 g / 10 ½ oz / 1 ¾ cup maris piper potatoes, peeled and cubed
2 tbsp olive oil
8 fresh scallops
2 tbsp chives, cut into short lengths
2 lemon wedges

Scallops and Potatoes with Mustard Cream
456

- Heat 200 ml of double cream with ½ crushed clove garlic and 1 tsp Dijon mustard until bubbling, then use it to dress the scallops and potatoes.

457

SERVES 4

Ackee and Saltfish

Salt Cod and Mango

458

- If you are unable to find canned ackee, use a large ripe mango instead. Peel and stone the mango and cut the flesh into large chunks.

Jerk Pork and Ackee

459

- Omit the salt cod and fry 400 g of pork tenderloin in strips with 2 tsp of jerk seasoning before adding it to the dish.

PREPARATION TIME 5 MINUTES

COOKING TIME 12 MINUTES

INGREDIENTS

3 tbsp olive oil
1 onion, sliced
1 red pepper, diced
1 red chilli, finely chopped
400 g / 14 oz / 2 cups salt cod, pre-soaked and cubed
400 g / 14 oz / 2 cups canned ackee, drained
1 tbsp fresh thyme leaves
1 lime, cut into wedges

- Heat the oil in a large sauté pan and fry the onion, peppers and chilli for 8 minutes or until softened.
- Dry the salt cod on some kitchen paper and add it to the pan with the drained ackee.
- Stir fry for 4 minutes or until cooked through then season with plenty of black pepper.
- Divide between 4 warm plates and serve with the lime wedges to be squeezed over at the table.

460

SERVES 4

Mushrooms and Walnuts Penne

- Cook the penne in boiling salted water according to the packet instructions or until al dente. Drain well.
- Meanwhile, melt the butter in a frying pan and cook the mushrooms with a pinch of salt for 10 minutes or until any liquid that comes out of them has evaporated and they start to brown.
- Tip the drained pasta into the pan and add the avocado, walnuts and parsley.
- Toss well then divide between 4 warm bowls and serve.

PREPARATION TIME 2 MINUTES

COOKING TIME 25 MINUTES

INGREDIENTS

400 g / 14 oz penne
2 tbsp butter
200 g / 7 oz / 2 ¾ cup chestnut mushrooms, sliced
1 avocado, peeled, stoned and cubed
75 g / 2 ½ oz / ⅔ cup walnut halves
2 tbsp curly parsley, finely chopped

Penne with Mushrooms and Stilton

461

- Replace the avocado with 100 g of cubed Stilton.

462

SERVES 2

Tagliatelle with Mushrooms and Parmesan

- Cook the tagliatelle in boiling salted water according to the packet instructions or until al dente.
- Meanwhile, fry the mushrooms with a pinch of salt in the oil for 10 minutes or until any liquid that comes out of them has evaporated and they start to colour.
- Add the garlic and cook for 1 more minute then take off the heat.
- Stir the Parmesan into the beaten egg.
- Reserve 1 ladleful of the pasta cooking water and drain the rest.
- Return the pasta to the pan and add the mushrooms and parmesan mixture. Stir well and add enough of the pasta water to make a thick sauce.
- Divide the pasta between 2 warm bowls and sprinkle with parsley and freshly ground black pepper.

PREPARATION TIME 2 MINUTES

COOKING TIME 14 MINUTES

INGREDIENTS

200 g / 7 oz / 2 cups tagliatelle
200 g / 7 oz / 2 cups mushrooms, sliced
4 tbsp olive oil
3 cloves garlic, crushed
50 g / 1 ¾ oz / ½ cup Parmesan, finely grated
1 egg, beaten
3 tbsp flat leaf parsley, chopped

Tagliatelle with Mushrooms and Walnuts

463

- Add 75 g of roughly chopped walnuts to the pan after cooking the mushrooms.

464

SERVES 4

Rice Salad

PREPARATION TIME 5 MINUTES

COOKING TIME 20 MINUTES

INGREDIENTS

200 g / 7 oz / ¾ cup long grain rice
75 g / 2 ½ oz / ½ cup green beans, chopped
75 g / 2 ½ oz / ½ cup frozen peas, defrosted
1 red pepper, cubed
1 yellow pepper, cubed

FOR THE DRESSING
1 tsp runny honey
½ lemon, juiced
3 tbsp olive oil

- Put the rice in a saucepan and add enough water to cover it by 1 cm.
- Bring the pan to the boil then cover and turn down the heat to its lowest setting.
- Cook for 10 minutes then turn off the heat and leave to stand, without lifting the lid, for 10 minutes.
- Meanwhile, blanch the beans and peas in boiling salted water for 4 minutes or until tender. Drain well.
- Whisk the honey with the lemon juice then whisk in the olive oil.
- Combine the rice with the vegetables and dressing and season well with salt and pepper.

Rice Salad with Ham
465

- Add 150 g of cooked ham in small cubes when you stir in the vegetables.

466

SERVES 4

Fusilli with Broccoli and Artichokes

PREPARATION TIME 2 MINUTES

COOKING TIME 12 MINUTES

INGREDIENTS

400 g / 14 oz / 4 cups fusilli tricolore
4 tbsp olive oil
4 cloves garlic, crushed
1 small head broccoli, broken into florets
1 jar preserved baby artichokes, drained
30 g / 1 oz / ¼ cup Parmesan, grated

- Cook the fusilli in boiling salted water according to the packet instructions or until al dente.
- While the pasta is cooking, heat the olive oil in a large frying pan and cook the garlic and broccoli for 5 minutes, stirring occasionally.
- Stir in the artichokes and warm through.
- Reserve 1 ladle of the pasta cooking water and drain the rest then stir the pasta into the frying pan.
- If it looks a bit dry, add some of the cooking water and shake the pan to emulsify.
- Divide the pasta between 4 warm bowls and top with freshly grated Parmesan.

Fusilli with Artichokes and Prosciutto
467

- Stir through 100 g of shredded prosciutto just before serving.

468

SERVES 4

Lentil, Tuna and Red Onion Salad

Puy Lentil and Poached Salmon Salad

469

- Poach 2 salmon fillet portions for 8 minutes or until just cooked in the centre, then flake into the salad in place of the tuna.

Puy Lentil and Roasted Squash Salad

470

- Peel a small butternut squash and cut it into cubes. Drizzle with olive oil and roast at 190°C for 30 minutes then use in place of the tuna.

PREPARATION TIME 5 MINUTES

COOKING TIME 30 MINUTES

INGREDIENTS

400 g / 14 oz / 2 cups puy lentils
1 small red onion, sliced
225 g / 8 oz / 1 cup white tuna in olive oil, drained
1 tbsp flat leaf parsley, finely chopped
1 tbsp chives, chopped
½ tsp ground cumin

FOR THE DRESSING

1 tsp runny honey
1 tsp Dijon mustard
2 tbsp white wine vinegar
4 tbsp olive oil

- Cook the lentils in simmering, unsalted water for 20 - 30 minutes or until tender, then drain and plunge into cold water to stop the cooking. Drain well.
- Meanwhile, make the dressing. Whisk the honey and mustard into the vinegar then incorporate the oil. Season to taste with salt and pepper.
- Mix the lentils with the onion and tuna and spoon over the dressing.
- Sprinkle with a little ground cumin then scatter over the herbs.

471

SERVES 2

Maccheroncini and Chicken Salad

PREPARATION TIME 5 MINUTES

COOKING TIME 12 MINUTES

....

INGREDIENTS

200 g / 7 oz / 2 cups maccheroncini
pasta
1 tbsp lemon juice
3 tbsp extra virgin olive oil
100 g / 3 ½ oz / ¾ cup cooked
chicken breast, cubed
50 g / 1 ¾ oz / ⅓ cup cucumber,
halved and sliced
½ red pepper, thinly sliced
½ green pepper, thinly sliced
50 g / 1 ¾ oz / ⅓ cup black olives,
pitted and sliced
2 tbsp flat leaf parsley, chopped

- Cook the maccheroncini in boiling salted water according to the packet instructions or until al dente.
- Plunge it into cold water to stop the cooking then drain well.
- Whisk the lemon juice into the oil with a pinch of salt and toss it with the pasta.
- Stir in the chicken, cucumber, peppers, olives and parsley and serve at room temperature.

Maccheroncini and Tuna Salad 472

- Replace the chicken with a jar of good quality white Tuna in oil.

473

SERVES 4

Farfalle with Spiced Winter Vegetables

PREPARATION TIME 5 MINUTES

COOKING TIME 12 MINUTES

....

INGREDIENTS

2 carrots, cut into chunks
½ cauliflower, broken into florets
½ head broccoli, broken into florets
400 g / 14 oz / 4 cups farfalle pasta
4 tbsp olive oil
4 cloves garlic, crushed
½ tsp ground cumin
½ tsp ground coriander
½ tsp chilli flakes

- Bring a very large saucepan of water to the boil with half a tablespoon of salt.
- Add the carrots and cook for 2 minutes then add the cauliflower and broccoli and cook for a further 4 minutes.
- Remove the vegetables from the pan with a slotted spoon and leave to drain in a colander.
- Add the farfalle to the saucepan and cook according to the packet instructions or until al dente.
- While the pasta is cooking, heat the olive oil in a large sauté pan and cook the garlic and spices for 2 minutes, stirring regularly.
- Add the drained vegetables and toss to coat in the spiced oil. Add half a ladle of the pasta cooking water and simmer over a low heat.
- Drain the pasta and stir it into the sauté pan then divide it between 4 warm bowls.

Farfalle and Spiced Vegetable Soup 474

- Add the pasta to the pan with enough of the cooking water to make a broth and

475

SERVES 4

Tuna Burgers

- Put the tuna in a food processor with the parsley, lemon zest and a pinch of salt and pepper and pulse until evenly mixed.
- Shape the mixture into 4 patties and chill in the fridge for 25 minutes or until firm.
- Preheat a griddle pan until smoking hot.
- Brush the burgers with oil and griddle for 8 minutes, turning them every 2 minutes.
- Serve the burgers with a lemon wedge on the side.

PREPARATION TIME 35 MINUTES

COOKING TIME 8 MINUTES

INGREDIENTS

450 g / 1 lb / 2 cups fresh tuna, chopped
2 tbsp flat leaf parsley, chopped
1 lemon, zest finely grated
2 tbsp olive oil
lemon wedges to serve

Moroccan Tuna Burgers

476

- Replace the parsley with coriander leaves and add 1 tsp each of ras al hanout and harissa to the tuna before processing.

477

SERVES 2

Turkey Baked with Bacon and Lemon

- Preheat the oven to 200⁰C (180⁰ fan), 390 F, gas 6.
- Line a baking dish with greaseproof paper and put the turkey breast on top.
- Arrange the lemon slices over the turkey and lay the bacon rashers on top.
- Drizzle over the olive oil and season well with salt and freshly ground black pepper.
- Fold the edges of the greaseproof paper over the top and bake for 30 minutes, peeling the paper back for the final 10.

PREPARATION TIME 5 MINUTES

COOKING TIME 30 MINUTES

INGREDIENTS

1 turkey breast
1 lemon, sliced
4 rashers smoked streaky bacon
3 tbsp olive oil

Turkey Breast
with Lemon and Herbs

478

- Omit the bacon and lay a few sprigs of fresh rosemary, thyme and sage on top of the

479

SERVES 2

Spaghetti with Roasted Vegetables

Spaghetti with Roasted Squash

480

- Replace the vegetables with a cubed butternut squash and substitute the goat's cheese with Gorgonzola.

Spaghetti with Watercress and Goat's Cheese

481

- Omit the roasted vegetable stage and use watercress instead of the rocket.

PREPARATION TIME 2 MINUTES

COOKING TIME 12 MINUTES

INGREDIENTS

1 courgette (zucchini), halved and sliced
½ aubergine, halved and sliced
1 red pepper, cut into strips
1 yellow pepper, cut into strips
4 tbsp olive oil
200 g / 7 oz / 2 cups spaghetti
100 g / 3 ½ oz / ⅔ cup fresh goat's cheese
30 g / 1 oz / 1 cup rocket leaves

- Preheat the oven to 220°C (200° fan), 430 F, gas 7.
- Rub the vegetables with oil and season well with salt and pepper then spread them out in a large roasting tin. Roast for 25 minutes, turning half way through.
- Once you've turned the vegetables, cook the spaghetti in boiling salted water according to the packet instructions or until al dente.
- Drain the pasta then stir it into the roasting tin to absorb some of the flavours.
- Divide the pasta and vegetables between 2 warm plates and crumble over the goat's cheese.
- Top with the rocket leaves and serve immediately.

482

SERVES 4

Pepper, Bacon and Mussel Kebabs

- Put 12 wooden skewers in a bowl of cold water and leave to soak for 20 minutes.
- Mix the oil with the oregano and drizzle it over the peppers, bacon and mussels. Leave to marinate for 20 minutes.
- Preheat the grill to its highest setting.
- Thread alternate pieces of red pepper, bacon and mussels onto the skewers.
- Grill the kebabs for 4 minutes on each side or until cooked and golden.
- Meanwhile, fry the mushrooms and oregano in the oil with a pinch of salt for 8 minutes or until any liquid that comes out has evaporated and they start to take on some colour.
- Serve the kebabs on a bed of fried mushrooms.

PREPARATION TIME 30 MINUTES

COOKING TIME 8 MINUTES

INGREDIENTS

4 tbsp olive oil
1 tsp dried oregano
3 red peppers, cut into large chunks
8 rashers streaky bacon, cut into large squares
450 g / 1 lb / 1 ½ cup cooked shelled mussels

FOR THE MUSHROOMS

300 g / 10 ½ oz / 4 cups mushrooms, sliced
1 tsp dried oregano
3 tbsp olive oil

Bacon, Mussel and Mushroom Kebabs

483

- Instead of serving the kebabs on a bed of mushrooms, thread the whole mushrooms onto the skewers and omit the peppers.

484

SERVES 4

Chicken, Pepper and Lemon Kebabs

- Put 12 wooden skewers in a bowl of water and leave to soak for 20 minutes.
- Meanwhile, stir the paprika into the oil and toss it with the chicken, lemon and vegetables.
- Leave to marinate for 20 minutes.
- Preheat the grill to its highest setting.
- Thread alternate chunks of chicken, lemon and vegetables onto the skewers and spread them out on a large grill tray.
- Grill the kebabs for 4 minutes on each side or until they are golden brown and cooked through.
- Garnish with thyme before serving.

PREPARATION TIME 20 MINUTES

COOKING TIME 8 MINUTES

INGREDIENTS

½ tsp smoked paprika
4 tbsp olive oil
6 skinless chicken breasts, cubed
1 lemon, sliced
1 red pepper, cubed
1 green pepper, cubed
1 onion, cut into chunks
12 cherry tomatoes
a few thyme sprigs to garnish

Lamb, Pepper and Lemon Kebabs

485

- Replace the chicken with 450 g of cubed lamb neck fillet.

Lamb and Vegetable Kebabs

486

SERVES 4

PREPARATION TIME 5 MINUTES

COOKING TIME 8 MINUTES

INGREDIENTS

1 tsp dried herbs de Provence
4 tbsp olive oil
900 g / 2 lb / 4 cups boneless lamb leg, cubed
1 green pepper, cubed
12 salad onions, trimmed
36 cherry tomatoes
12 button mushrooms, halved

- Preheat the grill to its highest setting.
- Stir the herbs into the oil and toss it with the lamb and vegetables.
- Thread alternate chunks of lamb and vegetables onto 12 metal skewers and spread them out on a large grill tray.
- Grill the kebabs for 4 minutes on each side or until they are golden brown and cooked through.

Duck and Vegetable Kebabs

487

- Replace the lamb with 4 large duck breasts that have been skinned and cubed.

488

SERVES 4

Lamb Burgers with Roasted Vegetables

PREPARATION TIME 2 MINUTES

COOKING TIME 45 MINUTES

INGREDIENTS

450 g / 1 lb / 2 cup minced lamb
1 tsp dried oregano
1 courgette (zucchini), cubed
½ aubergine, cubed
1 red pepper, cubed
4 charlotte potatoes, peeled and cubed
6 tbsp olive oil
2 tbsp chives, chopped

- Preheat the oven to 220°C (200° fan), 430 F, gas 7.
- Rub the vegetables with 4 tablespoons of the oil and season well with salt and pepper then spread them out in a large roasting tin. Roast for 35 minutes, turning half way through.
- Put the mince in a bowl with the oregano and plenty of salt and pepper, and knead with your hands until well mixed and starting to get sticky.
- Divide the mixture into 4 and shape it into burgers, squeezing the patties firmly with your hands.
- Heat the rest of the oil in a large frying pan and cook the burgers for 8 minutes, turning them every 2 minutes.
- Divide the roasted vegetables between 4 warm plates and top each one with a burger and a sprinkling of chives.

Lamb Burgers with Hummus

489

- Serve the lamb burgers in warm pitta bread, topped with hummous.

490

SERVES 2

Tuna Steaks with Tomato and Olive Sauce

Rib-Eye with Tomato and Olive Sauce

491

- Replace the tuna steaks with 2 good quality rib-eye steaks.

Tuna Steaks with Tomato and Caper Sauce

492

- Replace the olives with 2 tbsp capers.

PREPARATION TIME 10 MINUTES

COOKING TIME 15-20 MINUTES

INGREDIENTS

200 g / 7 oz / 1 cup tomatoes
6 tbsp extra virgin olive oil
1 onion, quartered and sliced
1 tbsp red wine vinegar
50 g / 1 ¾ oz / ⅓ cup black olives, pitted
2 tuna steaks
a few sprigs oregano

- Score a cross in the top of the tomatoes and blanch them in boiling water for 30 seconds. When the skin of the tomatoes starts to curl up, remove them with a slotted spoon and dunk in a bowl of cold water.

- Peel off and discard the skins then finely chop the tomato flesh.

- Meanwhile, heat 4 tablespoons of the oil in a frying pan and fry the onion for 5 minutes or until softened. Add a pinch of salt and the vinegar and bubble away almost to nothing.

- Add the tomatoes and olives and cook over a low heat while you cook the tuna.

- Preheat a griddle pan until smoking hot.

- Brush the tuna steaks with the rest of the oil and season well with salt and pepper.

- Griddle the steaks for 8 minutes, turning every 2 minutes or until cooked to your liking.

- Spoon the tomato sauce onto a serving plate and arrange the tuna steaks on top.

- Garnish with oregano and serve.

493

SERVES 4

Lamb Chops with Potatoes and Gravy

PREPARATION TIME 2 MINUTES

COOKING TIME 20 MINUTES

INGREDIENTS

800 g / 1 lb 12 oz / 4 ½ cup maris
piper potatoes
8 lamb chops
2 tbsp olive oil
a few sprigs oregano

FOR THE GRAVY
1 large onion, finely chopped
2 tbsp butter
2 tbsp Madeira
250 ml / 9 fl. oz / 1 cup lamb stock

- Preheat the grill to its highest setting.
- Boil the potatoes in salted water for 12 minutes then drain well and leave to steam dry for 2 minutes.
- Meanwhile, fry the onion in the butter for 10 minutes or until starting to caramelise.
- Add the Madeira and a pinch of salt and bubble away almost to nothing.
- Add the beef stock and simmer gently until reduced and slightly thickened.
- Brush the chops with oil and season with salt and pepper then grill for 3 minutes on each side.
- Arrange the potatoes on 4 warm plates and add 2 lamb chops to each.
- Strain the gravy through a sieve to get rid of the onions and spoon it around the plate.
- Garnish the plates with oregano sprigs.

494

SERVES 2

Prawn, Coconut and Lime Leaf Skewers

PREPARATION TIME 5 MINUTES

COOKING TIME 4 MINUTES

INGREDIENTS

20 raw king prawns, peeled
8 frozen lime leaves, defrosted
1 tbsp vegetable oil
30 g / 1 oz / ¼ cup creamed coconut
block, grated

- Preheat a griddle pan until smoking hot.
- Thread the prawns and lime leaves onto 8 metal skewers.
- Stir the oil into the creamed coconut and brush it over the prawns then griddle the skewers for 2 minutes on each side or until the prawns turn opaque.

495

SERVES 4

Lamb Kebabs with Cucumber Salad

- Soak 4 wooden skewers in cold water for 20 minutes.
- Stir the oregano into the oil and toss it with the lamb and peppers. Leave to marinate for 15 minutes.
- Meanwhile, toss the cucumber with the vinegar, oil and sesame seeds. Season well with salt and pepper and leave to drain in a sieve for 15 minutes.
- Preheat the grill to its highest setting.
- Thread alternate chunks of lamb and peppers onto the skewers and spread them out on a large grill tray.
- Grill the kebabs for 4 minutes on each side or until they are golden brown and cooked through.
- Split open the pita breads and fill them with cucumber salad.
- Top each one with a kebab and serve.

PREPARATION TIME 25 MINUTES

COOKING TIME 8 MINUTES

INGREDIENTS

1 tsp dried oregano
4 tbsp olive oil
450 g / 1 lb / 2 cup lamb leg, cubed
½ green pepper, cubed
½ red pepper, cubed
½ yellow pepper cubed
4 pitta breads

FOR THE CUCUMBER SALAD
½ cucumber, julienned
2 tbsp white wine vinegar
1 tbsp olive oil
1 tsp sesame seeds

Duck with Onions and Honey

496

SERVES 2

PREPARATION TIME 2 MINUTES

COOKING TIME 18 MINUTES

INGREDIENTS

2 small duck breasts, skin pierced
6 large spring onions, trimmed
a few sprigs rosemary
1 tbsp white wine vinegar

3 tbsp white wine
1 tbsp runny honey
½ tsp pink peppercorns, crushed

- Preheat the oven to 200⁰C (180⁰ fan), 390 F, gas 6.
- Put the duck breast, skin side down, in a cold oven-proof frying pan, then put the pan on the hob and turn the heat up high.
- Cook the duck without disturbing for 8 minutes. When the skin side is golden brown, turn the duck over, add the onions and rosemary to the pan. Season well then transfer to the oven for 6 minutes.
- Leave the duck, onions and all but 1 sprig of rosemary to rest on a warm plate, covered with a double layer of foil.
- Pour off all but 1 tbsp of the duck fat into a ramekin, then put the pan back on the heat and add the vinegar and wine. Reduce the liquid by half then stir in the honey.
- Finely chop the rosemary and add it to the sauce.
- Put the duck breasts on 2 warm plates and divide the onions and crisp rosemary sprigs between them.
- Spoon over the sauce and sprinkle with pink peppercorns.

Monkfish and Pepper Kebabs

497

SERVES 4

PREPARATION TIME 20 MINUTES

COOKING TIME 8 MINUTES

INGREDIENTS

450 g / 1 lb / 2 ¼ cups monkfish,
boned
and cubed

½ green pepper, cubed
½ red pepper, cubed
½ yellow pepper cubed
2 tbsp flat leaf parsley, chopped

- Soak 4 wooden skewers in cold water for 20 minutes.
- Preheat the grill to its highest setting.
- Thread alternate chunks of monkfish and peppers onto the skewers and spread them out on a large grill tray.
- Grill the kebabs for 4 minutes on each side or until they are golden brown and cooked through.
- Sprinkle with parsley and serve.

Steak with Garlic Sauce and Parsnip Chips

498

SERVES 2

PREPARATION TIME 10 MINUTES

COOKING TIME 12 MINUTES

INGREDIENTS

2 skirt steaks
1 tbsp olive oil

FOR THE SAUCE

1 tbsp butter
2 cloves garlic, finely chopped
½ tsp cracked black peppercorns
1 tbsp brandy
200 ml / 7 fl. oz / ¾ cup double cream

FOR THE PARSNIP CHIPS

3 parsnips, cut into long chips
2 - 3 litres / 3 ½ pints – 5 pints / 8-12 cups sunflower oil

- Heat the oil in a deep fat fryer, according to the manufacturer's instructions, to a temperature of 130°C. Fry the parsnips for 10 minutes without browning.
- Brush the steaks with oil and season. Fry in a smoking hot frying pan for 2 minutes on each side. Transfer the steaks to a warm plate, wrapped in a double layer of foil.
- Pull up the fryer basket and increase the temperature to 190°C. Cook the chips for 2 - 3 minutes at the hotter temperature or until crisp and golden brown.
- Tip the chips into a bowl with kitchen paper to remove oil. Return the pan to the heat and add the butter.
- Fry the garlic and peppercorns for 1 minute then add the brandy and cream and bubble for 1 minute.
- Transfer the steaks to 2 warm plates and stir any juices into the sauce.
- Arrange the parsnips next to the steaks and spoon the sauce over the top.

Parsnip Chips

499

- To accompany the steak, cut 3 parsnips into chips and deep-fry for 10 minutes at 130°C, then increase the temperature to 190°C and cook until golden and crisp.

Cod with Prosciutto and Cabbage

500

SERVES 2

PREPARATION TIME 5 MINUTES

COOKING TIME 10 MINUTES

INGREDIENTS

2 tbsp olive oil
2 thick portions cod fillet
2 slices prosciutto
2 tbsp flat leaf parsley, chopped
½ small hispi cabbage, sliced
1 tbsp butter

- Preheat the oven to 200°C (180° fan), 390 F, gas 6 and bring a large pan of salted water to the boil.
- Heat the oil in an oven proof frying pan. Season the cod with salt and pepper and fry, skin side down, for 4 minutes.
- Turn the pieces of cod over and sprinkle with parsley and lay the prosciutto slices next to them in the pan.
- Transfer the pan to the oven and cook for 5 minutes or until the prosciutto is crisp and the cod is just cooked in the centre.
- Boil the cabbage for 3 minutes or until tender then drain well. Stir in the butter and season with salt and pepper.
- Divide the cabbage between 2 warm plates and top with the cod and crispy prosciutto.

Chicken with Prosciutto and Cabbage

501

- Replace the cod with 2 skin-on chicken breasts.

502

SERVES 4

Boudin Blanc with Caramelised Apples

- Heat the oil in a large frying pan and fry the sausages over a low heat for 15 minutes, turning occasionally.
- Halfway through the cooking time, add the apples to the pan, turning them once.
- Remove the sausages from the pan and keep warm.
- Stir the vinegar into the honey then add it to the pan with the apples and bubble to a sticky glaze.
- Transfer the apples to a serving plate and top with the boudin blanc.

PREPARATION TIME 2 MINUTES

COOKING TIME 20 MINUTES

INGREDIENTS

2 tbsp olive oil
4 boudin blanc sausages
2 eating apples, cored and sliced
1 tbsp cider vinegar
1 tbsp runny honey

Fennel Sausages with Caramelised Pears

503

- Substitute Italian-style fennel sausages for the boudin blanc and replace the apples with pears.

504

SERVES 2

Sea Bass Fillet with Potato and Thyme

- Boil the potatoes in salted water for 8 minutes then drain well and leave to steam dry for 2 minutes.
- Heat 4 tbsp of the oil in a large sauté pan.
- Season the potatoes then fry for 10 minutes, shaking the pan and stirring occasionally.
- Meanwhile, heat the rest of the oil in a frying pan. Season the sea bass and lower the fillets into the pan, skin side down.
- Cook for 4 minutes or until the skin is golden brown and crisp, then turn them over and sprinkle in the thyme.
- Cook for 2 minutes or until the centre is just cooked.
- Transfer the bass to 2 warm plates and spoon over the potatoes.
- Wrap the lime halves in muslin to catch any pips and put them on the side of the plates.

PREPARATION TIME 5 MINUTES

COOKING TIME 25 MINUTES

INGREDIENTS

6 tbsp olive oil
400 g / 14 oz / 2 ¼ cup charlotte potatoes, peeled and cubed
1 large sea bass, filleted and pin boned
2 tbsp fresh thyme leaves
1 lime, halved

Barbequed Bream with Sautéed Potatoes

505

- Serve the potatoes with sea bream that have been barbequed whole.

506

SERVES 2

Lamb Chops with Summer Vegetables

Spicy Griddled Vegetables

507

- Mix 1 tbsp harissa paste with the oil before tossing with the vegetables.

Griddled Vegetables with Cheese

508

- Cut 100 g of Taleggio into cubes and scatter over the vegetables for the last minute of cooking time.

PREPARATION TIME 10 MINUTES

COOKING TIME 10-12 MINUTES

....

INGREDIENTS

4 lamb chops
2 tbsp olive oil
a few sprigs thyme

FOR THE VEGETABLES

1 shallot, cut into wedges
1 courgette (zucchini), sliced
1 yellow pepper, sliced
½ head broccoli, broken into small florets
100 g / 3 ½ oz / 1 cup sugar snap peas
4 tbsp olive oil

- Preheat the grill to its highest setting and heat a griddle pan until smoking hot.
- Toss the vegetables with the oil and season well with salt and pepper.
- Griddle the vegetables in 2 batches for 5 minutes on each side or until softened and nicely marked.
- When you put the second batch on to cook, brush the lamb chops with oil, sprinkle with thyme and season with salt and pepper.
- Grill the chops for 3 minutes on each side or until golden brown.
- Arrange the potatoes on 2 warm plates and add 2 lamb chops to each.
- Divide the vegetables between 2 warm plates and serve 2 chops per person.

509

SERVES 2

Tuna Steaks with Herb Salsa

- Preheat a griddle pan until smoking hot.
- Brush the tuna steaks with the oil and season well with salt and pepper.
- Griddle the steaks for 4 minutes then turn them over and cook for another 4 minutes or until done to your liking.
- Meanwhile, chop the onion finely then add the herbs and capers to the board and chop them all together to create a coarse salsa.
- Stir in the lemon juice and olive oil and season with salt and pepper.
- Serve the tuna with a simple tomato and cucumber salad and the salsa spooned on top.

PREPARATION TIME 5 MINUTES

COOKING TIME 8 MINUTES

INGREDIENTS

2 tuna steaks
1 tbsp olive oil

FOR THE SALSA
1 onion, peeled
a small bunch flat leaf parsley
1 tbsp mint leaves
1 tbsp capers
½ lemon, juiced
2 tbsp olive oil

Lamb Steaks with Herb Salsa   510

- Replace the tuna with lamb leg steaks.

511

SERVES 4

Lamb Tikka Skewers

- Mix the marinade ingredients together with a pinch of salt. Put the lamb in a large freezer bag, add the marinade and massage it into the meat. Leave to marinade for 30 minutes.
- Meanwhile, soak 12 wooden skewers in cold water for 20 minutes and preheat the grill to its highest setting.
- Thread the lamb onto the skewers and grill for 4 minutes on each side or until they are golden brown and cooked through.

PREPARATION TIME 40 MINUTES

COOKING TIME 8 MINUTES

INGREDIENTS

900 g / 2 lb / 4 cups boneless lamb leg, cubed

FOR THE MARINADE
4 tbsp Greek yoghurt
1 tbsp tomato puree
1 clove garlic, crushed
1 tbsp curry powder
1 tbsp mango chutney
1 tbsp coriander leaves, chopped

Monk Fish Tikka Skewers   512

- Replace the lamb with an equal weight of monkfish and reduce the cooking time to 3 minutes on each side.

513

SERVES 4

Pork Belly with Fennel and Chestnuts

PREPARATION TIME 5 MINUTES

COOKING TIME 40 MINUTES

....

INGREDIENTS

2 fennel bulbs, thickly sliced
200 g / 7 oz / 1 ⅔ cups whole
chestnuts, cooked and peeled
1 tbsp olive oil
800 g / 1 lb 12 oz / 5 cups boneless
pork belly, skin scored
30 g / 1 oz / ¼ cup fresh white
breadcrumbs

- Preheat the oven to 230°C (210° fan), 450 F, gas 8.
- Rub the fennel and chestnuts with oil and arrange them in a roasting tin.
- Put the pork on top, skin side up, and roast for 35 minutes.
- Take the pork out and leave it to rest in a warm place for 5 minutes.
- Meanwhile, sprinkle the fennel and chestnuts with breadcrumbs and return them to the oven for 5 minutes.
- Cut the pork into 4 thick slices and serve with the fennel and chestnuts.

Roast Pork with Red Onions

514

- Replace the fennel with 2 large sliced red onions and a few sprigs of rosemary. Omit the chestnuts.

515

SERVES 4

Crusted Lamb with Fondant Potatoes

PREPARATION TIME 2 MINUTES

COOKING TIME 20 MINUTES

....

INGREDIENTS

1 tbsp hazelnuts, chopped
1 tsp coriander seeds
2 tbsp flat leaf parsley
3 tbsp Parmesan, grated
1 - 2 tbsp olive oil
8 lamb chops
150 g / 5 ½ oz / 1 cup frozen peas

FOR THE POTATOES
1 large baking potato, peeled
2 tbsp butter
250 ml / 9 fl. oz / 1 cup lamb stock

- Mix the hazelnuts, coriander seeds, parsley and parmesan and stir in enough oil to make a stiff paste.
- Spread the paste onto the lamb and preheat the grill to its highest setting.
- Cut the ends off the potato then cut it into 4 thick slices. Melt the butter in a small frying pan and fry the potatoes for 3 minutes on one side or until browned.
- Cook for 3 minutes on the other side, then pour in the lamb stock. Cover the pan and cook for 5 minutes then turn the potatoes and cook uncovered for 5 minutes.
- Meanwhile, spread the lamb out on a grill tray and season. Grill the chops for 3 minutes on each side.
- Boil the peas for 4 minutes then drain. Arrange the potatoes and chops on 4 plates.
- Divide the peas between the plates and drizzle over any stock left in the potato pan.

Crusted Pork Chops

516

- Use pork chops instead of lamb chops and replace the parsley in the crust with sage leaves.

517

SERVES 2

Griddled Pork and Aubergine

Griddled Gammon and Aubergines

518

- Soak 2 gammon steaks in pineapple juice for 20 minutes then blot them dry and use in place of the pork.

Griddled Pork and Courgettes

519

- Use 4 sliced courgettes instead of the aubergine, adding them to the griddle pan half way through the cooking time.

PREPARATION TIME 5 MINUTES

COOKING TIME 8 MINUTES

INGREDIENTS

1 aubergine (eggplant), sliced lengthways
2 pork fillet steaks
2 tomatoes, halved
4 tbsp olive oil
a few sprigs thyme
½ tsp pink peppercorns, crushed

- Sprinkle the aubergine slices with salt and leave them for 5 minutes to draw the moisture out.
- Blot them well with kitchen paper.
- Preheat a large griddle pan until smoking hot.
- Brush the aubergine, pork and tomatoes with oil and sprinkle over the thyme and pink peppercorns.
- Season everything with sea salt at the last minute then griddle for 4 minutes on each side or until nicely marked.

520

SERVES 2

Mustard Mackerel with Carrots

PREPARATION TIME 5 MINUTES

COOKING TIME 8 - 10 MINUTES

INGREDIENTS

10 baby carrots, peeled
2 mackerel fillets
1 tbsp plain flour
2 tbsp olive oil
1 tbsp balsamic vinegar
2 tbsp white wine
1 tsp runny honey
2 tsp wholegrain mustard
2 sprigs sage

- Boil the carrots in salted water for 6 minutes.
- Meanwhile, season the mackerel fillets with salt and pepper and dust them with flour. Heat the oil in a large frying pan and fry the fillets, skin side down for 4 minutes.
- Turn them over and turn off the heat then leave them to cook in the heat of the pan for 2 minutes.
- Transfer the mackerel and carrots to 2 warm plates and turn the heat back on under the pan.
- Stir the vinegar, wine, honey and mustard into the pan and bubble for 1 minute then spoon the sauce over the fish and carrots.
- Garnish the plates with sage.

Mustard Mackerel with Mange Tout

521

- Use mange tout instead of the carrots, but reduce the cooking time to 3 minutes.

522

SERVES 2

Wasabi Salmon with Cucumber Ribbons

PREPARATION TIME 10 MINUTES

COOKING TIME 6 MINUTES

INGREDIENTS

1 egg white, beaten
1 tbsp cornflour
2 portions salmon fillet, skinned
50 g / 1 ¾ oz / ⅓ cup wasabi peas, crushed
2 tbsp olive oil
1 cucumber, peeled
1 tsp caster (superfine) sugar
1 tbsp rice wine vinegar

- Mix the egg white with the cornflour and brush a thin layer onto the skinned side of the salmon. Dip the salmon in the crushed wasabi peas, pressing down firmly so they stick in an even layer.
- Heat half the oil in a large frying pan and cook the salmon, wasabi side down, for 4 minutes.
- Meanwhile, use a vegetable peeler to slice the cucumber into long ribbons.
- Stir the caster (superfine) sugar into the vinegar with a pinch of salt until dissolved, then pour the dressing over the cucumber and toss to coat.
- Turn the salmon over, turn off the heat and let the other side cook in the residual heat of the pan for 2 minutes.
- Serve the salmon wasabi side up with a bundle of cucumber ribbons on the side.

Wasabi-crusted Tuna

523

- Substitute tuna steaks for the salmon portions.

524

SERVES 4

Tuna and Melon with Lime Mayonnaise

- Put 8 wooden kebab skewers in a bowl of water and leave to soak for 20 minutes.
- Preheat a griddle pan until smoking hot.
- Thread the pieces of tuna onto the skewers and season well with salt and pepper.
- Brush the tuna and melon with oil and griddle for 2 minutes on each side or until nicely marked.
- Meanwhile, stir the lime juice and zest into the mayonnaise and divide it between 4 small bowls.
- Serve 2 tuna skewers per person with some of the melon and a bowl of mayonnaise.

PREPARATION TIME 20-25 MINUTES

COOKING TIME 8 MINUTES

INGREDIENTS

2 fresh tuna steaks, thickly sliced
1 orange-fleshed melon, cut into thin wedges
2 tbsp olive oil
4 tbsp mayonnaise
1 lime, juiced and zest finely grated

Griddled Tuna and Pineapple   525

- Cut a whole pineapple into slices with the skin on and griddle in place of the melon.

526

SERVES 4

Turkey and Green Pepper Kebabs

- Put 12 wooden skewers in a bowl of water and leave to soak for 20 minutes.
- Meanwhile, stir the basil and crushed peppercorns into the oil and toss it with the turkey and peppers.
- Leave to marinate for 20 minutes.
- Preheat the grill to its highest setting.
- Thread alternate chunks of turkey and pepper onto the skewers and spread them out on a large grill tray.
- Sprinkle with salt and grill for 4 minutes on each side or until they are golden brown and cooked through.

PREPARATION TIME 30 MINUTES

COOKING TIME 8 MINUTES

INGREDIENTS

2 tbsp basil leaves, finely chopped, plus extra to garnish
½ tsp pink peppercorns, crushed
2 tbsp olive oil
450 g / 1 lb / 2 cups turkey breast, cubed
2 green peppers, cubed

Tofu and Green Pepper Kebabs   527

- Replace the turkey with firm tofu for a vegetarian version of these kebabs.

528

SERVES 4

Scallops with Udon Noodle Soup

Prawns with Udon Noodle Soup

529

- Use 12 large raw peeled king prawns instead of the scallops.

Red Mullet with Udon Soup

530

- Replace the scallops with 12 small red mullet fillets

PREPARATION TIME 2 MINUTES

COOKING TIME 10 MINUTES

INGREDIENTS

300 g / 10 ½ oz / 2 ½ cups udon noodles
1 litre / 1 pint 15 fl. oz / 4 cups good quality fish stock
2 tsp yellow miso paste
2 tbsp olive oil
6 scallops, halved horizontally
sprigs of tarragon and coriander to serve

- Cook the noodles in boiling water according to the packet instructions or until just al dente.
- Meanwhile, bring the fish stock to a simmer and stir in the yellow miso paste.
- Heat the olive oil in a large frying pan until smoking hot and season the scallops at the last minute with salt and pepper.
- Sear the scallops for 1 minute on each side until golden brown.
- Divide the drained noodles between 4 bowls and ladle over the stock.
- Top each bowl with 3 scallop slices and garnish with herbs.

SERVES 4

Spiced Turkey Kebabs with Yoghurt Sauce

- Put 8 wooden skewers in a bowl of water and leave to soak for 20 minutes.
- Meanwhile, stir the spices into the oil and toss it with the turkey and peppers.
- Leave to marinate for 20 minutes.
- Preheat the grill to its highest setting.
- Thread alternate chunks of turkey and pepper onto the skewers and spread them out on a large grill tray.
- Sprinkle with salt and grill for 4 minutes on each side or until they are golden brown and cooked through.
- While the kebabs are cooking, mix the sauce ingredients together in a bowl.
- Serve 2 kebabs per person and drizzle over the yoghurt sauce.

PREPARATION TIME 20 MINUTES

COOKING TIME 8-10 MINUTES

INGREDIENTS

½ tsp coriander seeds, crushed
½ tsp ground cumin
½ tsp chilli flakes
a pinch ground turmeric
2 tbsp olive oil
450 g / 1 lb / 2 cups turkey breast, cubed
1 green pepper, cubed
1 red pepper, cubed

FOR THE SAUCE
4 tbsp natural yoghurt
1 lime, juiced
½ clove garlic, minced to a paste
1 tsp runny honey
boiled rice, to serve

Lamb Kebabs with Mint Yoghurt 532
- Replace the turkey with cubes of lamb neck fillet and add 2 tbsp of chopped mint to the sauce.

 533

SERVES 2

Sardine and Cherry Tomato Skewers

- Put 8 wooden skewers in a bowl of water and leave to soak for 20 minutes.
- Preheat the grill to its highest setting.
- Cut the heads off the sardines and thread them onto the skewers with the tomatoes.
- Brush them with oil and sprinkle with salt and pepper then grill for 4 minutes on each side or until cooked through.

PREPARATION TIME 20 MINUTES

COOKING TIME 8 MINUTES

INGREDIENTS

8 sardines
8 cherry tomatoes
2 tbsp olive oil

Sardine and Lemon Skewers 534
- Replace the tomatoes with rolled up slices of lemon.

535

SERVES 2

Swordfish with Onions and Thyme

PREPARATION TIME 5 MINUTES

COOKING TIME 15 MINUTES

INGREDIENTS

2 tbsp fresh thyme leaves
2 tbsp olive oil
2 swordfish steaks

FOR THE ONIONS

3 tbsp olive oil
2 onions, sliced
½ tsp pink peppercorns, crushed
½ lemon, juiced

- Heat the oil in a large sauté pan and fry the onions and peppercorns over a low heat with a pinch of salt for 15 minutes or until soft and sweet. Stir in the lemon juice.
- Meanwhile, preheat a griddle pan until smoking hot.
- Stir the thyme into the oil and brush it over the swordfish.
- Griddle the fish for 3 minutes on each side or until nicely marked.
- Divide the onions between 2 warm plates and serve the swordfish on top.

Liver with Onions and Thyme   536

- Replace the Swordfish with 2 portions of fresh calf's liver and reduce the cooking time to 2 minutes on each side.

537

SERVES 2

Lamb Chops with Roasted Vegetables

PREPARATION TIME 5 MINUTES

COOKING TIME 30 MINUTES

INGREDIENTS

2 tbsp fresh thyme leaves
4 tbsp olive oil
4 lamb chops
1 red pepper, sliced
1 yellow pepper, sliced
½ aubergine, sliced

- Preheat the oven to 220°C (200° fan), 430 F, gas 7.
- Stir the thyme into the oil and massage it into the lamb and vegetables.
- Arrange them in a large roasting tin in a single layer and season with salt and pepper.
- Roast for 30 minutes, turning the lamb over half way through.

Chicken Wings with   538
Roasted Vegetables

- Replace the lamb chops with chicken wings.

539

SERVES 4

Griddled Lamb Chops and Potatoes

Lamb with
Rosemary Mash

540

- Boil the potatoes for 4 more minutes or until completely tender then mash with 5 tbsp of olive oil and a little finely chopped rosemary. Season with salt and pepper.

Griddled Kidneys
and Potatoes

541

- Replace the lamb chops with 12 trimmed lamb's kidneys.

PREPARATION TIME 5 MINUTES

COOKING TIME 20 MINUTES

···

INGREDIENTS

800 g / 1 lb 12 oz / 4 ½ cup maris piper potatoes, halved
8 lamb chops
4 tbsp olive oil
a few sprigs rosemary

- Boil the potatoes in salted water for 12 minutes or until tender then drain well and leave to steam dry for 2 minutes.
- Meanwhile, heat a griddle pan until smoking hot.
- Brush the chops and potatoes with oil and season with salt and pepper then arrange them on the griddle with the rosemary.
- Griddle for 3 minutes on each side or until cooked to your liking.
- Arrange the potatoes on 4 warm plates and add 2 lamb chops to each. Garnish with the rosemary.

542

SERVES 2

Chicken Escalope with Sautéed Vegetables

PREPARATION TIME 5 MINUTES

COOKING TIME 15 MINUTES

....

INGREDIENTS

2 tbsp fresh thyme leaves
2 tbsp olive oil
2 chicken escallops

FOR THE VEGETABLES

2 tbsp olive oil
100 g / 3 ½ oz / 1 cup baby button onions, peeled
100 g / 3 ½ oz / ½ cup lardons
100 g / 3 ½ oz / 1 cup baby button mushrooms
100 g / 3 ½ oz / 1 cup sugar snap peas
½ lemon, juiced

- Mix the thyme with the oil and some freshly ground black pepper and brush it over the chicken. Leave to marinade for 10 minutes.
- Heat the oil in a large sauté pan and fry the onions and lardons for 5 minutes. Add the mushrooms and cook for another 5 minutes, then add the sugar snap peas and cook for a final 3 minutes. Stir in the lemon juice.
- Meanwhile, preheat a griddle pan until smoking hot.
- Griddle the chicken for 3 minutes on each side or until nicely marked.
- Divide the vegetables between 2 warm plates and serve the chicken on top.

Turkey Escalope with Sautéed Vegetables

543

- Replace the chicken with turkey and use finely shredded sage leaves instead of thyme.

544

SERVES 4

Steak Skewers with Corn on the Cob

PREPARATION TIME 20 MINUTES

COOKING TIME 15 MINUTES

....

INGREDIENTS

1 tsp orange zest, finely grated
1 tbsp flat leaf parsley, finely chopped
2 tbsp olive oil
4 minute steaks, halved lengthways
4 sweetcorn cobs, snapped in half

- Soak 8 wooden skewers in cold water for 20 minutes.
- Stir the orange zest and parsley into the oil with plenty of freshly ground black pepper and brush it over the steak. Leave to marinate for 15 minutes.
- Meanwhile, boil the sweetcorn in salted water for 8 minutes. Drain well.
- Preheat a large griddle pan until smoking hot.
- Thread each piece of steak onto a skewer and arrange on the griddle with the corn.
- Cook for 3 minutes on each side or until nicely marked.

Satay Beef Skewers

545

- Mix 2 tbsp of crunchy peanut butter with 1 tbsp of soy sauce and 1 tsp each of honey and Chinese 5 spice and massage into the beef instead of the orange and parsley.

546

SERVES 4 Red Mullet with Salad

- Put the couscous and garlic in a bowl and pour over 100 ml of boiling water.
- Cover the bowl with clingfilm and let it stand for 5 minutes then fluff up the grains with a fork.
- Season the couscous with salt and pepper and stir in the pine nuts and mint.
- Preheat a grill to its highest setting.
- Stuff the stomach cavities of the mullet with the couscous mixture and arrange them on a large grill tray.
- Grill the fish for 4 minutes on each side or until cooked through.
- Meanwhile, whisk together the honey, lemon juice and oil with a pinch of salt and use it to dress the onion and tomatoes.
- Divide the salad between 4 plates and top each one with 2 mullet.

PREPARATION TIME 10 MINUTES

COOKING TIME 8 MINUTES

INGREDIENTS

100 g / 3 ½ oz / ⅔ cup couscous
½ clove garlic, crushed
1 tbsp pine nuts
1 tbsp mint, chopped
8 red mullet, gutted

FOR THE SALAD

1 tsp runny honey
½ lemon, juiced
3 tbsp olive oil
1 red onion, sliced
2 tomatoes, cut into wedges

Stuffed Sea Bream 547

- Use the couscous to stuff 1 small sea bream per person. You may need to increase the cooking time to 5 minutes per side.

548

SERVES 4 Chicken and Rosemary Skewers

- Heat the oil in a sauté pan and fry the leeks, celery and courgettes for 10 minutes to soften. Add the garlic and cook for 2 more minutes, then stir in the wine and cook until almost evaporated.
- Meanwhile, preheat the grill to its highest setting.
- Strip most of the leaves off the rosemary sprigs and thread the chicken onto the woody stems like a skewer.
- Brush the chicken with oil and season with salt and pepper then grill for 4 minutes on each side or until cooked through.
- Divide the vegetables between 4 warm bowls and top each one with 2 chicken skewers. Garnish with chervil.

PREPARATION TIME 20 MINUTES

COOKING TIME 30 MINUTES

INGREDIENTS

8 woody sprigs of rosemary
2 skinless chicken breasts, cubed
2 tbsp olive oil
a few sprigs of chervil to garnish

FOR THE VEGETABLES

4 tbsp olive oil
1 leek, cleaned and chopped
2 sticks celery, cubed
2 courgettes (zucchini), cubed
2 cloves of garlic, crushed
100 ml / 3 ½ fl. oz / ½ cup white wine

Lamb and Rosemary Skewers 549

- Replace the chicken with chunks of lamb neck fillet, making the holes with a metal skewer first before threading it onto the rosemary.

550

SERVES 4

Duck and Apricot Kebabs

Duck and Date Kebabs

551

- Replace the dried apricots with pitted medjool dates.

Duck and Fig Kebabs

552

- Replace the apricots with pre-soaked dried figs and the peppers with quarters of fresh fig.

PREPARATION TIME 5 MINUTES

COOKING TIME 8 MINUTES

··

INGREDIENTS

1 tbsp fresh thyme leaves
4 tbsp olive oil
2 large duck breasts, cubed
24 dried apricots
1 green pepper, cubed
1 red pepper, cubed

- Preheat the grill to its highest setting.
- Stir the thyme into the oil and toss it with the duck, apricots and peppers.
- Thread the pieces onto 8 metal skewers and spread them out on a large grill tray.
- Sprinkle the kebabs with salt and grill for 4 minutes on each side or until they are golden brown and cooked through.
- Serve with a simple green salad.

553
SERVES 2 Baked Chicken with Squash and Carrots

- Preheat the oven to 200°C (180° fan), 390 F, gas 6.
- Stir the seeds into the oil and massage it into the chicken and vegetables.
- Arrange them in an oven-proof griddle pan or roasting tin and season well with salt and pepper.
- Bake for 35 – 40 minutes or until the chicken is cooked through.

PREPARATION TIME 5 MINUTES

COOKING TIME 35-40 MINUTES

INGREDIENTS

1 tsp coriander seeds, crushed
1 tsp mustard seeds
3 tbsp olive oil
2 chicken thigh quarters
2 chicken wings
½ onion squash, cut into wedges
8 baby carrots, peeled

Baked Chicken with Parsnips   554

- Replace the squash and carrots with 3 small parsnips, cut into quarters.

555
SERVES 4 Fusilli with Roasted Vegetables

- Preheat the oven to 220°C (200° fan), 430 F, gas 7.
- Rub the vegetables with oil and season well with salt and pepper then spread them out in a large roasting tin. Roast for 25 minutes, turning half way through.
- Once you've turned the vegetables, cook the fusilli in boiling salted water according to the packet instructions or until al dente.
- Drain the pasta then stir it into the roasting tin to absorb some of the flavours.
- Divide the pasta and vegetables between 4 warm bowls and sprinkle over the basil leaves.
- Use a vegetables peeler to shave over some Parmesan and serve.

PREPARATION TIME 2 MINUTES

COOKING TIME 25 MINUTES

INGREDIENTS

2 courgettes (zucchini), cut into chunks
1 green pepper, cut into chunks
1 red pepper, cut into chunks
1 yellow pepper, cut into chunks
4 tbsp olive oil
400 g / 14 oz / 4 cups spaghetti
2 tbsp Greek basil leaves
30 g / 1 oz / ⅓ cup Parmesan

Fusilli and Vegetable Salad   556

- Leave the pasta and vegetables to cool to room temperature then stir in 2 tbsp each of mayonnaise and pesto.

557

MAKES 6

Mediterranean Chicken Burgers

PREPARATION TIME 35 MINUTES

COOKING TIME 12 MINUTES

INGREDIENTS

600 g / 1 lb 5 oz / 2 ⅔ cup chicken
thigh, chopped
1 clove of garlic, crushed
1 tbsp lemon zest, finely grated
25 g Parmesan, finely grated
a small bunch basil, chopped
2 tbsp olive oil

- Put all of the ingredients except the oil into a food processor and pulse until finely chopped and evenly mixed.
- Shape the mixture into 6 thin patties and layer between sheets of greaseproof paper.
- Chill for 30 minutes to firm up.
- Heat the oil in a large frying pan and fry the burgers in 2 batches for 3 minutes on each side or until cooked through and golden brown.

Mediterranean Mackerel Burgers 558

- Replace the chicken with an equal weight of boneless, skinless mackerel fillet.

559

SERVES 4

Rack of Lamb with Peas

PREPARATION TIME 2 MINUTES

COOKING TIME 20 MINUTES

INGREDIENTS

2 x 6-bone racks of lamb
2 tbsp olive oil
150 g / 5 ½ oz / 1 ½ cups sugar snap
peas
150 g / 5 ½ oz / 1 cup fresh peas,
podded
a few sprigs fresh coriander (cilantro)

FOR THE GRAVY

1 large onion, finely chopped
2 tbsp butter
2 tbsp Madeira
250 ml / 9 fl. oz / 1 cup good quality
lamb stock

- Preheat the oven to 220ºC (200º fan), 430 F, gas 7 and heat a frying pan until smoking hot.
- Brush the lamb with oil and sear it all over in the frying pan, then season and roast in the oven for 10 minutes. Leave the lamb to rest for 5 minutes.
- Meanwhile, fry the onion in the butter for 10 minutes.
- Add the Madeira and a pinch of salt and bubble away almost to nothing. Add the beef stock and simmer gently until reduced and slightly thickened.
- While the gravy is cooking, boil the sugar snaps and peas for 4 minutes or until al dente.
- Cut the lamb into individual chops and serve 3 per person on a bed of peas and sugar snaps.
- Strain the gravy through a sieve to get rid of the onions and spoon it around the plate.
- Garnish the lamb with coriander (cilantro).

Rack of Lamb with Onion Gravy 560

- Thinly slice the onions instead of chopping them and don't strain the gravy.

561

SERVES 2

Salmon with Peppers and Tartar Sauce

Mackerel with Peppers and Tartare Sauce

562

- Substitute the salmon with whole grilled mackerel.

Poached Salmon with Tartare Sauce

563

- Poach the salmon instead of frying it and serve without the pepper garnish.

PREPARATION TIME 4 MINUTES

COOKING TIME 6 MINUTES

....

INGREDIENTS

2 portions salmon fillet
2 tbsp olive oil
1 jar roasted pepper in oil, drained
1 tbsp walnuts, chopped
1 tbsp fresh dill, chopped

FOR THE TARTAR SAUCE
3 tbsp mayonnaise
2 gherkins, finely chopped
1 tsp baby capers
½ shallot, finely chopped
2 tsp lemon juice

- Preheat a frying pan until smoking hot.
- Brush the salmon fillets with the oil and season with salt and pepper.
- Fry the salmon for 3 minutes on each side.
- Meanwhile, mix the peppers with the walnuts and dill and season with salt and pepper.
- To make the tartar sauce, stir the ingredients together with a little freshly ground black pepper.
- Serve the salmon on a bed of red peppers with a spoonful of tartar sauce on the side.

564

SERVES 4

Steak Kebabs and Chips

PREPARATION TIME 20 MINUTES

COOKING TIME 10 MINUTES

INGREDIENTS

400 g / 14 oz / 2 ⅓ cups oven chips
450 g / 1 lb / 2 cups sirloin steak, cubed
1 green pepper, cubed
1 onion, cubed
2 tbsp olive oil
1 lettuce, sliced
12 cherry tomatoes, halved

- Put 8 wooden skewers in a bowl of water and leave to soak for 20 minutes.
- Preheat the oven to 200°C (180° fan), 390 F, gas 6.
- Spread the chips out on a baking tray and cook for 10 minutes or according to the packet instructions.
- Meanwhile, preheat a griddle pan until smoking hot.
- Thread alternate chunks of steak, pepper and onion onto the skewers, brush with oil and season with salt and pepper.
- Griddle the kebabs for 4 minutes on each side or until cooked through.
- Sprinkle the chips with salt and pepper and divide between 4 warm plates. Serve 2 kebabs per person and arrange the lettuce and tomatoes on the side.

565

SERVES 4

Chicken Tikka Skewers with Rice Salad

PREPARATION TIME 15 MINUTES

COOKING TIME 20 MINUTES

INGREDIENTS

450 g / 1 lb / 2 cups chicken breast, cubed

FOR THE MARINADE
4 tbsp Greek yoghurt
1 clove of garlic, crushed
1 tbsp curry powder
1 tbsp mango chutney

FOR THE RICE
200 g / 7 oz / 1 cup long grain rice
1 stick celery, finely chopped
1 red pepper, finely chopped
1 yellow pepper, finely chopped

FOR THE DRESSING
1 tsp runny honey
½ lemon, juiced
3 tbsp olive oil

- Mix the marinade ingredients together with a pinch of salt. Put the lamb in a large freezer bag, add the marinade and massage it into the meat. Leave to marinade for 30 minutes.
- Meanwhile, soak 4 wooden skewers in cold water for 20 minutes.
- While the meat is marinating, put the rice in a saucepan and add enough water to cover it by 1 cm.
- Bring the pan to the boil then cover and turn down the heat to its lowest setting.
- Cook for 10 minutes then turn off the heat and leave to stand, without lifting the lid, for 10 minutes.
- Preheat the grill to its highest setting.
- Thread the lamb onto the skewers and grill for 4 minutes on each side or until they are golden brown and cooked through.
- Whisk the honey with the lemon juice then whisk in the olive oil.
- Combine the rice with the vegetables and dressing and season well with salt and pepper.
- Serve the skewers on a bed of rice salad with a simple green salad on the side.

566

SERVES 2

Steak with Couscous and Radish Leaves

- Preheat a grill to its highest setting.
- Brush the steaks with oil and season liberally with salt and pepper.
- Grill the steaks for 4 minutes on each side or until slightly charred.
- Meanwhile, put the couscous, garlic and lemon zest in a bowl and pour over 200 ml of boiling water.
- Cover the bowl with clingfilm and let it stand for 5 minutes then fluff up the grains with a fork.
- Season the couscous with salt and pepper and stir in the radish leaves.
- Serve the steaks on a bed of couscous.

PREPARATION TIME 5 MINUTES

COOKING TIME 8 MINUTES

INGREDIENTS

2 thick rump steaks
2 tbsp olive oil
200 g / 7 oz / 1 ¼ cups couscous
½ clove of garlic, crushed
1 tsp lemon zest, finely grated
a bunch of radish leaves, washed

Chicken and Asparagus Salad

567

SERVES 2

PREPARATION TIME 2 MINUTES

COOKING TIME 10 MINUTES

6 asparagus spears
½ small red onion, sliced
small bunch of young radish leaves

INGREDIENTS

2 large skinless chicken breasts
2 slices sourdough bread
6 tbsp olive oil
1 tbsp sherry vinegar

- Preheat a large griddle pan until smoking hot.
- Brush the chicken and sourdough with oil and season with salt and pepper.
- Cook the chicken for 4 minutes on each side or until cooked through but still juicy.
- Boil the asparagus in salted water for 4 minutes or until al dente, then slice each spear in half lengthways.
- Griddle the sourdough for 1 minute on each side or until nicely toasted.
- Cut it into quarters and put in the bottom of 2 bowls.
- Mix the rest of the oil with the vinegar and a little salt and pepper to make a dressing.
- Toss the asparagus, onion and radish leaves with the dressing and arrange on top of the toasted sourdough.
- Cut each chicken breast into 3 pieces and position on top of the salad.

Chicken Kebabs with Rice

568

SERVES 4

PREPARATION TIME 20 MINUTES

COOKING TIME 28 MINUTES

2 chicken breasts, cubed
1 green pepper, cubed
1 onion, cubed
2 tbsp olive oil

INGREDIENTS

200 g / 7 oz / 1 cup long grain rice
1 chicken stock cube, crumbled
1 tbsp flat leaf parsley, finely chopped

- Put 8 wooden skewers in a bowl of water and leave to soak for 20 minutes.
- Meanwhile, put the rice, stock cube and parsley in a saucepan and add enough water to cover it by 1 cm.
- Bring the pan to the boil then cover and turn down the heat to its lowest setting.
- Cook for 10 minutes then turn off the heat and leave to stand, without lifting the lid, for 10 minutes.
- Preheat a griddle pan until smoking hot.
- Thread alternate chunks of chicken, pepper and onion onto the skewers. Brush with oil and sprinkle with salt then griddle for 4 minutes on each side or until they are golden brown and cooked through.
- Fluff up the rice with a fork then divide it between 4 warm plates and top with the kebabs.

SERVES 4 569

Roasted Vegetable Crustless Quiche

PREPARATION TIME 2 MINUTES

COOKING TIME 40-45 MINUTES

....

INGREDIENTS

1 courgette, cut into chunks
1 aubergine (eggplant) , cut into chunks
1 red pepper, cut into chunks
1 yellow pepper, cut into chunks
2 tbsp olive oil
6 eggs
1 tbsp basil, finely shredded

- Preheat the oven to 180°C (160° fan), 355 F, gas 4.
- Rub the vegetables with oil and season with salt and pepper then roast for 20 minutes.
- Lightly beat the eggs and stir in the vegetables.
- Pour the mixture into a small baking dish and bake in the oven for 20 – 25 minutes or until just set in the centre.
- Sprinkle with basil and serve warm or at room temperature.

Roasted Onion Crustless Quiche   570

- Replace the vegetables with 2 red onions, cut into eighths.

571

SERVES 4

Pea and White Asparagus Crustless Quiche with Shrimp and Tomato Salsa

PREPARATION TIME 5 MINUTES

COOKING TIME 20-25 MINUTES

....

INGREDIENTS

6 free-range eggs
100 g / 3 ½ oz / ⅔ cup frozen peas, defrosted
1 jar white asparagus, drained

FOR THE SALSA
1 shallot, finely chopped
1 mild green chilli, chopped
3 tomatoes, diced
100 g / 3 ½ oz / ½ cup cooked brown shrimp, peeled

- Preheat the oven to 180°C (160° fan), 355 F, gas 4.
- Lightly beat the eggs and mix them with the peas then season well with salt and black pepper.
- Pour the mixture into a small baking dish and lay the asparagus across the top then bake in the oven for 20 – 25 minutes or until just set in the centre.
- Meanwhile, mix together the salsa ingredients and season to taste with salt and black pepper.

Shrimp and Tomato Bruschetta   572

- Use the salsa to top slices of toasted sourdough bread.

573

SERVES 4

Crispy Sesame and Poppy Seed Sole

- Mix the poppy seeds and sesame seeds together in a bowl then put the cornflour and egg white in 2 separate bowls.
- Dip the sole fillets first in the cornflour, then in egg white, then in the seeds.
- Heat the oil in a deep fat fryer, according to the manufacturer's instructions, to a temperature of 180°C.
- Lower the sole in the fryer basket and cook for 4 – 5 minutes or until crisp and golden brown.
- Line a large bowl with a thick layer of kitchen paper and when they are ready, tip them into the bowl to remove any excess oil.
- Sprinkle with a little sea salt to taste and serve immediately with the mixed leaves and petals.

PREPARATION TIME 10 MINUTES

COOKING TIME 4-5 MINUTES

INGREDIENTS

50 g / 2 ½ oz / 1 cup poppy seeds
50 g / 2 ½ oz sesame seeds
4 tbsp cornflour
1 egg white, beaten
12 small sole fillets
2 - 3 litres / 3 ½ pints – 5 pints / 8-12 cups sunflower oil
mixed salad leaves and flower petals to serve

Beer-Battered Sole

574

- Make a simple batter for the sole instead: stir enough fizzy beer into 50 g of plain (all purpose) flour to make it the consistency of double cream and use immediately.

575

SERVES 4

Farfalle, Broad Bean and Pesto Salad

- Cook the farfalle in boiling salted water according to the packet instructions or until al dente.
- 6 minutes before the end of cooking time, add the broad beans to the pot.
- Drain the pasta and broad beans and toss it with the tomato, pesto and olive oil.
- Use a vegetable peeler to shave over some Parmesan and garnish with sprigs of basil.

PREPARATION TIME 2 MINUTES

COOKING TIME 12 MINUTES

INGREDIENTS

400 g / 14 oz / 4 cups farfalle pasta
200 g / 7 oz / 1 ¾ cup broad beans, podded weight
1 tomato, diced
4 tbsp pesto
3 tbsp olive oil
30 g / 1 oz Parmesan
a few sprigs basil

Farfalle, Asparagus and Pesto Salad

576

- Replace the broad beans with asparagus spears, cut into short lengths.

577

SERVES 4

Lotus Root Stir-fry

Lotus and Vegetable Soup

578

- Add 800 ml of boiling vegetable stock to the wok before stirring in the cornflour mixture. Bring back to a simmer and serve immediately.

Lotus and Chicken Stir-fry

579

- Add a thinly sliced chicken breast to the wok when you add the lotus root.

PREPARATION TIME 15 MINUTES

COOKING TIME 6 MINUTES

....

INGREDIENTS

15 g / ½ oz dried black fungus
3 tbsp vegetable oil
2 cloves garlic, finely chopped
1 tbsp root ginger, finely chopped
1 lotus root, peeled and sliced
8 asparagus spears, trimmed and halved
100 g / 3 ½ oz / 1 cup mange tout, trimmed
½ tsp cornflour
2 tbsp rice wine or dry sherry
1 tsp caster (superfine) sugar
1 tbsp light soy sauce
75 g / 2 ½ oz / ¾ cup bean sprouts

- Pour 200 ml boiling water over the dried fungus and leave to soak for 15 minutes.
- Heat the oil in a large wok and fry the garlic and ginger for 30 seconds.
- Add the lotus root and asparagus and stir-fry for 2 minutes then add the mange tout and drained black fungus and stir-fry for another 2 minutes.
- Mix the cornflour with the rice wine, sugar and soy and add it to the wok with the bean sprouts.
- Stir-fry for 1 more minute then serve immediately.

580

SERVES 4

Penne with Provolone, Seeds and Petals

- Cook the penne in boiling salted water according to the packet instructions or until al dente. Drain well.
- Meanwhile, squash the clove of garlic and put it in a frying pan with the oil. Heat gently for 2 minutes to infuse the oil, then remove and discard the garlic.
- Add the seeds to the pan and cook until toasted and golden.
- Drain the pasta and stir it into the frying pan.
- Stir in the cheese and petals and serve immediately.

PREPARATION TIME 5 MINUTES

COOKING TIME 12 MINUTES

INGREDIENTS

400 g / 14 oz / 4 cups penne
1 clove of garlic, skin on
3 tbsp olive oil
50 g / 1 ¾ oz / 1 ¼ cups pumpkin seeds
50 g / 1 ¾ oz / 1 ¼ cups sesame seeds
150 g / 5 ½ oz / 1 ¼ cups Provolone, cubed
a big handful calendula petals

Penne with Provolone and Squash   581

- Add roasted cubes of butternut squash to the pasta to complement the pumpkin seeds.

582

SERVES 4

Baked King Prawns, Cherry Tomatoes and Samphire

- Preheat the oven to 220°C (200° fan), 430 F, gas 7.
- Mix the onion and tomatoes with the oil and spread them out in a large baking dish.
- Bake for 30 minutes or until the onions are starting to caramelise and the tomatoes are soft.
- Stir in the prawns (shrimp), samphire, chilli and almonds and return to the oven for 10 minutes or until the prawns (shrimp) are just opaque.
- Garnish with watercress just before serving.

PREPARATION TIME 12-15 MINUTES

COOKING TIME 4 MINUTES

INGREDIENTS

1 red onion, cut into thin wedges
250 g / 9 oz cherry tomatoes
4 tbsp olive oil
150 g / 5 ½ oz / 1 cup raw king prawns (shrimp), peeled leaving tails intact
100 g / 3 ½ oz / ¾ cup raw prawns (shrimp), peeled
200 g / 7 oz / 2 cups samphire, washed
1 mild red chilli, thinly sliced
50 g / 1 ¾ oz / ⅓ cup blanched almonds
watercress to garnish

Baked Scallops and Samphire   583

- Replace the prawns (shrimp) with 12 scallops.

584

SERVES 2

Mushrooms with Bacon and Chestnuts

PREPARATION TIME 5 MINUTES

COOKING TIME 18 MINUTES

INGREDIENTS

200 g / 7 oz / 2 cups mixed wild
mushrooms (to include chanterelles,
cepes and wood blewits)
1 tbsp olive oil
2 shallots, finely chopped
2 thick rashers streaky bacon, sliced
10 g / 1 tbsp butter
1 clove of garlic, crushed
100 g / 3 ½ oz / ¾ cup whole
chestnuts, cooked and peeled
1 tbsp flat leaf parsley, chopped

- Pick over the mushrooms and brush away any soil with
  a pastry brush. Cut the bigger mushrooms into bite-
  sized pieces.
- Heat the olive oil in a large sauté pan and fry the
  shallots and bacon for 4 minutes.
- Add the mushrooms to the pan with the butter, season
  with salt and pepper and cook for 10 minutes, stirring
  occasionally.
- When all of the liquid that comes out of the
  mushrooms has evaporated and they start to colour,
  add the garlic, chestnuts and parsley and cook for
  another minute or two.

Wild Mushrooms with Walnuts   585

- Replace the chestnuts with 75 g of
  walnut halves.

586

SERVES 4

Stir-Fried Beef with Vegetables

PREPARATION TIME 5 MINUTES

COOKING TIME 12 MINUTES

INGREDIENTS

4 tbsp vegetable oil
1 aubergine (eggplant) , peeled and
cubed
2 cloves garlic, finely chopped
1 tbsp root ginger, finely chopped
200 g / 7 oz / 1 ¼ cups sirloin steak,
thinly sliced
75 g / 2 ½ oz / ½ cup baby sweetcorn,
chopped
1 carrot, julienned
1 courgette, julienned
1 red pepper, julienned
½ tsp cornflour
2 tbsp rice wine or dry sherry
1 tsp caster (superfine) sugar
1 tbsp light soy sauce
75 g / 2 ½ oz / ¾ cup bean sprouts
a few sprigs coriander (cilantro)

- Heat half the oil in a large wok and stir-fry the
  aubergine (eggplant) for 4 minutes or until golden.
  Remove from the wok with a slotted spoon and reserve.
- Heat the rest of the oil and fry the garlic and ginger for
  30 seconds.
- Add the steak and stir-fry for 2 minutes then add the
  baby corn and carrot and stir-fry for another 2 minutes.
- Add the courgette (zucchini)and pepper and return
  the aubergine (eggplant) to the pan. Stir-fry for 2 more
  minutes.
- Mix the cornflour with the rice wine, sugar and soy and
  add it to the wok with the bean sprouts.
- Stir-fry for 1 more minute then serve immediately,
  garnished with the coriander (cilantro).

Stir-Fried Duck with Vegetables   587

- Replace the beef with a thinly sliced
  duck breast.

588

SERVES 4

Stir-Fried Pork with Peppers and Cabbage

Two Cabbage Stir-Fry

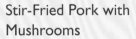

589

- Omit the pork and add ¼ a thinly shredded red cabbage to the wok when you add the Chinese cabbage.

Stir-Fried Pork with Mushrooms

590

- Replace the cabbage and peppers with 300 g of sliced button mushrooms.

PREPARATION TIME 5 MINUTES

COOKING TIME 8 MINUTES

INGREDIENTS

3 tbsp vegetable oil
2 cloves garlic, finely chopped
1 tbsp root ginger, finely chopped
200 g / 7 oz / 1 ¼ cups pork steak, thinly sliced
1 carrot, julienned
1 red pepper, julienned
1 yellow pepper, julienned
½ Chinese cabbage, chopped
2 tbsp oyster sauce
1 tbsp light soy sauce
75 g / 2 ½ oz / ¾ cup bean sprouts

- Heat the oil in a large wok and fry the garlic and ginger for 30 seconds.
- Add the pork and stir-fry for 2 minutes then add the carrots and peppers and stir-fry for another 2 minutes.
- Add the cabbage and stir-fry for 2 more minutes.
- Mix the oyster sauce with the soy and 2 tablespoons of water and add it to the wok with the bean sprouts.
- Stir-fry for 1 more minute then serve immediately.

591

SERVES 2 # Sautéed Wild Mushrooms

PREPARATION TIME 1 MINUTES

COOKING TIME 12 MINUTES

INGREDIENTS

300 g / 10 ½ oz / 3 cups mixed wild mushrooms (to include chanterelles, cepes and wood blewits)
1 tbsp olive oil
2 tbsp butter
1 clove of garlic, crushed
1 tbsp flat leaf parsley, chopped

- Pick over the mushrooms and brush away any soil with a pastry brush. Cut the bigger mushrooms into bite-sized pieces.
- Heat the olive oil and butter in a large sauté pan until sizzling.
- Add the mushrooms, season with salt and pepper and cook for 10 minutes, stirring occasionally.
- When all of the liquid that comes out of the mushrooms has evaporated and they start to colour, add the garlic and parsley and cook for another minute or two.
- Serve immediately with toasted sourdough or soft polenta.

Creamy Wild Mushrooms with Bacon

592

- Add 4 rashers of chopped bacon to the pan with the mushrooms and stir through 2 tbsp of crème

593

SERVES 4 # Rice Noodles with Beef and Sugar Snaps

PREPARATION TIME 5 MINUTES

COOKING TIME 10 MINUTES

INGREDIENTS

200 g / 7 oz / 2 cups sugar snap peas
200 g / 7 oz / 2 cups Pho or Pad Thai rice noodles
3 tbsp vegetable oil
2 cloves garlic, finely chopped
1 tbsp root ginger, julienned
1 red chilli, finely chopped
200 g / 7 oz / 1 ¼ cups sirloin steak, thinly sliced
2 tbsp oyster sauce
1 tbsp light soy sauce

- Bring a small saucepan of water to the boil and cook the sugar snaps for 3 minutes or until al dente.
- Put the rice noodles into a heatproof bowl and strain the sugar snap water over them.
- Plunge the sugar snaps into cold water and cover the noodle bowl with cling film. Leave to soften for 3 minutes.
- Drain the noodles and plunge into cold water with the mange tout to stop the cooking.
- Heat the oil in a large wok and fry the garlic and ginger for 30 seconds.
- Add the steak and stir-fry for 2 minutes then add the sugar snaps and noodles.
- Mix the oyster sauce with the soy and 2 tablespoons of water and add it to the wok.
- Stir-fry for 1 more minute then serve immediately.

Rice Noodles with Prawns and Sugar Snaps

594

- Replace the beef with 200 g of raw, peeled prawns (shrimp).

595

SERVES 4

Pork with Haricot Beans and Sweetcorn

- Heat the oil in a large sauté pan and stir-fry the pork, onion and green pepper for 5 minutes or until the pork is nicely browned.
- Add the beans and sweetcorn to the pan and cook for 3 more minutes then stir in the lemon juice and honey and season with salt and pepper.
- Cook for a further minute to glaze the pork then serve in warm bowls with the tortillas on the side.

PREPARATION TIME 2 MINUTES

COOKING TIME 10 MINUTES

INGREDIENTS

2 tbsp olive oil
450 g / 1 lb / 3 cups pork fillet, cubed
1 onion, sliced
½ green pepper, chopped
200 g / 7 oz / ¾ cup canned haricot beans, drained
200 g / 7 oz / ¾ cup canned sweetcorn, drained
½ lemon, juiced
1 tsp runny honey
4 flour tortillas

Pork with Kidney Beans and Sweetcorn

596

- Replace the haricot beans with kidney beans.

597

SERVES 4

Aubergine with Chilli Beef

- Preheat the oven to 200°C (180° fan), 390 F, gas 6.
- Rub the aubergine (eggplant) with half of the oil and season well with salt and pepper.
- Roast for 30 minutes or until golden brown and softened.
- 10 minutes before the end of cooking time, heat the rest of the oil and fry the garlic, ginger and chilli for 30 seconds.
- Add the mince and stir-fry for 4 minutes or until nicely browned then add the peas.
- Mix the cornflour with the rice wine, sugar and soy and add it to the wok.
- Stir-fry for 4 more minutes or until it has reduced to a sticky glaze.
- Toss the beef mixture with the roasted aubergine (eggplant) and serve, garnished with lettuce.

PREPARATION TIME 5 MINUTES

COOKING TIME 30 MINUTES

INGREDIENTS

1 aubergine (eggplant) , cut into large chunks
4 tbsp vegetable oil
2 cloves garlic, finely chopped
1 tbsp root ginger, finely chopped
2 red chillies, finely chopped
200 g / 7 oz / 1 cup minced beef
75 g / 2 ½ oz / ½ cup frozen peas, defrosted
½ tsp cornflour
2 tbsp rice wine or dry sherry
1 tsp caster (superfine) sugar
1 tbsp light soy sauce
lettuce to garnish

Aubergine with Chilli Pork

598

- Replace the minced beef with minced pork.

599

SERVES 4

Spiced Broccoli and Cauliflower

Spice-Roasted Broccoli and Cauliflower

600

- Rub the raw vegetables with the oil and spices and roast for 25 minutes at 190°C.

Spicy Broccoli and Cauliflower Soup

601

- When the vegetables are ready, add 800 ml of vegetable stock and simmer for 5 minutes. Blend to a smooth soup in a liquidiser.

PREPARATION TIME 5 MINUTES

COOKING TIME 6-8 MINUTES

....

INGREDIENTS

1 small cauliflower, broken into florets
1 small head broccoli, broken into florets
2 tbsp olive oil
½ tsp pink peppercorns
½ tsp ground cumin
½ tsp ground coriander (cilantro)

- Steam the cauliflower and broccoli for 5 minutes or until tender.
- Heat the oil in a frying pan and add the vegetables, spices and a sprinkle of sea salt and stir-fry for 2 minutes.

602

SERVES 4

Pork with Bean Sprouts and Noodles

- Put the noodles in a pan of boiling water and turn off the heat. Cover and leave to soften for 10 minutes before draining.
- To make the crispy shallots, heat the vegetable oil in a saucepan and fry the shallots for 5 minutes or until golden brown. Add the lime zest and continue to cook until the shallots are crisp.
- Remove from the pan with a slotted spoon and leave to drain on kitchen paper.
- Heat the oil in a large wok and fry the garlic, ginger and shallots for 1 minute.
- Add the pork and stir-fry for 3 minutes. Add the soy sauce and bean sprouts and stir-fry for 2 more minutes.
- Serve the pork on a bed of glass noodles, sprinkled with crispy shallots and garnished with coriander (cilantro).

Stir-Fried Turkey with Bean Sprouts

603

- Substitute sliced turkey breast for the pork.

PREPARATION TIME 5 MINUTES

COOKING TIME 20 MINUTES

INGREDIENTS

400 g / 14 oz / 4 cups dried glass noodles
3 tbsp vegetable oil
2 cloves garlic, thinly sliced
1 tbsp root ginger, thinly sliced
2 shallots, cut into wedges
200 g / 7 oz / 1 ½ cups pork steak, thinly sliced
2 tbsp light soy sauce
75 g / 2 ½ oz / ¾ cup bean sprouts
coriander (cilantro) (cilantro)leaves to garnish

FOR THE CRISPY SHALLOTS

150 ml / 5 ½ fl. oz / ⅔ cup vegetable oil
2 shallots, finely sliced
1 tsp lime zest, finely pared

604

SERVES 4

Chicken and Vegetable Stir-fry

- Heat the oil in a large wok and fry the garlic, ginger and onion for 30 seconds.
- Add the chicken and stir-fry for 2 minutes then add the mange tout and mushrooms and stir-fry for another 2 minutes.
- Mix the cornflour with the rice wine, sugar and soy and add it to the wok.
- Stir-fry for 1 more minute then serve immediately.

PREPARATION TIME 5 MINUTES

COOKING TIME 6 MINUTES

INGREDIENTS

3 tbsp vegetable oil
2 cloves garlic, finely chopped
1 tbsp root ginger, finely chopped
1 onion, thinly sliced
200 g / 7 oz / 1 ½ cups chicken breast, cubed
100 g / 3 ½ oz / 1 cup mange tout, trimmed
100 g / 3 ½ oz / 1 cup mushrooms, sliced
½ tsp cornflour
2 tbsp rice wine or dry sherry
1 tsp caster (superfine) sugar
1 tbsp light soy sauce

Chicken and Baby Corn Stir-fry

605

- Replace the mange tout with baby sweetcorn, halved lengthways.

606

SERVES 4

Chicken with Pineapple and Tomatoes

PREPARATION TIME 5 MINUTES

COOKING TIME 6-8 MINUTES

INGREDIENTS

3 tbsp vegetable oil
2 cloves garlic, finely chopped
1 tbsp root ginger, finely chopped
225 g / 8 oz / 1 ½ cups chicken breast, sliced
½ fresh pineapple, peeled and cut into chunks
2 tbsp rice wine or dry sherry
1 tsp caster (superfine) sugar
1 tbsp light soy sauce
100 g / 3 ½ oz / ¾ cup cherry tomatoes, halved
4 spring onions (scallions), sliced diagonally

- Heat the oil in a large wok and fry the garlic and ginger for 30 seconds.
- Add the chicken and stir-fry for 2 minutes then add the pineapple and stir-fry for another 2 minutes.
- Mix the rice wine, sugar and soy together and add it to the wok with the tomatoes and spring onion.
- Stir-fry for 2 more minutes then serve immediately.

Duck with Pineapple and Tomatoes

607

- Replace the chicken with duck breast.

608

SERVES 4

Stir-Fried Squid with Chilli and Spinach

PREPARATION TIME 2 MINUTES

COOKING TIME 4 MINUTES

INGREDIENTS

100 g / 3 ½ oz / 3 ¼ cup baby leaf spinach
2 tbsp vegetable oil
2 cloves garlic, finely chopped
2 red chillies, thinly sliced
300 g / 10 ½ oz / 2 cups raw squid rings
½ lemon, juiced
2 tsp light soy sauce

- Heat a large saucepan on the hob then wash the spinach and put it in the pan. Cover and leave to wilt for 2 minutes, then stir well and drain in a sieve.
- Heat the oil in a large wok and fry the garlic and chilli for 30 seconds.
- Add the squid rings and cook for 1 minute or until they just turn opaque then stir in the spinach, lemon and soy. Serve immediately.

Stir-Fried Squid with Oyster Sauce

609

- Omit the spinach and replace the soy sauce with 3 tbsp of oyster sauce.

610

SERVES 4

Pork with Mushrooms and Cream

Creamy Pork Tagliatelle   611

- Use the dish to dress a large bowl of tagliatelle.

Pork with Mushrooms and Spinach   612

- Add 100 g baby spinach leaves with the cream and cook until wilted.

PREPARATION TIME 5 MINUTES

COOKING TIME 20 MINUTES

....

INGREDIENTS

2 tbsp olive oil
450 g / 1 lb / 3 cups pork fillet, cubed
200 g / 7 oz / 2 cups mushrooms, sliced
1 tbsp butter
100 ml / 3 ½ fl. oz / ½ cup white wine
200 ml / 7 fl. oz / ¾ cup double cream
1 tbsp chives, chopped

- Heat the oil in a large sauté pan and stir-fry the pork for 5 minutes or until nicely browned. Remove from the pan with a slotted spoon and reserve.
- Add the mushrooms to the pan with the butter and a pinch of salt and fry for 10 minutes or until any liquid that comes out of them has evaporated and they start to colour.
- Add the wine and bubble for 2 minutes then return the pork to the pan.
- Stir in the cream and chives and season with freshly ground black pepper, then bubble for 2 more minutes.

613

SERVES 4

Chicken, Honey and Sesame Stir-fry

PREPARATION TIME 5 MINUTES

COOKING TIME 8 MINUTES

....

INGREDIENTS

3 tbsp vegetable oil
2 cloves garlic, finely chopped
1 tbsp root ginger, finely chopped
225 g / 7 oz / 1 ½ cups chicken breast, cubed
2 tbsp sesame seeds
1 carrot, thinly sliced lengthways
100 g / 3 ½ oz / 1 cup sugar snap peas, trimmed
100 g / 3 ½ oz / ¾ cup baby sweetcorn
8 spring onions (scallions), trimmed
2 tbsp rice wine or dry sherry
2 tbsp runny honey
1 tbsp light soy sauce
100 g / 3 ½ oz / 1 cup canned white asparagus, drained

- Heat the oil in a large wok and fry the garlic and ginger for 30 seconds.
- Add the chicken and sesame seeds and stir-fry for 2 minutes then add the carrot, sugar snaps, sweetcorn and spring onions and stir-fry for another 2 minutes.
- Mix the rice wine with the honey and soy and add it to the wok with the asparagus.
- Stir-fry for 2 more minutes then serve immediately.

Beef, Honey and Sesame Stir-fry

614

- Replace the chicken with thinly sliced sirloin steak.

615

SERVES 4

Stir-Fried Salmon with Vegetables

/ 1 cup
PREPARATION TIME 5 MINUTES

COOKING TIME 8 MINUTES

....

INGREDIENTS

3 tbsp vegetable oil
2 cloves garlic, finely chopped
1 tbsp root ginger, finely chopped
150 g / 5 ½ oz / 1 cup baby carrots, peeled
150 g / 5 ½ oz / 1 ½ cups asparagus spears
300 g / 10 ½ oz / 2 cups salmon fillet, cubed
1 red pepper, julienned
1 yellow pepper, julienned
1 green pepper, julienned
2 tbsp rice wine or dry sherry
1 tsp caster (superfine) sugar
1 tbsp light soy sauce
1 tbsp sesame seeds

- Heat the oil in a large wok and fry the garlic and ginger for 30 seconds.
- Add the carrots and asparagus and stir-fry for 2 minutes then add the salmon and peppers and stir-fry for another 2 minutes.
- Mix the rice wine, sugar and soy together and add it to the wok with the sesame seeds.
- Stir-fry for 2 more minutes then serve immediately.

Stir-Fried Sword Fish

616

- Replace the salmon with cubes of fresh swordfish steak.

617

SERVES 4

Cumin Beef with Stir-Fried Vegetables

- Heat half the oil in a large wok and stir-fry the steak with the cumin seeds for 4 minutes. Remove from the wok with a slotted spoon and reserve.
- Heat the rest of the oil and fry the garlic and ginger for 30 seconds.
- Add the baby corn and carrot and stir-fry for 2 minutes then add the mange tout and stir-fry for another minute.
- Mix the rice wine, sugar and soy together and add it to the wok with the bean sprouts.
- Stir-fry for 2 more minutes then divide between 4 warm bowls and top with the cumin beef.

PREPARATION TIME 5 MINUTES

COOKING TIME 10 MINUTES

INGREDIENTS

4 tbsp vegetable oil
225 g / 8 oz / 1 ½ cups sirloin steak, thinly sliced
1 tsp cumin seeds
2 cloves garlic, finely chopped
1 tbsp root ginger, finely chopped
75 g / 2 ½ oz / ¾ cup baby sweetcorn, chopped
1 carrot, sliced
100 g / 3 ½ oz / 1 cup mange tout, trimmed
2 tbsp rice wine or dry sherry
1 tsp caster (superfine) sugar
1 tbsp light soy sauce
100 g / 3 ½ oz / 1 cup bean sprouts

Coriander Beef with Stir-Fried Vegetables

618

- Substitute the cumin for crushed coriander (cilantro) (cilantro)seeds.

619

SERVES 4

Chicken and Mange Tout in Oyster Sauce

- Heat the oil in a large wok and fry the shallots, garlic and ginger for 30 seconds.
- Add the chicken and stir-fry for 2 minutes then add the mange tout and stir-fry for another 2 minutes.
- Mix the oyster sauce with the soy and 2 tablespoons of water and add it to the wok with the spring onions.
- Stir-fry for 2 more minutes then serve immediately.

PREPARATION TIME 5 MINUTES

COOKING TIME 8 MINUTES

INGREDIENTS

3 tbsp vegetable oil
2 shallots, thinly sliced
2 cloves garlic, finely chopped
1 tbsp root ginger, finely chopped
300 g / 10 ½ oz / 2 cups chicken breast, thinly sliced
200 g / 7 oz / 2 cups mange tout
2 tbsp oyster sauce
1 tbsp dark soy sauce
2 spring onions, finely chopped

Chicken and Straw Mushrooms

 620

- Replace the mange tout with a drained can of Chinese straw mushrooms.

Omelette with Broccoli and Noodles

Chinese Omelette Fried Rice

622

- Omit the noodles and add 4 portions of cooked rice to the wok before returning the omelette pieces.

Tofu with Broccoli and Noodles

623

- Omit the omelette and use silken tofu instead.

PREPARATION TIME 5 MINUTES

COOKING TIME 12 MINUTES

....

INGREDIENTS

200 g / 7 oz / 2 cups thin egg noodles
½ head broccoli, broken into florets
2 tbsp vegetable oil
2 cloves of garlic, thinly sliced
1 tbsp root ginger, thinly sliced
3 large eggs, beaten
2 tbsp light soy sauce

- Cook the noodles in boiling salted water according to the packet instructions or until al dente, then drain well.
- Meanwhile, blanch the broccoli for 4 minutes then plunge into cold water and drain well.
- Heat the oil in a large wok and fry the garlic and ginger for 1 minute.
- Pour the eggs into the pan and shake it while it sets into a thin omelette.
- Use a fish slice to remove the omelette from the pan and cut it into squares.
- Put the wok back on the heat and add the omelette, soy sauce, noodles and broccoli and stir-fry for 2 more minutes.

624

SERVES 2 Salt and Pepper Prawns with Holy Basil

- Heat the oil in a wok and fry the garlic cloves and chilli for 1 minute.
- Add the prawns (shrimp) and stir-fry over a very high heat until just opaque then stir in the pepper, salt, sugar and basil.
- Serve immediately.

PREPARATION TIME 2 MINUTES

COOKING TIME 5-8 MINUTES

INGREDIENTS

2 tbsp vegetable oil
2 cloves of garlic, skin on, squashed
1 red chilli, finely chopped
16 raw king prawns (shrimp), peeled leaving tails intact
1 tsp Szechwan peppercorns, crushed
½ tsp sea salt flakes
1 tsp granulated sugar
a small bunch holy basil, leaves only

Salt and Pepper Squid   625

- Replace the prawns (shrimp) with pieces of squid that have been dusted with cornflour.

626

SERVES 4 Stir-Fried Brussels Sprouts

- Steam the Brussels sprouts for 5 minutes or until just tender.
- Heat the oil in a large wok and fry the chilli and garlic for 30 seconds. Add the carrot, spring onions and sprouts and stir-fry for 3 minutes.
- Mix the rice wine with the honey and soy and add it to the wok, then stir-fry for 2 more minutes.
- Divide between 4 warm bowls and serve.

PREPARATION TIME 5 MINUTES

COOKING TIME 12 MINUTES

INGREDIENTS

300 g / 10 ½ oz / 3 cups Brussels sprouts
3 tbsp olive oil
1 red chilli, finely chopped
1 clove of garlic, crushed
1 carrot, thinly sliced
100 g / 3 ½ oz / 1 cup spring onions (scallions), cut into short lengths
2 tbsp rice wine or dry sherry
1 tbsp runny honey
1 tbsp light soy sauce

Stir-Fried Sprouts with Chilli Pork   627

- Omit the carrots and add 200 g of pork mince to the wok. Fry until crispy.

628

SERVES 4

Prawn Fried Rice

PREPARATION TIME 2 MINUTES

COOKING TIME 10 MINUTES

INGREDIENTS

3 tbsp olive oil
1 red chilli, finely chopped
1 clove of garlic, crushed
20 raw king prawns (shrimp), peeled
200 g / 7 oz / 2 cups sugar snap peas, trimmed
1 red pepper, sliced
300 g / 10 ½ oz / 1 ¼ cups mixed basmati, red and wild rice, cooked and cooled
2 tbsp soy sauce
50 g / 1 ¾ oz / ½ cup bean sprouts

- Heat the oil in a large wok and fry the chilli and garlic for 30 seconds.
- Add the prawns (shrimp), sugar snaps and peppers and stir-fry for 3 minutes or until the prawns (shrimp) turn opaque.
- Add the rice and stir-fry until piping hot – this should take about 4 minutes.
- Add the soy and bean sprouts and cook for 1 more minute then serve immediately.

Beef Fried Rice   629

- Replace the prawns (shrimp) with 150 g of very thinly sliced sirloin steak.

630

SERVES 4

Special Fried Rice

PREPARATION TIME 12 MINUTES

COOKING TIME 15-20 MINUTES

INGREDIENTS

15 g / ½ oz dried black fungus
3 tbsp vegetable oil
1 clove of garlic, crushed
1 tbsp root ginger, finely chopped
1 large egg
20 raw king prawns (shrimp), peeled with tails left intact
100 g / 3 ½ oz / ¾ cup frozen peas, defrosted
300 g / 10 ½ oz / 1 ¾ cup long grain rice, cooked and cooled
2 tbsp soy sauce

FOR THE PORK BALLS

2 - 3 litres / 3 ½ pints – 5 pints / 8-12 cups sunflower oil
4 tbsp cornflour
1 tsp Chinese five spice powder
200 g / 7 oz / 1 ½ cups pork belly, cubed
1 egg white, beaten

- Put the fungus in a bowl and pour over 200 ml of boiling water. Cover the bowl with film and leave to soak for 10 minutes then drain and thinly slice.
- Heat the sunflower oil in a deep fat fryer, to a temperature of 180°C.
- Mix the cornflour with the five spice and a pinch of salt and use half of it to coat the pork. Dip the pork in egg white then coat in the cornflour again.
- Deep-fry the pork for 4 – 5 minutes until crispy.
- Heat the vegetable oil in a large wok and fry the garlic and ginger for 30 seconds. Add the egg and scramble.
- Add the prawns and peas and fry for 3 minutes. Add the rice and fry for 4 minutes.
- Add the soy and black fungus and cook for 1 more minute then divide between 4 warm bowls and top with the pork balls.

Chicken Special Fried Rice   631

- Replace the pork with chicken and the peas with sweetcorn.

SERVES 4

Prawn Stir-fry with Vegetables

Stir-Fried Prawns with Baby Corn

633

- Replace the bean sprouts with sliced baby sweetcorn, adding them to the wok with the mange tout.

Stir-Fried Tofu with Mange Tout

634

- Replace the prawns with an equal weight of firm tofu cubes and double the quantity of mange tout.

PREPARATION TIME 5 MINUTES

COOKING TIME 5 MINUTES

INGREDIENTS

3 tbsp olive oil
1 red chilli, finely chopped
1 clove of garlic, crushed
20 raw king prawns (shrimp), peeled leaving tails intact
200 g / 7 oz / 2 cups mange tout, trimmed
100 g / 3 ½ oz / ¾ cup canned straw mushrooms, drained
2 tbsp soy sauce
100 g / 3 ½ oz / 1 cup bean sprouts

- Heat the oil in a large wok and fry the chilli and garlic for 30 seconds.
- Add the prawns (shrimp), mange tout and mushrooms and stir-fry for 3 minutes or until the prawns (shrimp) turn opaque.
- Add the soy and bean sprouts and cook for 1 more minute then serve immediately.

635

SERVES 2

Salt and Pepper Chicken with Holy Basil

PREPARATION TIME 2 MINUTES

COOKING TIME 4 MINUTES

INGREDIENTS

2 tbsp vegetable oil
1 onion, sliced
200 g / 7 oz / 1 ½ cups chicken breast, sliced
½ tsp cayenne pepper
1 tsp ground Szechwan pepper
½ tsp caster (superfine) sugar
a small bunch holy basil, leaves only

- Heat the oil in a wok and fry the onion and chicken for 4 minutes or until the chicken is cooked through.
- Add the Cayenne, Szechwan pepper and sugar with a pinch of salt then stir in the basil and cook until wilted.
- Serve immediately.

636

SERVES 4

Stir-Fried Chicken with Almonds

PREPARATION TIME 2 MINUTES

COOKING TIME 6 MINUTES

INGREDIENTS

2 tbsp vegetable oil
1 onion, sliced
3 chicken breasts, sliced
1 tsp Chinese five spice powder
50 g / 1 ¾ oz / ½ cup flaked (slivered) almonds
2 tbsp soy sauce

- Heat the oil in a wok and fry the onion and chicken for 4 minutes or until the chicken is cooked through.
- Add the five spice, almonds and soy and stir-fry for 2 more minutes, then serve immediately.

637

SERVES 4

Stir-Fried Turkey with Peppers

- Heat the oil in a large wok and fry the garlic and ginger for 30 seconds.
- Add the turkey and peppers and stir-fry for 4 minutes or until the turkey is cooked through.
- Mix the rice wine, sugar and soy together and add it to the wok.
- Stir-fry for 2 more minutes then serve immediately.

PREPARATION TIME 5 MINUTES

COOKING TIME 8 MINUTES

INGREDIENTS

3 tbsp vegetable oil
2 cloves garlic, finely chopped
1 tbsp root ginger, finely chopped
300 g / 10 ½ oz / 1 ¾ cup turkey breast, cubed
1 red pepper, julienned
1 yellow pepper, julienned
1 green pepper, julienned
2 tbsp rice wine or dry sherry
1 tsp caster (superfine) sugar
1 tbsp light soy sauce

Chicken with Honey and Ginger

638

SERVES 4

PREPARATION TIME 5 MINUTES

COOKING TIME 6 MINUTES

INGREDIENTS

3 tbsp vegetable oil
1 clove of garlic, thinly sliced
2 tbsp root ginger, thinly sliced
4 chicken breasts, cubed

2 tbsp rice wine or dry sherry
2 tbsp runny honey
1 tbsp light soy sauce
a handful of rocket (arugula) leaves

- Heat the oil in a large wok and fry the garlic and ginger for 30 seconds.
- Add the chicken and stir-fry for 4 minutes or until cooked through.
- Mix the rice wine with the honey and soy and add it to the wok.
- Stir-fry for 1 more minute then serve immediately, garnished with rocket (arugula).

Pork, Honey and Sesame Stir-fry

639

SERVES 4

PREPARATION TIME 2 MINUTES

COOKING TIME 8 MINUTES

INGREDIENTS

3 tbsp vegetable oil
1 onion, thinly sliced
2 cloves of garlic, finely chopped
225 g / 8 oz / 1 ½ cups pork steak, sliced

2 tbsp sesame seeds
1 red pepper, julienned
2 tbsp rice wine or dry sherry
2 tbsp runny honey
1 tbsp dark soy sauce

- Heat the oil in a large wok and fry the onion for 2 minutes.
- Add the garlic, pork and sesame seeds and stir-fry for 2 more minutes then add the peppers.
- Stir-fry for 2 minutes then mix the rice wine with the honey and soy and add it to the wok.
- Stir-fry until it reduced to a sticky glaze then serve immediately.

640

SERVES 2

Stir-Fried Pork and Pineapple

PREPARATION TIME 5 MINUTES

COOKING TIME 8 MINUTES

INGREDIENTS

3 tbsp vegetable oil
2 cloves garlic, finely chopped
1 tbsp root ginger, finely chopped
225 g / 8 oz / 1 ½ cups pork belly, cubed
300 g / 10 ½ oz / 1 ½ cups canned pineapple rings, drained and halved
2 tbsp rice wine or dry sherry
1 tsp caster (superfine) sugar
1 tbsp light soy sauce
a small bunch of chives, cut into short lengths

- Heat the oil in a large wok and fry the garlic and ginger for 30 seconds.
- Add the pork and stir-fry for 2 minutes then add the pineapple and stir-fry for another 2 minutes.
- Mix the rice wine, sugar and soy together and add it to the wok.
- Stir-fry for 2 more minutes then serve immediately, garnished with chives

Stir-Fried Pork and Mandarin | 641

- Replace the canned pineapple with canned mandarin segments, drained of the juice.

642

SERVES 4

Chicken, Noodle and Broccoli Stir-fry

PREPARATION TIME 5 MINUTES

COOKING TIME 12 MINUTES

INGREDIENTS

200 g / 7 oz / 2 cups thin egg noodles
½ head broccoli, broken into florets
3 tbsp vegetable oil
2 cloves of garlic, thinly sliced
1 tbsp root ginger, thinly sliced
2 shallots, sliced
4 chestnut mushrooms, thinly sliced
200 g / 7 oz chicken breast, thinly sliced
2 tbsp light soy sauce
lemon slices to garnish

- Cook the noodles in boiling salted water according to the packet instructions or until al dente, then drain well.
- Meanwhile, blanch the broccoli for 4 minutes then plunge into cold water and drain well.
- Heat the oil in a large wok and fry the garlic, ginger, shallots and mushrooms for 2 minutes.
- Add the chicken and stir-fry for 3 minutes or until just cooked through.
- Add the soy sauce, noodles and broccoli and stir-fry for 2 more minutes.
- Serve immediately, garnished with lemon slices.

Spicy Chicken Noodle Stir-fry | 643

- Add 2 finely chopped red chillies and 1 tsp of crushed Szechwan peppercorns to the frying onions.

644

SERVES 2 # Stir-Fried Prawns and Pineapple

- Heat the oil in a large wok and fry the garlic and ginger for 30 seconds.
- Add the prawns (shrimp) and pineapple and stir-fry for 2 minutes or until the prawns (shrimp) turn opaque.
- Mix the rice wine, sugar and soy together and add it to the wok.
- Stir-fry for 2 more minutes then serve immediately, garnished with chives

PREPARATION TIME 5 MINUTES

COOKING TIME 5 MINUTES

INGREDIENTS

3 tbsp vegetable oil
2 cloves of garlic, thinly sliced
1 tbsp root ginger, thinly sliced
200 g / 7 oz / 1 cup raw prawns (shrimp), peeled with tails left intact
300 g / 10 ½ oz / 1 ½ cups canned pineapple rings, drained and halved
2 tbsp rice wine or dry sherry
1 tsp caster (superfine) sugar
1 tbsp light soy sauce
a small bunch of chives, cut into short lengths

Prawns with Pineapple and Chicken

645

- Slice a chicken breast into thin strips and add to the wok along with the garlic. Once cooked through, add the prawns.

646

SERVES 4 # Stir-Fried Beef with Peppers

- Heat the oil in a large wok and fry the garlic and ginger for 30 seconds.
- Add the steak, peppers and spring onions and stir-fry for 4 minutes or until the beef is cooked through.
- Mix the rice wine, sugar and soy together and add it to the wok.
- Stir-fry for 2 more minutes then serve immediately, garnished with coriander (cilantro).

PREPARATION TIME 5 MINUTES

COOKING TIME 8 MINUTES

INGREDIENTS

3 tbsp vegetable oil
2 cloves garlic, finely chopped
1 tbsp root ginger, finely chopped
300 g / 10 ½ oz / 2 cups sirloin steak, sliced
1 yellow pepper, julienned
1 green pepper, julienned
4 spring onions (scallions), chopped
2 tbsp rice wine or dry sherry
1 tsp caster (superfine) sugar
1 tbsp light soy sauce
coriander (cilantro) (cilantro)leaves to garnish

Stir-Fried Beef with Red Peppers

 647

- Replace the green and yellow peppers with red peppers and add a handful of bean sprouts in place of the spring onions. Garnish with holy basil instead of coriander (cilantro).

648

SERVES 4

Duck with Orange and Honey

Duck with Apple and Chilli

649

- Add a peeled, sliced apple and 6 dried birds-eye chillies to the wok with the duck and omit the orange slices.

Duck with Honey and Lime

650

- Replace the orange juice and orange slices with lime juice and lime slices.

PREPARATION TIME 2 MINUTES

COOKING TIME 6 MINUTES

INGREDIENTS

3 tbsp vegetable oil
2 duck breasts, thinly sliced
2 tbsp orange juice
2 tbsp runny honey
1 tbsp light soy sauce
orange slices to garnish

- Heat the oil in a large wok and stir-fry the duck for 4 minutes or until cooked through.
- Mix the orange juice with the honey and soy and add it to the wok then stir-fry until the liquid has reduced to a sticky glaze.
- Serve immediately, garnished with orange slices.

651

SERVES 4

Beef with Ginger, Peppers and Tomato

- Heat the oil in a large wok and fry the garlic and ginger for 30 seconds.
- Add the steak, peppers and tomatoes and stir-fry for 4 minutes or until the beef is cooked through.
- Mix the rice wine, sugar and soy together and add it to the wok.
- Stir-fry for 2 more minutes then serve immediately, garnished with coriander (cilantro).

PREPARATION TIME 5 MINUTES

COOKING TIME 8 MINUTES

INGREDIENTS

3 tbsp vegetable oil
2 cloves garlic, thinly sliced
1 tbsp root ginger, sliced
300 g / 10 ½ oz / 2 cups sirloin steak, cubed
1 red pepper, julienned
100 g / 3 ½ oz / ¾ cup cherry tomatoes, halved
2 tbsp rice wine or dry sherry
1 tsp caster (superfine) sugar
1 tbsp light soy sauce
coriander (cilantro) (cilantro)leaves to garnish

Beef with Ginger and Spring Onions

652

- Replace the red pepper with green pepper and omit the tomatoes in favour of a bunch of chopped spring onions.

653

SERVES 4

Monkfish and Lemongrass Curry

- Heat the oil in a wok and fry the garlic, lemongrass and curry paste for 2 minutes.
- Sprinkle the monkfish with cumin, then add to the wok and stir-fry for 2 minutes.
- Pour in the coconut milk and bring to a simmer then stir in the sugar, fish sauce and lime slices.
- Serve with jasmine rice.

PREPARATION TIME 2 MINUTES

COOKING TIME 10 MINUTES

INGREDIENTS

2 tbsp vegetable oil
1 clove of garlic, skin on
1 lemongrass stem, thinly sliced
2 tbsp Thai yellow curry paste
1 monkfish tail, boned and cubed
½ tsp ground cumin
400 ml / 14 fl. oz / 1 ⅔ cups coconut milk
1 tsp caster (superfine) sugar
1 tbsp fish sauce
1 lime, sliced

Salmon and Lemongrass Curry

654

- Replace the monk fish with skinless salmon fillet and replace the cumin with ground coriander (cilantro).

655

SERVES 4

Stir-Fried Beef with Winter Vegetables

PREPARATION TIME 5 MINUTES

COOKING TIME 10 MINUTES

INGREDIENTS

½ head broccoli, broken into florets
½ cauliflower, broken into florets
2 carrots, cut into batons
100 g / 3 ½ oz / ¾ cup green beans
3 tbsp vegetable oil
2 cloves of garlic, thinly sliced
1 tbsp root ginger, thinly sliced
200 g / 7 oz / 1 ¼ cups sirloin steak,
thinly sliced
2 tbsp light soy sauce
chives to garnish

- Blanch the vegetables for 4 minutes then plunge into cold water and drain well.
- Heat the oil in a large wok and fry the garlic and ginger for 30 seconds.
- Add the beef and stir-fry for 3 minutes or until just cooked through.
- Add the soy sauce and vegetables and stir-fry for 2 more minutes.
- Serve immediately, garnished with chives.

Beef and Vegetables in Oyster Sauce
656

- Replace the soy sauce with 3 tbsp of oyster sauce mixed with an equal quantity of water.

657

SERVES 4

Pork with Coconut, Lime and Paprika

PREPARATION TIME 35 MINUTES

COOKING TIME 8 MINUTES

INGREDIENTS

1 clove of garlic, crushed
1 tsp root ginger, grated
½ tsp paprika
1 lime, juiced and zest finely grated
400 g / 14 oz / 2 ½ cups pork
shoulder, cubed
2 tbsp cornflour
2 tbsp vegetable oil
200 ml / 7 fl. oz coconut milk
paprika, lime slices and holy basil
to garnish

- Mix the garlic, ginger and paprika with the lime juice and zest and massage it into the pork.
- Leave to marinate for 30 minutes.
- Pat the pork dry with kitchen paper and dust it with cornflour.
- Heat the oil in a wok and stir-fry the pork over a high heat for 4 minutes or until golden brown and cooked through.
- Pour in the coconut milk and bubble until reduced and thick.
- Spoon onto a serving plate and sprinkle with paprika. Garnish with lime and holy basil.

Chicken with Coconut, Lime and Paprika
658

- Replace the pork belly with pieces of boneless, skinless chicken thigh.

659

SERVES 4

Beef and Noodle Stir-fry

Egg Fried Noodles

 660

- Replace the beef with 2 beaten eggs. Stir-fry until scrambled.

Crispy Lamb Noodles 661

- Shred 200 g of leftover roast lamb and deep fry at 190°C until crisp, then add it to the noodles in place of the beef.

PREPARATION TIME 5 MINUTES

COOKING TIME 10 MINUTES

INGREDIENTS

200 g / 7 oz / 2 cups thin egg noodles
3 tbsp vegetable oil
2 cloves of garlic, thinly sliced
1 tbsp root ginger, thinly sliced
2 small dried chillies
200 g / 7 oz / 1 ¼ cups sirloin steak, thinly sliced
2 tbsp light soy sauce
2 tbsp peanuts, roughly chopped
2 tbsp mint leaves
2 tbsp coriander (cilantro) (cilantro) leaves

- Cook the noodles in boiling salted water according to the packet instructions or until al dente, then drain well.
- Heat the oil in a large wok and fry the garlic, ginger, and dried chillies for 30 seconds.
- Add the beef and stir-fry for 3 minutes or until just cooked through.
- Add the soy sauce, noodles and peanuts and stir-fry for 2 more minutes.
- Serve immediately, garnished with herbs.

662

SERVES 4

Lamb and Shrimp Biryani

PREPARATION TIME 5 MINUTES

COOKING TIME 30 MINUTES

INGREDIENTS

2 tbsp vegetable oil
1 onion, finely chopped
2 cloves of garlic, finely chopped
2 tsp root ginger, grated
2 lamb neck fillets, sliced
1 tbsp mild curry powder
200 g / 7 oz / 1 cup long grain rice
4 tbsp coriander (cilantro) (cilantro)
leaves, roughly chopped
400 ml / 14 fl. oz / 1 ⅔ cups vegetable
stock
100 g / 3 ½ oz / ¾ cup cooked brown
shrimps
1 lime, juiced
red onion slices to garnish

- Heat the oil in a large saucepan and fry the onion, garlic and ginger for 2 minutes.
- Add the lamb and stir-fry until it starts to colour then stir in the curry powder and a pinch of salt.
- Stir in the rice and half the coriander (cilantro) (cilantro)and cook for 1 minute.
- Pour in enough stock to cover the rice by 1 cm and bring to the boil.
- Put the lid on and turn the heat down to its lowest setting.
- Cook the rice for 10 minutes then turn off the heat and leave to stand for 10 minutes without removing the lid.
- Stir in the brown shrimps, lime juice and the rest of the coriander (cilantro) (cilantro)then divide between 4 warm bowls and garnish with onion slices.

Lamb and Apricot Biryani

 663

- Replace the shrimps with an equal weight of chopped dried apricots.

664

SERVES 4

Chicken and Mango Stir-fry

PREPARATION TIME 5 MINUTES

COOKING TIME 8 MINUTES

INGREDIENTS

3 tbsp vegetable oil
2 cloves garlic, finely chopped
1 tbsp root ginger, finely chopped
1 red chilli, halved and sliced
200 g / 7 oz / 1 ¼ cups chicken breast,
sliced
1 carrot, julienned
1 mango, peeled, stoned and cut
into strips
2 tbsp rice wine or dry sherry
2 tbsp runny honey
1 tbsp light soy sauce

- Heat the oil in a large wok and fry the garlic, ginger and chilli for 30 seconds.
- Add the chicken and carrot and stir-fry for 2 minutes then add the mango and stir-fry for another 2 minutes.
- Mix the rice wine with the honey and soy and add it to the wok.
- Stir-fry for 2 more minutes then serve immediately.

Monk Fish and Mango Stir-fry

665

- Replace the chicken with an equal weight of monk fish, cut into chunks.

666 SERVES 4 — Mussels with Chilli and Lemongrass

- Heat the oil in a wok and fry the garlic, chilli, lemongrass and curry paste for 2 minutes.
- Add the mussels, stock and sugar to the pan and put on the lid.
- Cook for 5 minutes or until the mussels have steamed open.
- Stir in the lime juice and chives and serve immediately.

PREPARATION TIME 2 MINUTES

COOKING TIME 8 MINUTES

INGREDIENTS

2 tbsp vegetable oil
1 clove of garlic, skin on
1 red chilli, halved and thinly sliced
1 lemongrass stem, thinly sliced
1 tbsp Thai yellow curry paste
900 g / 2 lb / 4 ½ cups live mussels, cleaned
400 ml / 14 fl. oz / 1 ⅔ cups fish stock
1 tsp caster (superfine) sugar
1 lime, juiced
1 tbsp chives, chopped

Mussels with Ginger and Coconut — 667

- Replace the lemongrass with 1 tbsp of thinly sliced root ginger and use coconut milk instead of the fish stock.

668 SERVES 4 — Kumquat-Marinated Chicken Thigh

- Put all of the ingredients except the chicken into a food processor and blend to a puree.
- Spread the mixture over the skin of the chicken thighs and leave to marinate for 30 minutes.
- Preheat the grill to its highest setting.
- Grill the chicken thighs for 8 minutes, turning half way through.

PREPARATION TIME 35 MINUTES

COOKING TIME 8 MINUTES

INGREDIENTS

8 kumquats
2 tbsp honey
2 tbsp dark soy sauce
1 clove of garlic, crushed
1 tbsp root ginger, grated
1 tsp sesame oil
4 boneless chicken thighs

Kumquat-Marinated Pork Belly — 669

- Use the marinade to flavour a 600 g piece of pork belly and roast at 220°C for 40 minutes.

SERVES 4

Barbeque Pork Belly

670

Barbeque Chicken Wings

671

- Use the marinade to coat 12 chicken wings and reduce the cooking time to 20 minutes.

Barbeque Spare Ribs

672

- Gently poach 1 kg of spare ribs in chicken stock for 30 minutes, then drain and dry with kitchen towel before brushing with the marinade and barbequing.

PREPARATION TIME 40 MINUTES

COOKING TIME 25 MINUTES

....

INGREDIENTS

½ onion, finely grated
2 cloves garlic, crushed
2 tbsp soy sauce
1 tbsp tomato ketchup
1 tbsp dark brown sugar
1 tsp Worcester sauce
1 tsp Chinese five spice powder
800 g / 1 lb 12 oz / 5 cups boneless
pork belly, skin removed

- Mix the onion, garlic, soy, ketchup, sugar, Worcester sauce and five spice together and massage it into the pork. Leave to marinate for 20 minutes.

- Prepare a barbeque or preheat the grill to its highest setting.

- Grill or barbeque the pork for 25 minutes, turning and basting occasionally, until the meat is cooked through and tender.

- Cut into slices and serve hot or at room temperature.

673

SERVES 4

Chicken with Asparagus and Holy Basil

- Heat the oil in a wok and fry the curry paste for 1 minute.
- Add the chicken and asparagus and stir-fry for 2 minutes, then add the red pepper and stir-fry for 4 minutes.
- Pour in the coconut milk and bubble until reduced almost to nothing.
- Stir in the spring onions and holy basil and serve immediately.

PREPARATION TIME 2 MINUTES

COOKING TIME 10 MINUTES

INGREDIENTS

1 tbsp vegetable oil
1 tbsp Thai green curry paste
400 g / 14 oz / 2 cups chicken breast, sliced
400 g / 14 oz / 4 cups asparagus tips
½ red pepper, sliced
100 ml / 3 ½ fl. oz / ½ cup coconut milk
2 spring onions, thinly sliced
a small bunch holy basil, leaves only

Prawns with Asparagus and Holy Basil

674

- Replace the chicken with 200 g of peeled prawns, adding them at the red pepper stage.

675

SERVES 4

Chicken Satay

- Put 12 wooden skewers in a bowl of water and leave to soak for 20 minutes.
- Meanwhile, mix together the peanut butter, honey, soy, spice and garlic and massage it into the chicken pieces.
- Leave to marinate for 20 minutes.
- Preheat the grill to its highest setting.
- Thread the chicken onto the skewers then cook them under the grill for 4 minutes on each side or until they are golden brown and cooked through.
- Serve with red onion marmalade.

PREPARATION TIME 20 MINUTES

COOKING TIME 8 MINUTES

INGREDIENTS

4 tbsp crunchy peanut butter
1 tbsp runny honey
2 tbsp dark soy sauce
1 tsp Chinese five spice powder
1 clove of garlic, crushed
6 skinless chicken breasts, cubed
red onion marmalade to serve

Tofu Satay

676

- Replace the chicken with 600 g of firm tofu cubes.

677

SERVES 4

Chicken with Caramelised Peaches

PREPARATION TIME 5 MINUTES

COOKING TIME 12 MINUTES

INGREDIENTS

3 tbsp vegetable oil
2 chicken breasts
2 peaches, peeled, stoned and sliced
2 cloves garlic, finely chopped
1 tbsp root ginger, finely chopped
100 g / 3 ½ oz / ⅔ cup baby carrots, peeled
100 g / 3 ½ oz / ⅓ cup sugar snap peas, trimmed
50 g / 1 ¾ oz / 1 ½ cups baby spinach leaves, washed
2 tbsp rice wine or dry sherry
2 tbsp runny honey
1 tbsp light soy sauce
1 tbsp coriander (cilantro) (cilantro) leaves, chopped

- Heat 2 tablespoons of the oil in a wok and fry the chicken and peaches for 4 minutes on each side.
- Remove from the pan with a slotted spoon and reserve.
- Add the rest of the oil to the wok and fry the garlic and ginger for 30 seconds.
- Add the carrots and sugar snaps and stir-fry for 2 minutes. Slice the chicken and add it to the wok with the spinach leaves.
- Mix the rice wine with the honey and soy and add it to the wok with the peaches then stir-fry for 1 more minute.
- Serve immediately, sprinkled with coriander (cilantro).

Stir-Fried Duck with Peaches   678

- Replace the chicken breasts with duck breasts.

679

SERVES 4

Grilled Prawns with Stir-Fried Noodles

PREPARATION TIME 5 MINUTES

COOKING TIME 10 MINUTES

INGREDIENTS

200 g / 7 oz / 2 cups thin egg noodles
16 raw king prawns (shrimp)
3 tbsp vegetable oil
2 cloves of garlic, julienned
1 tbsp root ginger, julienned
1 carrot, julienned
50 g / 1 ¾ oz / ½1 cup green beans, thinly sliced lengthways
¼ pineapple, peeled, cored and thinly sliced
2 tbsp light soy sauce
50 g / 1 ¾ oz / ½ cup bean sprouts
a few sprigs coriander (cilantro)

- Cook the noodles in boiling salted water according to the packet instructions or until al dente, then drain well.
- Preheat the grill to its highest setting.
- Spread the prawns (shrimp) out on a large grill tray and grill
  for 2 minutes on each side or until opaque.
- Meanwhile, heat the oil in a large wok and fry the garlic and ginger for 30 seconds.
- Add the carrot, beans and pineapple and stir-fry for 2 minutes then add the soy, beansprouts and noodles and cook for 2 minutes.
- Serve the noodles in warm bowls, garnished with coriander (cilantro), with the prawns (shrimp) on the side.

Butterflied Prawns with Noodles   680

- De-head and peel the prawns leaving the tails intact. Carefully run a knife down their backs, without cutting all the way through, so they open out like a book. Grill as before.

681

SERVES 4

Spicy Crab Pancakes

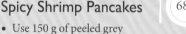

Spicy Shrimp Pancakes   **682**

- Use 150 g of peeled grey shrimp instead of the crab.

Spicy Coconut Pancakes   **683**

- Omit the crab and add 100 g of freshly grated coconut to the batter.

PREPARATION TIME 5 MINUTES

COOKING TIME 20 MINUTES

INGREDIENTS

125 g / 4 ½ oz / ¾ cup plain (all purpose) flour
1 tsp baking powder
1 large egg
150 ml / 5 ½ fl. oz / ⅔ cup milk
15 g / ½ oz butter, melted
1 red chilli, finely chopped
1 clove of garlic, crushed
1 tsp root ginger, grated
100 g / 3 ½ oz / ½ cup fresh crab meat
2 spring onions, thinly sliced

- Mix the flour and baking powder in a bowl and make a well in the centre. Break in the egg and pour in the milk then use a whisk to gradually incorporate all of the flour from round the outside.
- Melt the butter in a small frying pan then whisk it into the batter.
- Stir in the chilli, garlic, ginger and crab meat.
- Put the buttered frying pan back over a low heat. Add a quarter of the pancake batter to the pan and cook for 2 minutes or until small bubbles start to appear on the surface.
- Turn the pancake over with a spatula and cook the other side until golden brown and cooked through.
- Repeat with the rest of the mixture to make another 3 large pancakes.
- Serve the pancakes sprinkled with spring onion.

684

SERVES 4

Stir-Fried Vegetables

PREPARATION TIME 2 MINUTES

COOKING TIME 6 MINUTES

....

INGREDIENTS

2 tbsp vegetable oil
2 cloves garlic, finely chopped
1 tbsp root ginger, finely chopped
1 fennel bulb, thinly sliced
½ Chinese cabbage, shredded
1 courgette, diced
1 red pepper, julienned
2 tomatoes, cut into wedges
2 tbsp rice wine or dry sherry
1 tsp caster (superfine) sugar
1 tbsp light soy sauce

- Heat the oil in a large wok and fry the garlic and ginger for 30 seconds.
- Add the vegetables and stir-fry for 4 minutes.
- Mix the rice wine, sugar and soy together and add it to the wok.
- Stir-fry for 1 more minute then serve immediately.

Stir-Steamed Vegetables   685

- For a fat-free version of this dish, use water instead of oil at the beginning, adding extra splashes of water whenever the vegetables get too dry.

686

SERVES 4

Chicken, Noodle and Shitake Stir-fry

PREPARATION TIME 5 MINUTES

COOKING TIME 15 MINUTES

....

INGREDIENTS

200 g / 7 oz / 2 cups Pho or Pad Thai rice noodles
3 tbsp vegetable oil
2 cloves of garlic, thinly sliced
1 tbsp root ginger, thinly sliced
2 shallots, sliced
100 g / 3 ½ oz / 1 cup shitake mushrooms, thinly sliced
200 g / 7 oz / 1 ¼ cups chicken breast, thinly sliced
2 tbsp light soy sauce
chopped coriander (cilantro) (cilantro)to garnish

- Cook the noodles in boiling salted water according to the packet instructions or until al dente, then drain well.
- Heat the oil in a large wok and fry the garlic, ginger, shallots and mushrooms for 2 minutes.
- Add the chicken and stir-fry for 3 minutes or until just cooked through.
- Add the soy sauce and noodles and stir-fry for 2 more minutes.
- Serve immediately, garnished with coriander (cilantro).

Chicken and Shitake Fried Rice   687

- Replace the cooked noodles with cooked long grain rice.

688
SERVES 4

Chicken and Pea Thai Green Curry

- Heat the oil in a wok and fry the curry paste and shallots for 2 minutes.
- Add the chicken to the wok and stir-fry for 4 minutes then add the coconut milk and peas and bring to a simmer.
- Season to taste with the caster (superfine) sugar and fish sauce before serving in warm bowls, garnished with holy basil.
- Serve with jasmine rice.

PREPARATION TIME 5 MINUTES

COOKING TIME 12 MINUTES

INGREDIENTS

2 tbsp vegetable oil
2 tbsp Thai green curry paste
2 shallots, chopped
2 skinless chicken breasts,
cut into chunks
400 ml / 14 fl. oz / 1 ⅔ cups coconut milk
200 g / 7 oz / 1 ⅓ cup frozen peas, defrosted
1 tsp caster (superfine) sugar
1 tbsp fish sauce
a few sprigs holy basil

Chicken and Bamboo Shoot Curry
689

- Replace the peas with 200 g of canned bamboo shoots.

690
SERVES 4

Prawn and Chicken Rice

- Heat the oil in a large wok and fry the ginger and garlic for 30 seconds.
- Add the chicken and mushrooms and stir-fry for 3 minutes then add the prawns (shrimp) and fry for another 2 minutes.
- Add the rice and stir-fry until piping hot – this should take about 4 minutes.
- Add the soy, sesame oil and coriander (cilantro) (cilantro)and cook for 1 more minute then serve immediately.

PREPARATION TIME 2 MINUTES

COOKING TIME 12 MINUTES

INGREDIENTS

3 tbsp olive oil
1 tsp root ginger, grated
1 clove of garlic, crushed
200 g / 7 oz / 1 ¼ cups chicken breast, thinly sliced
150 g / 5 ½ oz / 1 ½ cups mushrooms, sliced
150 g / 5 ½ oz / 1 cup raw prawns (shrimp), peeled
300 g / 10 ½ oz / 1 ¾ cup long grain rice, cooked and cooled
2 tbsp light soy sauce
1 tsp sesame oil
a small bunch coriander (cilantro), leaves only

Fried Rice with Chicken and Mushrooms
691

- Omit the prawns and add 3 tbsp of soaked, sliced wood ear fungus when you add the mushrooms.

692

SERVES 2

Prawns with Red and Szechwan Pepper

Szechwan King Prawn Noodles

693

- Add 150 g of cooked noodles to the wok and 2 tbsp soy sauce when you add the prawns (shrimp). Serve without rice.

Stir-Fried Szechwan Chicken

694

- Replace the prawns (shrimp) with 250 g of thinly sliced chicken thigh.

PREPARATION TIME 5 MINUTES

COOKING TIME 4-6 MINUTES

INGREDIENTS

2 tbsp vegetable oil
1 red pepper, thinly sliced
1 red chilli, finely chopped
1 clove of garlic, crushed
16 raw king prawns (shrimp), peeled leaving tails intact
1 tsp Szechwan peppercorns, crushed
1 tbsp coriander (cilantro) (cilantro) leaves, chopped
boiled rice to serve

- Heat the oil in a wok and fry the red pepper with a pinch of salt for 5 minutes or until softened and starting to caramelise.

- Add the chilli and garlic and stir-fry for 30 seconds then add the prawns (shrimp) and Szechwan pepper and stir-fry for 2 minutes or until the prawns (shrimp) turn opaque.

- Stir in the coriander (cilantro) (cilantro)and serve on a bed of rice.

695

SERVES 4

Minced Pork Fried Rice

- Heat the oil in a large wok and fry the chilli and garlic for 30 seconds.
- Add the pork mince and stir-fry for 3 minutes or until it starts to colour.
- Add the rice and stir-fry until piping hot – this should take about 4 minutes.
- Add the soy, coconut milk and coriander (cilantro) (cilantro)leaves and cook for 1 more minute then serve immediately.

PREPARATION TIME 5 MINUTES

COOKING TIME 10 MINUTES

INGREDIENTS

3 tbsp olive oil
1 red chilli, finely chopped
1 clove of garlic, crushed
150 g / 5 ½ oz / ¾ cup minced pork
300 g / 10 ½ oz / 1 ¾ cup long grain rice, cooked and cooled
2 tbsp soy sauce
4 tbsp coconut milk
2 tbsp coriander (cilantro) (cilantro) leaves

Shitake Fried Rice

696

- Replace the minced pork with finely chopped shitake mushrooms.

697

SERVES 2

Fillet of Lamb with Garlic Sauce

- Put the lamb stock in a small saucepan with the garlic cloves and rosemary and bring to a simmer.
- Cook for 30 minutes or until the liquid has reduced by half and the garlic is soft.
- Remove the garlic and rosemary from the pan with a slotted spoon, then squeeze the softened garlic out of its skins and stir it back into the stock.
- Use an emersion blender to emulsify the sauce and season to taste with salt and pepper.
- Meanwhile, heat a frying pan until smoking hot then add the oil and butter.
- Season the lamb all over with salt and pepper, then fry the medallions for 2 minutes on each side.
- Leave to rest somewhere warm, covered with foil, for 4 minutes then serve with the garlic sauce.

PREPARATION TIME 2 MINUTES

COOKING TIME 35 MINUTES

INGREDIENTS

400 ml / 14 fl. oz / 1 ⅔ cups lamb stock
1 large bulb of garlic, separated into unpeeled cloves
1 sprig rosemary
1 tbsp olive oil
1 tbsp butter
1 fillet of lamb, cut into 6 medallions

Rib-Eye Steak with Garlic Sauce

698

- Replace the lamb stock with beef stock and use the sauce to dress 2 thick rib-eye steaks that have been char-grilled on the barbeque.

699

SERVES 4

Haddock and Butternut Squash Gratin

PREPARATION TIME 10 MINUTES

COOKING TIME 35 MINUTES

INGREDIENTS

450 g / 1 lb / 3 cups butternut squash, peeled and cubed
600 ml / 1 pint / 2 ½ cups whole milk
450 g / 1 lb / 2 ¼ cups smoked haddock
3 tbsp butter
1 tbsp plain (all purpose) flour
2 tbsp flat leaf parsley, chopped
15 g / ½ oz breadcrumbs

- Cook the squash in boiling salted water for 12 minutes then drain well.
- Bring the milk to a simmer then pour over the haddock. Cover the dish with film and leave for 10 minutes. Drain off and reserve the milk and flake the haddock, discarding any skin and bones.
- When the squash is ready, mash it until smooth with 1 tablespoon of the butter and a little of the haddock milk.
- Heat 1 tablespoon of the butter in a saucepan and stir in the flour. Gradually incorporate the rest of the haddock milk. Stir until it starts to bubble then stir in the parsley and flaked haddock.
- Preheat the grill to its highest setting. Pour the haddock mixture into a dish and top with the mashed squash.
- Dot 1 tbsp of butter over the top and sprinkle with breadcrumbs then grill for 5 minutes until golden.

Haddock and Sweet Potato Gratin
700

- Replace the squash with an equal weight of sweet potato.

701

SERVES 2

Rib-eye Steak with Niçoise Vegetables

PREPARATION TIME 5 MINUTES

COOKING TIME 25-30 MINUTES

INGREDIENTS

2 ribeye steaks
2 tbsp olive oil
½ tsp smoked paprika

FOR THE VEGETABLES
200 g / 7 oz / 1 ¼ cups baby new potatoes
200 g / 7 oz / 1 cup vine cherry tomatoes
2 tbsp olive oil
75 g / 2 ½ oz / ½ cup black Niçoise olives

- Preheat the oven to 200°C (180° fan), 390 F, gas 6.
- Boil the potatoes in boiling salted water for 12 minutes or until tender. Drain well.
- Arrange the potatoes and tomatoes in a roasting tin, drizzle with oil and season with salt and pepper.
- Roast for 25 minutes, then add the olives and roast for 5 more minutes.
- Meanwhile, brush the steaks with oil and season liberally with salt, pepper and paprika.
- Heat a large frying pan until smoking hot then fry the steaks for 6 minutes, turning them every 2 minutes.
- Transfer the steaks to a warm plate and cover with foil, then leave to rest for 5 minutes.
- Divide the steaks and vegetables between 2 warm plates and serve immediately.

Lamb Chops with Niçoise Vegetables
702

- Replace the steaks with 3 lamb chops per person.

703

SERVES 2

Baked Chicken with Vegetables

Lemon Baked Chicken   704

- Replace the lime juice and slices with lemon.

Orange Baked Chicken   705

- Replace the lime juice and slices with orange.

PREPARATION TIME 10 MINUTES

COOKING TIME 35 MINUTES

INGREDIENTS

1 lime, juiced
1 tsp runny honey
2 chicken breasts
1 large tomato
1 courgette, sliced
3 tbsp olive oil
2 tbsp breadcrumbs
1 tsp flat leaf parsley, finely chopped
lime slices and parsley to garnish

- Mix the lime juice with the honey and a pinch of salt and pour it over the chicken. Leave to marinate for 10 minutes.
- Preheat the oven to 200°C (180° fan), 390 F, gas 6.
- Rub the vegetables with oil and drizzle any that's left over the chicken.
- Arrange them in a baking dish and season well with salt and pepper.
- Bake for 25 minutes then stack up the courgette (zucchini)slices and sprinkle the tomatoes and courgette (zucchini)stack with breadcrumbs and parsley.
- Return to the oven for 10 minutes or until the chicken is cooked through.
- Garnish the chicken with lime slices and parsley before serving.

706

SERVES 2

Sea Bass with Tomato and Caper Salsa

PREPARATION TIME 10 MINUTES

COOKING TIME 8 MINUTES

....

INGREDIENTS

2 tbsp olive oil
2 thick portions sea bass fillet
mixed salad leaves to serve

FOR THE SALSA

2 tomatoes
1 shallot, finely chopped
1 tbsp baby capers
1 tbsp balsamic vinegar
3 tbsp extra virgin olive oil

- Score a cross in the top of the tomatoes and blanch them in boiling water for 30 seconds.
- Plunge them into cold water then peel off the skins.
- Cut the tomatoes in half and remove the seeds, then cut the flesh into small cubes.
- Stir the shallot and capers into the tomato then whisk in the balsamic and oil. Season to taste with salt and pepper.
- Heat the oil in an oven-proof frying pan. Season the sea bass with salt and pepper and fry, skin side down, for 4 minutes.
- Turn the fillets over then turn off the heat and leave them to cook in the heat of the pan for 2 minutes.
- Serve the sea bass with some mixed salad leaves and the salsa spooned around.

707

SERVES 4

Seared Salmon with Vegetable Broth

PREPARATION TIME 2 MINUTES

COOKING TIME 10 MINUTES

....

INGREDIENTS

1 litre / 1 pint 15 fl. oz / 4 cups good
quality fish stock
2 tsp yellow miso paste
1 carrot, peeled and cubed
1 courgette, cubed
2 tomatoes, peeled and cubed
4 spring onions, chopped
2 tbsp olive oil
8 slices salmon fillet

TO SERVE

2 tbsp candied orange peel, finely
chopped
2 tbsp chives, finely chopped
1 tbsp light soy sauce
1 tsp sesame oil

- Bring the fish stock to a simmer and stir in the yellow miso paste, carrots and courgette. Simmer for 4 minutes then add the tomatoes and spring onion and simmer for another 2 minutes.
- Meanwhile, heat the olive oil in a large frying pan until smoking hot and season the salmon at the last minute with salt and pepper.
- Sear the salmon slices for 1 minute on each side or until golden brown.
- Ladle the vegetable broth into 4 warm bowls and top each one with 2 slices of salmon.
- Mix the candied peel with the chives, soy sauce and sesame oil and spoon it over the salmon.

708

SERVES 4

Red Mullet Crostini with Tomato Salsa

- Score a cross in the top of the tomatoes and blanch them in boiling water for 30 seconds.
- Plunge them into cold water then peel off the skins.
- Cut the tomatoes in half and remove the seeds, then cut the flesh into small cubes.
- Stir the shallot and herbs into the tomato then whisk in the vinegar and oil. Season to taste with salt and pepper.
- Heat the oil in an oven proof frying pan. Season the red mullet fillets with salt and pepper and fry, skin side down, for 2 minutes.
- Turn the fillets over then turn off the heat and leave them to cook in the heat of the pan for 1 minute.
- While the fish is cooking, toast the bread.
- Arrange the mullet on top of the crostini and drizzle over the vinaigrette. Garnish with mixed salad leaves.

PREPARATION TIME 10 MINUTES

COOKING TIME 5 MINUTES

INGREDIENTS

2 tbsp olive oil
8 red mullet fillets
4 slices baguette
mixed salad leaves to serve

FOR THE SALSA
2 tomatoes
1 shallot, finely chopped
1 tbsp chives, finely chopped
1 tbsp flat leaf parsley, finely chopped
1 tbsp white wine vinegar
3 tbsp extra virgin olive oil

Chicken with Vine Tomatoes

709

SERVES 4

Miso Tuna with Rice Noodles

710

SERVES 4

PREPARATION TIME 10 MINUTES

COOKING TIME 35 MINUTES

INGREDIENTS

4 chicken breasts
4 small cherry tomato vines
3 tbsp olive oil

- Preheat the oven to 200°C (180° fan), 390 F, gas 6.
- Rub the chicken and tomatoes with oil and arrange in a baking dish. Season well with salt and pepper.
- Bake for 30 minutes or until the chicken is cooked through and the tomatoes have softened and wrinkled.

PREPARATION TIME 2 MINUTES

COOKING TIME 10 MINUTES

INGREDIENTS

2 tbsp yellow miso paste
1 tbsp runny honey
125 ml / 4 ½ fl. oz / ½ cup rice wine vinegar (mirin)

1 tsp sesame oil
2 thick tuna steaks, halved
200 g / 7 oz / 2 cups mange tout, trimmed
200 g / 7 oz / 2 cups Pho or Pad Thai rice noodles
4 spring onions, sliced diagonally

- Mix the miso paste with the honey and gradually incorporate the rice wine vinegar. Stir in the sesame oil and brush half of the mixture over the tuna steaks. Preheat the grill as hot as it will go.
- Bring a saucepan of water to the boil and cook the mange tout for 2 minutes. Put the noodles into a heatproof bowl and strain the mange tout water over them. Cover and leave for 3 minutes.
- Drain the noodles and plunge into cold water with the mange tout to stop the cooking. Drain again and mix with the spring onions.
- Cook the tuna steaks under the grill for 2 minutes on each side, basting with more miso dressing half way through. The steaks should be a little caramelised on the outside, but still pink in the centre.
- Divide the noodle salad between 4 plates and top each one with a tuna steak.
- Brush over the rest of the miso dressing to glaze.

711

SERVES 2

Pork Chops with Potatoes

PREPARATION TIME 10 MINUTES

COOKING TIME 20 MINUTES

....

INGREDIENTS

10 new potatoes, halved
2 woody sprigs of rosemary
2 pork chops
4 tbsp olive oil
2 tbsp thyme leaves
2 courgettes

- Boil the potatoes in salted water for 12 minutes or until tender. Drain well.
- Meanwhile, preheat the grill to its highest setting and put a griddle pan on the hob to heat.
- Strip most of the leaves off the rosemary sprigs and thread the potatoes onto the woody stems like a skewer.
- Brush the pork and potatoes with half the oil and season with salt, pepper and thyme leaves.
- Grill for 4 minutes on each side, or until the pork is cooked through.
- Meanwhile, cut the courgettes into thin ribbons with a vegetable peeler and brush them with oil.
- Griddle the ribbons for 2 minutes on each side or until nicely marked.
- Divide the pork, potatoes and courgettes between 2 warm plates and serve immediately.

Potato and Mushroom Rosemary Skewers

712

- Halve the quantity of potatoes and thread alternately onto the rosemary skewers with whole chestnut mushrooms.

713

SERVES 4

Tofu and Vegetable Kebabs

PREPARATION TIME 20 MINUTES

COOKING TIME 8 MINUTES

....

INGREDIENTS

1 tbsp dried herbs de Provence
3 tbsp olive oil
400 g / 14 oz / 2 ½ cups firm tofu, cubed
1 yellow pepper, cubed
1 large courgette, quartered and sliced
12 cherry tomatoes

- Put 12 wooden skewers in a bowl of water and leave to soak for 20 minutes.
- Meanwhile, stir the herbs into the oil and toss with the tofu and vegetables.
- Leave to marinate for 20 minutes.
- Preheat the grill to its highest setting.
- Thread the tofu and vegetables onto the skewers and spread them out on a large grill tray.
- Grill the kebabs for 4 minutes on each side or until they are golden brown and cooked through.

Tofu and Pineapple Kebabs

714

- Replace the courgette (zucchini) with chunks of fresh pineapple

715

SERVES 2 # Steak with Balsamic Peppers and Crisps

- Mix the balsamic vinegar with the honey and stir it into the peppers. Leave to marinate for 10 minutes.
- Preheat the oven to 200°C (180° fan), 390 F, gas 6.
- Rinse the potatoes under cold water then dry well.
- Rub the potatoes with oil and season then spread them out on a large non-stick baking tray.
- Crisp the potatoes in the oven for 15 minutes, turning half way through. Meanwhile, preheat a griddle pan until smoking hot.
- Brush the steaks with the oil and season well. Griddle the steaks for 4 minutes then turn them over and cook for another 4 minutes.
- Transfer the steaks to a warm plate, wrap in foil, and leave to rest for 5 minutes.
- Transfer the steaks to warm plates and spoon over the peppers. Top with rocket and serve crisps on the side.

PREPARATION TIME 12 MINUTES

COOKING TIME 15 MINUTES

INGREDIENTS

2 tbsp balsamic vinegar
2 tsp runny honey
1 jar roasted red peppers in oil, drained
2 small sirloin steaks
1 tbsp olive oil
a handful rocket (arugula) leaves

FOR THE POTATOES
2 maris piper potatoes, peeled and very thinly sliced
4 tbsp olive oil

Pan-Fried Cod with Griddled Peppers

716

- Use the balsamic peppers and rocket to dress 2 portions of pan-fried cod fillet.

717

SERVES 4 # Grilled Belly Pork with Honey and Lime

- Squeeze the lime quarters into a bowl and put them on one side.
- Stir the honey, soy and five spice into the lime juice then pour it over the pork steaks and empty lime quarters. Leave to marinate for 25 minutes.
- Preheat the grill to its highest setting.
- Arrange the pork belly and lime on a large grill tray and grill for 4 minutes on each side or until the glaze is golden and sticky and the pork is cooked through.
- Serve with steamed jasmine rice.

PREPARATION TIME 30 MINUTES

COOKING TIME 8 MINUTES

INGREDIENTS

2 limes, quartered
2 tbsp runny honey
2 tbsp dark soy sauce
½ tsp Chinese five spice powder
4 pork belly steaks, skin removed

Grilled Liver with Honey and Lime

718

- Replace the pork belly with strips of pork liver and reduce the cooking time to 2 minutes on each side.

719

SERVES 4

Grilled Salmon with Honey and Lime

Grilled Prawns with Honey and Lime

720

- Replace the salmon with raw king prawns (shrimp) and reduce the cooking time to 1 minute on each side.

Grilled Tuna with Honey and Lime

721

- Substitute the salmon with fresh tuna steaks and reduce the cooking time to 2 minutes on each side.

PREPARATION TIME 30 MINUTES

COOKING TIME 6 MINUTES

....

INGREDIENTS

2 tbsp runny honey
2 tbsp light soy sauce
2 limes, sliced
4 portions salmon fillet, skinned

- Mix the honey with the soy and stir in the limes then pour it over the salmon. Leave to marinate for 25 minutes.
- Preheat the grill to its highest setting.
- Arrange the salmon and lime slices on a large grill tray and grill for 3 minutes on each side or until the glaze is golden and sticky and the salmon is just cooked in the centre.

722

SERVES 4

Honey and Orange Spare Rib Chops

- Stir together the orange juice, honey and soy and pour it over the spare rib chops. Leave to marinate for 25 minutes.
- Meanwhile, boil the potatoes in salted water for 12 minutes or until tender then drain well.
- Preheat the grill to its highest setting and heat a griddle pan until smoking hot.
- Mix the oil with the rosemary and rub it into the potatoes and baby corn.
- Grill the pork for 4 minutes on each side or until the glaze is golden and sticky and the pork is cooked through.
- While the pork is cooking, griddle the potatoes and baby corn for 8 minutes, turning once.
- Divide the pork and vegetables between 4 warm plates and serve immediately.

PREPARATION TIME 30 MINUTES

COOKING TIME 8 MINUTES

INGREDIENTS

1 orange, juiced
2 tbsp runny honey
2 tbsp light soy sauce
8 pork spare rib chops

FOR THE GRIDDLED VEGETABLES
400 g / 14 oz / 2 ¼ cups new potatoes, halved
2 tbsp olive oil
2 tsp fresh rosemary, chopped
8 baby sweetcorn

Honey and Orange Duck Breasts   723

- Replace the spare rib chops with 1 small duck breast per person.

724

SERVES 2

Grilled Swordfish with Sprouting Seeds

- Mix together the dressing ingredients and pour them over the shallots. Leave to macerate for 20 minutes.
- Preheat the grill to its highest setting.
- Brush the swordfish with oil then grill it for 3 minutes on each side or until cooked to your liking.
- Transfer the fish to 2 warm plates and spoon over the dressing, then garnish with the sprouts and chives.

PREPARATION TIME 25 MINUTES

COOKING TIME 6 MINUTES

INGREDIENTS

2 swordfish steaks
2 tbsp olive oil
50 g / 1 ¾ oz / 1 cup alfalfa sprouts
50 g / 1 ¾ oz / ½ cup bean sprouts
4 chives

FOR THE DRESSING
2 tbsp soy sauce
1 tbsp rice wine vinegar
½ tsp caster (superfine) sugar
1 tsp sesame oil
a pinch chilli powder
½ tsp Szechwan peppercorns, crushed
4 small shallots, peeled

Grilled Tuna with Sprouting Seeds   725

- Replace the swordfish with fresh tuna steaks.

726

SERVES 4

Penne Salad with Goats' Cheese

PREPARATION TIME 5 MINUTES

COOKING TIME 12 MINUTES

INGREDIENTS

400 g / 14 oz / 4 cups penne
100 g / 3 ½ oz / ¾ cup fresh peas
8 tomatoes, cut into wedges
4 slices prosciutto, chopped
100 g / 3 ½ oz / ⅔ cup goats' cheese, crumbled
a small bunch basil, leaves only
4 tbsp extra virgin olive oil

- Cook the penne in boiling salted water according to the packet instructions or until al dente.
- 4 minutes before the end of cooking time, add the peas to the pot.
- Drain the pasta and peas and toss with the tomato, prosciutto, goats' cheese and basil.
- Dress the salad with olive oil and serve warm or at room temperature.

Penne Salad with Stilton and Chorizo

727

- Replace the Goats' Cheese with Stilton and the Parma Ham with Chorizo.

728

SERVES 2

Tagliatelle a la Carbonara

PREPARATION TIME 5 MINUTES

COOKING TIME 14 MINUTES

INGREDIENTS

200 g / 7 oz / 2 cups tagliatelle
100 g / 3 ½ oz / ¾ cup guanciale or pancetta, thinly sliced
3 cloves of garlic, crushed
4 tbsp olive oil
50 g / 1 ¾ oz / ½ cup Parmesan, finely grated
1 egg, beaten

- Cook the tagliatelle in boiling salted water according to the packet instructions or until al dente.
- Meanwhile, fry the pancetta and garlic in the oil for 2 minutes or until golden brown.
- Stir the Parmesan into the beaten egg.
- Reserve 1 ladleful of the pasta cooking water and drain the rest.
- Return the pasta to the pan and add the pancetta and parmesan mixture. Stir well and add enough of the pasta water to make a thick sauce.
- Divide the pasta between 2 warm bowls and sprinkle with freshly ground black pepper.

Mushroom Carbonara

729

- Finely slice 6 closed cup mushrooms and add to the pancetta.

730

SERVES 4

Pork and Brie Roulades

- Preheat the oven to 200°C (180° fan), 390 F, gas 6
- Put the pork between 2 sheets of clingfilm and bash it flat with a rolling pin.
- Peel off the cling film.
- Lay the prosciutto slices out on a chopping board and top with the basil leaves.
- Top each one with a piece of pork then lay the Brie on top.
- Roll them up into roulades and secure with a skewer or cocktail stick.
- Transfer the roulades to a roasting tin and cook in the oven for 25 – 30 minutes or until the pork is cooked in the centre.
- Serve with spaghetti or a green salad.

PREPARATION TIME 15 MINUTES

COOKING TIME 25-30 MINUTES

INGREDIENTS

4 pork escallops
4 slices prosciutto
12 large basil leaves
8 slices Brie

Rose Veal and Brie Roulades

731

- Replace the pork with rose veal.

732

SERVES 4

Penne with Broccoli and Garlic

- Cook the garlic cloves in a large saucepan of boiling salted water for 15 minutes.
- Add the penne to the pan and cook according to the packet instructions or until al dente.
- 4 minutes before the end of cooking time, add the broccoli to the pan.
- Reserve 1 ladle of the cooking water and drain the rest then toss the penne, broccoli and garlic cloves with the oil and season with salt and pepper.
- If the pasta looks a bit dry, add a little of the cooking water and shake the pan to emulsify.
- Divide the pasta between 4 warm bowls and use a vegetable peeler to shave over some Parmesan.
- The softened garlic can be squeezed out of the skins at the table and eaten with the pasta.

PREPARATION TIME 5 MINUTES

COOKING TIME 30 MINUTES

INGREDIENTS

1 bulb of garlic, cloves separated
400 g / 14 oz / 4 cups penne
1 small head broccoli, broken into florets
6 tbsp olive oil
30 g / 1 oz / ¼ cup Parmesan

Penne with Broccoli and Garlic Sauce

 733

- Cook pasta separately. When the garlic is cooked, squeeze it out of its skins into a food processor and blend with the broccoli and oil. Season well.

734

SERVES 4

Pasta with Spring Onion and Chickpeas

PREPARATION TIME 5 MINUTES

COOKING TIME 12 MINUTES

INGREDIENTS

400 g / 14 oz / 4 cups farfalle pasta
8 spring onions (scallions)
4 tbsp olive oil
200 g / 7 oz / 1 ½ cups canned chickpeas, drained
4 tbsp pesto
100 g / 3 ½ oz / ⅔ cup goats' cheese

- Cook the farfalle in boiling salted water according to the packet instructions or until al dente.
- While the pasta is cooking, finely chop the green parts of the spring onions and set aside.
- Thinly slice the white part lengthways then fry in the oil for 8 minutes or until starting to caramelise.
- 2 minutes before the pasta is ready, add the chickpeas to the pasta pan to warm through.
- Drain the pasta and chickpeas and toss with the pesto.
- Divide between 4 warm plates and crumble over the goats' cheese, then top with the caramelised spring onions and their oil and the chopped spring onion tops.

Farfalle with Spring Onions and Roquefort

735

- Omit the chickpeas and replace the goats' cheese with Roquefort.

736

SERVES 4

Baked Tomatoes with Parsley and

PREPARATION TIME 5 MINUTES

COOKING TIME 25 MINUTES

INGREDIENTS

4 beefsteak or marmande tomatoes
50 g / 1 ¾ oz / ⅔ cup breadcrumbs
50 g / 1 ¾ oz / ½ cup Parmesan, grated
1 clove of garlic, crushed
4 tbsp flat leaf parsley, roughly chopped
4 tbsp olive oil

- Preheat the oven to 200°C (180° fan), 390 F, gas 6.
- Cut the tops off the tomatoes and scoop out a 1 cm layer of the inside.
- Mix the breadcrumbs and Parmesan with the garlic and parsley and a good grind of black pepper, then pack the mixture into the tomato cavities.
- Arrange the tomatoes in a baking dish and drizzle over the oil.
- Bake for 25 minutes or until the topping is golden and the tomatoes are soft, but not collapsing.
- Serve with plenty of crusty bread to mop up the juices.

Baked Tomatoes with Parsley and Chorizo

737

- Add 75 g of finely chopped chorizo to the breadcrumb mixture.

738

SERVES 2

Butterflied Bream with Grilled Tomatoes

Bream Stuffed with Pesto

739

- Spread the inside of the bream with 3 tbsp pesto, then close them up and grill as before.

Butterflied Sea Bass with Grilled Tomatoes

740

- Replace the bream with 2 small sea bass.

PREPARATION TIME 5 MINUTES

COOKING TIME 5-8 MINUTES

INGREDIENTS

2 small sea bream, scaled, filleted and butterflied
1 large tomato, sliced
2 tbsp olive oil
1 tsp runny honey
1 tbsp white wine vinegar
2 tbsp walnut oil
1 tbsp flat leaf parsley, finely chopped
2 tbsp kalamata olives
2 tbsp caperberries

- Preheat the grill to its highest setting.
- Arrange the bream, skin side up, on a large grill pan and surround with the tomato slices.
- Brush the bream and tomatoes with olive oil and season well with salt and pepper, then grill for 3 minutes.
- Turn the fish and tomatoes over and grill for 2 more minutes.
- Meanwhile, whisk the honey and vinegar into the walnut oil and stir in the parsley.
- When the fish is ready, transfer it to 2 warm plates and garnish with the grilled tomato slices, olives and capers.
- Drizzle over the dressing and serve immediately.

741

SERVES 4

Chicken and Herb Savoury Pancakes

PREPARATION TIME 4 MINUTES

COOKING TIME 20 MINUTES

....

INGREDIENTS

2 tbsp butter
1 tbsp plain (all purpose) flour
300 ml / 10 ½ fl. oz / 1 ¼ cups milk
100 g / 3 ½ oz / 1 cup cooked chicken breast, chopped
2 tbsp flat leaf parsley, chopped
2 tbsp chives, chopped
8 ready-made pancakes
30 g / 1 oz / ¼ cup breadcrumbs

- Preheat the oven to 200°C (180° fan), 390 F, gas 6.
- Melt the butter in a large saucepan and stir in the flour. Gradually incorporate the milk, stirring continuously to avoid any lumps forming.
- When the mixture starts to bubble, stir in the chicken, herbs and a grind of salt and black pepper then take the pan off the heat.
- Lay the pancakes out on the work surface and divide the chicken mixture between them.
- Roll the pancakes up and transfer them to a baking dish then sprinkle with breadcrumbs.
- Bake the pancakes for 15 minutes or until the breadcrumbs are golden brown.
- Serve warm or at room temperature.

Smoked Salmon Savoury Pancakes

 742

- Replace the chicken with 100 g chopped smoked salmon.

743

SERVES 2

Tagliatelle with Chicken and Honey and Mustard Dressing

PREPARATION TIME 4 MINUTES

COOKING TIME 12 MINUTES

....

INGREDIENTS

200 g / 7 oz / 2 cups tagliatelle
1 tsp runny honey
1 tsp Dijon mustard
1 tbsp lemon juice
3 tbsp olive oil
100 g / 3 ½ oz / 1 cup cooked chicken breast, sliced
basil leaves to garnish

- Cook the tagliatelle in boiling salted water according to the packet instructions or until al dente.
- While the pasta is cooking, put the honey, mustard, lemon juice and oil in a jar with a pinch of salt and pepper and shake to emulsify.
- Drain the pasta and return it to the pan, then add the chicken and dressing and stir to coat.
- Divide between 2 warm bowls and garnish with basil leaves.

Tagliatelle, Salmon and Mustard Dressing

744

- Replace the cooked chicken with poached salmon.

745

SERVES 8

Savoury Vegetable Crumble

- Preheat the oven to 180°C (160° fan), 355 F, gas 4.
- Mix together the courgette, aubergine (eggplant) , spring onions and sundried tomatoes and arrange them in a baking dish.
- Rub the butter into the flour and stir in the ground almonds and Feta, then season with salt and pepper.
- Take a handful of the topping and squeeze it into a clump, then crumble it over the vegetables.
- Repeat with the rest of the crumble mixture then press down with your fingertips into an even layer. Bake the crumble for 40 minutes or until the topping is golden brown.

PREPARATION TIME 5 MINUTES

COOKING TIME 40 MINUTES

INGREDIENTS

1 courgette, chopped
1 aubergine (eggplant) , chopped
6 spring onions, chopped
100 g / 3 ½ oz / ½ cup sundried tomatoes in oil, drained
75 g / 2 ½ oz / ⅓ cup butter
50 g / 1 ¾ oz / ⅓ cup plain (all purpose) flour
25 g / 1 oz / ¼ cup ground almonds
40 g / 1 ½ oz / ½ cup Feta, crumbled

Savoury Vegetable Cobbler   746

- Add enough milk to the crumble mixture to bring it together into a soft dough. Shape it into small discs and arrange them round the outside of the baking dish before baking.

747

SERVES 4

Grilled Parmesan Polenta

- Bring 1 litre of water to the boil with a large pinch of salt then stir in the polenta.
- Continue to cook, stirring continuously, until the polenta is very thick.
- Beat in the butter and three quarters of the Parmesan, then scrape the mixture into a greased cake tin and level the top.
- Chill in the fridge for 15 minutes to set.
- Preheat the grill to its highest setting.
- Cut the polenta into wedges and spread them out on a grill tray.
- Sprinkle the polenta with the rest of the Parmesan then grill for 5 minutes or until toasted at the edges.

PREPARATION TIME 20 MINUTES

COOKING TIME 10 MINUTES

INGREDIENTS

225 g / 8 oz / 1 ¼ cups instant polenta
75 g / 2 ½ oz / ⅓ cup butter
75 g / 2 ½ oz / ¾ cup Parmesan, grated

Grilled Gorgonzola Polenta   748

- Stir 50 g of cubed Gorgonzola into the polenta with the Parmesan.

749

SERVES 1

Clam Omelette

Mussel Omelette   750

- Replace the clams with cooked, shelled mussels.

Sweetcorn Omelette   751

- Replace the clams with 100 g of canned sweetcorn.

PREPARATION TIME I MINUTE

COOKING TIME 4 MINUTES

INGREDIENTS

3 large eggs
10 g / 1 tbsp butter
50 g / 1 ¾ oz / ¼ cup cooked shelled clams
1 tbsp flat leaf parsley, finely chopped

- Break the eggs into a jug with a pinch of salt and pepper and beat them gently to break up the yolks.
- Heat the butter in a non-stick frying pan until sizzling then pour in the eggs.
- Cook over a medium heat until the eggs start to set around the outside. Use a spatula to draw the sides of the omelette into the centre and tilt the pan to fill the gaps with more liquid egg.
- Repeat the process until the top of the omelette is just set then sprinkle over the clams and parsley.
- Shake the omelette out onto a plate, folding it over as you go.

752

SERVES 1

Tofu and Spring Onion Omelette

- Break the eggs into a jug with a pinch of salt and pepper and beat them gently to break up the yolks.
- Stir in the tofu and spring onions.
- Heat the butter in a non-stick frying pan until sizzling then pour in the eggs.
- Cook over a medium heat until the eggs start to set around the outside. Use a spatula to draw the sides of the omelette into the centre and tilt the pan to fill the gaps with more liquid egg.
- Repeat the process until the top of the omelette is just set then fold in half and sprinkle over the parsley.

PREPARATION TIME 1 MINUTES

COOKING TIME 4 MINUTES

INGREDIENTS

3 large eggs
2 tbsp flat leaf parsley
1 tbsp butter
50 g / 1 ¾ oz / ¼ cup firm tofu, cubed
2 spring onions (scallions), chopped
flat leaf parsley to garnish

Halloumi and Spring Onion Omelette

753

- Replace the tofu with cubes of Halloumi.

754

SERVES 6

Savoury Tomato and Pesto Crumble

- Preheat the oven to 180°C (160° fan), 355 F, gas 4.
- Arrange the tomatoes in a baking dish and spread the pesto on top.
- Rub the butter into the flour and stir in the ground almonds, then season with salt and pepper.
- Take a handful of the topping and squeeze it into a clump, then crumble it over the vegetables.
- Repeat with the rest of the crumble mixture then press down with your fingertips into an even layer. Bake the crumble for 40 minutes or until the topping is golden brown.

PREPARATION TIME 5 MINUTES

COOKING TIME 40 MINUTES

INGREDIENTS

400 g / 14 oz / 2 cups canned tomatoes, drained
4 tbsp pesto
75 g / 2 ½ oz / ⅓ cup butter
50 g / 1 ¾ oz / ⅓ cup plain (all purpose) flour
25 g / 1 oz / ¼ cup ground almonds

Tomato and Tapenade Crumble

755

- Replace the pesto with black olive tapenade.

756

SERVES 4

Chicken and Potato Gratin

PREPARATION TIME 5 MINUTES

COOKING TIME 35 MINUTES

....

INGREDIENTS

450 g / 1 lb / 2 ½ cups maris piper potatoes, peeled and cubed
600 ml / 1 pint / 2 ½ cups whole milk
3 tbsp butter
1 tbsp plain (all purpose) flour
2 tbsp flat leaf parsley, chopped
450 g / 1 lb / 2 ¾ cups cooked chicken
15 g / ½ oz breadcrumbs

- Cook the potatoes in boiling salted water for 12 minutes, then drain well. Bring the milk to a simmer.
- When the potatoes are ready, mash them until smooth with 1 tablespoon of the butter and a little of the hot milk.
- Heat 1 tablespoon of the butter in a small saucepan and stir in the flour. Gradually incorporate the rest of the hot milk, stirring continuously to avoid any lumps forming. Continue to stir until it starts to bubble then stir in the parsley and chicken.
- Preheat the grill to its highest setting.
- Pour the chicken mixture into a baking dish and top with the mashed potato.
- Dot the final tablespoon of butter over the top and sprinkle with breadcrumbs then grill for 5 minutes or until the top is golden and bubbling.

Chicken and Parsnip Gratin

757

- Replace the potatoes with parsnips and puree until smooth with the butter in a food processor.

758

SERVES 6

Pot-Roasted Chicken with White Wine

PREPARATION TIME 5 MINUTES

COOKING TIME 40 MINUTES

....

INGREDIENTS

700 ml / 1 pint 5 oz / 3 ½ cups white wine
300 ml / 10 ½ fl. oz / 1 ¼ cups chicken stock
2 tbsp plain (all purpose) flour
1 tsp mustard powder
1 chicken, jointed
2 tbsp olive oil
2 tbsp butter
200 g / 7 oz / 2 cups pickling onions, peeled
2 tbsp flat leaf parsley, chopped

- Preheat the oven to 200°C (180° fan), 390 F, gas 6.
- Put the wine and stock in a saucepan and bring to the boil as you prepare the chicken.
- Mix the flour with the mustard powder and a pinch of salt and pepper and dust it over the chicken pieces.
- Heat the oil and butter in a large cast iron casserole pan then brown the chicken pieces all over in 2 batches.
- Arrange them all in the pot and add the onions, then pour over the hot wine and chicken stock.
- Transfer the dish to the oven and cook uncovered for 35 – 40 minutes.
- Pierce the thickest part of one of the chicken pieces – if the juices run clear, the meat is ready.
- Spoon the chicken and onions onto warm plates then stir the parsley into the reduced sauce before spooning it over the meat.

Coq au Vin

759

- Add 100 g of lardons when you fry the last batch of chicken pieces and use red wine instead of white wine.

760

SERVES 6 # Baked Chicken with Mustard and Lime

- Preheat the oven to 200°C (180° fan), 390 F, gas 6.
- Stir the mustard into the lime juice and zest and massage it into the chicken pieces.
- Arrange them in a roasting tin and season well with salt and pepper.
- Bake for 35 – 40 minutes or until the chicken is cooked through.
- Transfer the chicken to a warm serving dish and garnish with lime wedges and coriander (cilantro) (cilantro)sprigs.

PREPARATION TIME 5 MINUTES

COOKING TIME 35-40 MINUTES

INGREDIENTS

2 tbsp wholegrain mustard
1 lime, juiced and zest finely grated
1 chicken, jointed
lime wedges and fresh coriander
(cilantro) (cilantro)to serve

Quail Baked with Mustard and Lime   761

- Replace the chicken with 2 whole quail per person and educe the cooking time if necessary.

762

SERVES 2 # Stuffed Chicken Breasts

- Preheat the oven to 200°C (180° fan), 390 F, gas 6.
- Slice open the chicken breasts without cutting all the way through and stuff them with the tomato and Cambozola.
- Wrap a rasher of bacon round each one and secure underneath with a cocktail stick then transfer the chicken to a baking tray.
- Bake the chicken for 20 minutes or until the bacon is cooked and the cheese has melted.
- Serve with dauphinoise potatoes and a green salad.

PREPARATION TIME 10 MINUTES

COOKING TIME 20 MINUTES

INGREDIENTS

2 cooked skinless chicken breasts
1 tomato, sliced
4 slices Cambozola
2 rashers smoked bacon

Stuffed Pork Steaks   763

- Butterfly a pork leg steak then stuff and wrap as before. Check the pork is cooked through before serving.

764

SERVES 4

Chicken and Red Onion Pasta Bake

PREPARATION TIME 5 MINUTES

COOKING TIME 25 MINUTES

INGREDIENTS

400 g / 14 oz / 4 cups penne
4 tbsp olive oil
1 red onion, sliced
200 g / 7 oz / 1 ¼ cups chicken breast, sliced
2 tbsp flat leaf parsley, finely chopped
300 ml / 10 ½ fl. oz / 1 ¼ cups white wine
150 g / 5 ½ oz / 1 ½ cups mozzarella, cubed

- Preheat the oven to 220⁰C (200⁰ fan), 430 F, gas 7.
- Cook the penne in boiling salted water according to the packet instructions or until al dente. Drain well.
- Meanwhile, heat the oil in a frying pan and cook the onions with a pinch of salt for 5 minutes.
- Add the chicken and stir-fry for 3 minutes then sprinkle with parsley, pour in the wine, and bring to a simmer.
- Stir in the pasta and spoon it into a baking dish.
- Level the top and scatter over the mozzarella cubes then bake for 10 minutes or until the top is bubbling.

Chicken and Mushroom Pasta Bake

765

- Add 100 g of sliced button mushrooms when you fry the chicken.

766

SERVES 4

Chicken and Red Onion Hot Pot

PREPARATION TIME 5 MINUTES

COOKING TIME 40 MINUTES

INGREDIENTS

400 g / 14 oz maris piper potatoes, peeled and sliced
4 tbsp olive oil
1 red onion, sliced
200 g / 7 oz / 1 ¼ cups chicken breast, sliced
2 tsp Dijon mustard
300 ml / 10 ½ fl. oz / 1 ¼ cups white wine
50 g / 1 ¾ oz / ¼ cup butter, melted

- Preheat the oven to 220⁰C (200⁰ fan), 430 F, gas 7 and put a baking dish in to heat
- Cook the potatoes in boiling salted water for 10 minutes or until tender. Drain well.
- Meanwhile, heat the oil in a frying pan and cook the onions with a pinch of salt for 5 minutes.
- Add the chicken and stir-fry for 3 minutes then stir in the mustard, pour in the wine, and bring to a simmer.
- Spoon the chicken mixture into the preheated baking dish and arrange the potatoes on top.
- Brush the potatoes with melted butter and sprinkle with salt and pepper, then bake for 30 minutes or until the potatoes are golden.

Quick Lamb Hot Pot

767

- Replace the chicken with lamb neck fillet, cut into cubes.

768

SERVES 1

Wild Mushroom Omelette

Mushroom and Bacon Omelette

769

- Add 2 chopped rashers of smoked streaky bacon to the pan with the mushrooms.

Creamy Mushroom Omelette

770

- Add 2 tbsp of crème fraîche to the mushrooms for the last minute of cooking time.

PREPARATION TIME 1 MINUTES

COOKING TIME 4 MINUTES

INGREDIENTS

200 g / 8 oz / 2 cups mixed wild mushrooms (to include chanterelles and ceps)
1 tbsp olive oil
4 tbsp butter
3 large eggs
1 tbsp chives, chopped

- Pick over the mushrooms and brush away any soil with a pastry brush. Cut the bigger mushrooms into bite-sized pieces.
- Heat the olive oil and half the butter in a large sauté pan until sizzling.
- Add the mushrooms, season with salt and pepper and cook for 10 minutes, stirring occasionally.
- Break the eggs into a jug with a pinch of salt and pepper and beat them gently to break up the yolks.
- Heat the rest of the butter in a non-stick frying pan until sizzling then pour in the eggs.
- Cook over a medium heat until the eggs start to set around the outside. Use a spatula to draw the sides of the omelette into the centre and tilt the pan to fill the gaps with more liquid egg.
- Repeat the process until the top of the omelette is just set then fold it over and slide onto a warm plate.
- Spoon over the mushrooms and sprinkle with chives.

771
SERVES 4

Chicken and Mushroom Cannelloni

PREPARATION TIME 10 MINUTES

COOKING TIME 35 MINUTES

INGREDIENTS

50 g / 1 ¾ oz / ¼ cup butter
2 shallots, chopped
2 cloves garlic, crushed
200 g / 7 oz / 2 cups button
mushrooms, chopped
200 g / 7 oz / 1 ¼ cups cooked
chicken, sliced
2 tbsp plain (all purpose) flour
600 ml / 1 pint / 2 ½ cups milk
200 g / 7 oz / 2 cups Emmental,
grated
12 sheets ready-made fresh pasta
4 cherry tomatoes, halved
basil leaves to garnish

- Preheat the oven to 200°C (180° fan), 390 F, gas 6.
- Melt half the butter in a pan and fry the shallots and garlic for 5 minutes. Add the mushrooms with a pinch of salt and cook for 5 minutes. Stir in the chicken.
- Melt the rest of the butter in a saucepan. Stir in the flour then gradually add the milk, stirring continuously.
- When the mixture starts to bubble, stir in half the cheese and black pepper then remove from the heat.
- Add half of the sauce to the mushroom mixture and stir. Split the mushroom filling between the pasta sheets, then roll them up and pack them a baking dish.
- Pour over the rest of the sauce and sprinkle with the other half of the cheese.
- Arrange the cherry tomatoes on top and bake for 20 minutes or until golden brown.
- Garnish with basil leaves.

Mushroom and Tofu Cannelloni   772

- Replace the chicken for tofu pieces for a vegetarian option.

773
SERVES 4

Green Pepper and Bacon Crustless Quiche

PREPARATION TIME 5 MINUTES

COOKING TIME 30-35 MINUTES

INGREDIENTS

1 green pepper, very thinly sliced
2 rashers streaky bacon, very thinly
sliced
2 tbsp olive oil
6 eggs
1 tbsp basil, finely shredded

- Preheat the oven to 180°C (160° fan), 355 F, gas 4.
- Fry the peppers and bacon in the oil for 10 minutes or until softened.
- Lightly beat the eggs and stir in the peppers and bacon.
- Pour the mixture into a non-stick cake tin and bake in the oven for 20 – 25 minutes or until just set in the centre.
- Sprinkle with basil and serve warm or at room temperature.

Green Pepper and Haloumi   774
Crustless Quiche

- Replace the bacon with 100 g of cubed Haloumi.

775

SERVES 2 Spaghetti with Green Beans

- Cook the spaghetti in boiling salted water according to the packet instructions or until al dente.
- Meanwhile, blanch the green beans in boiling salted water for 3 – 4 minutes or until just tender. Drain well.
- Heat the oil in a sauté pan and fry the garlic for 2 minutes. Add the drained beans and cook, stirring occasionally, for 3 minutes so they can take on the flavour from the oil. Season to taste with salt and pepper.
- Reserve a couple of ladles of pasta water and drain the rest.
- Stir the pasta into the green bean pan with 3 tablespoons of the pasta water and shake to emulsify with the oil. If it looks a bit dry, add some more pasta water.
- Divide between 2 warm bowls and serve immediately.

PREPARATION TIME 2 MINUTES

COOKING TIME 12 MINUTES

INGREDIENTS

200 g / 7 oz / 1 cup spaghetti
200 g / 7 oz green beans
4 tbsp olive oil
3 cloves garlic, crushed
2 tbsp flat leaf parsley, finely chopped

Spaghetti with Green Beans and Pesto

776

- Stir 3 tbsp of pesto into the spaghetti at the end.

777

SERVES 4 Penne Salad with Roasted Squash

- Preheat the oven to 200°C (180° fan), 390 F, gas 6.
- Rub the squash and onion with oil and sprinkle with salt and pepper then roast for 30 minutes or until tender.
- Meanwhile, cook the penne in boiling salted water according to the packet instructions or until al dente.
- Rinse the pasta under cold water to cool then drain well.
- When the squash and onions are ready, toss the with the pasta, tomatoes, onion, spinach and walnuts then season with salt and pepper.

PREPARATION TIME 10 MINUTES

COOKING TIME 30 MINUTES

INGREDIENTS

½ butternut squash, peeled and cubed
1 red onion, sliced
2 tbsp olive oil
400 g / 14 oz / 4 cups penne
2 tomatoes, cubed
1 white onion, sliced
50 g / 1 ¾ oz / 2 cups baby spinach leaves, torn
2 tbsp walnuts, roughly chopped

Penne Salad with Squash and Roquefort

778

- Replace the Parmesan with 100 g of cubed Roquefort.

SERVES 2

Ravioli with Tomato, Basil and Pine Nuts

Ravioli with Mushrooms and Truffle Oil

780

- Dress the ravioli with 100 g of sliced mushrooms that have been fried in 20 g of butter. Add a few drops of truffle oil to the pan just before serving.

Ravioli with Gorgonzola Cream

781

- Dress the ravioli with 150 ml of double cream and 50 g of Gorgonzola that have been heated together in a small saucepan.

PREPARATION TIME 2 MINUTES

COOKING TIME 10 MINUTES

INGREDIENTS

250 g / 9 oz / 2 cups fresh ravioli
2 tbsp pine nuts
6 sundried tomatoes in oil, chopped
2 tbsp oil from the sundried tomato jar
a small bunch basil, shredded

- Cook the ravioli in boiling salted water according to the packet instructions or until al dente.
- Meanwhile, dry-fry the pine nuts in a frying pan until toasted.
- Take off the heat and stir in the sundried tomatoes and their oil.
- Drain the ravioli and split between 2 warm bowls then spoon over the sundried tomato mixture and sprinkle with basil.

782

SERVES 4

Fried Gnocchi with Tomato Sauce

- Heat the oil in a sauté pan and fry the onion for 5 minutes to soften. Add the garlic and cook for 2 more minutes, then stir in the tomatoes. Simmer for 15 minutes.
- Meanwhile, heat the oil in a large non-stick frying pan and fry the gnocchi for 5 minutes, turning once.
- Divide the gnocchi between 4 warm bowls and top with a spoonful of tomato sauce.

PREPARATION TIME 5 MINUTES

COOKING TIME 20 MINUTES

INGREDIENTS

4 tbsp olive oil
500 g / 1 lb 2 oz / 2 cups ready-made gnocchi

FOR THE SAUCE
4 tbsp olive oil
1 onion, sliced
2 cloves of garlic, crushed
400 g / 14 oz / 2 cups canned tomatoes, chopped

Fried Gnocchi with Dolcelatte Cream

783

- Replace the tomato sauce with a sauce made from 150ml of double cream and 50 g of

784

SERVES 4

Baked Maccheroncini with Pancetta and Mozzarella

- Preheat the oven to 220⁰C (200⁰ fan), 430 F, gas 7.
- Cook the penne in boiling salted water according to the packet instructions or until al dente. Drain well.
- Meanwhile, heat the oil in a frying pan and fry the pancetta for 5 minutes.
- Pour in the wine, bring to a simmer and cook for 5 minutes.
- Stir in the pasta and parsley and spoon it into a baking dish.
- Scatter over the mozzarella cubes then bake for 10 minutes or until the top is bubbling.

PREPARATION TIME 2 MINUTES

COOKING TIME 25 MINUTES

INGREDIENTS

400 g / 14 oz / 4 cups penne pasta
4 tbsp olive oil
200 g / 7 oz / 1 ¼ cups pancetta, cut into lardons
300 ml / 10 ½ fl. oz / 1 ¼ cups white wine
2 tbsp flat leaf parsley, finely chopped
150 g / 5 ½ oz / 1 ½ cups mozzarella, cubed

Baked Maccheroncini with Chorizo and Mozzarella

785

- Replace the pancetta with cubed chorizo.

786

SERVES 2

Ham, Pesto and Mozzarella Open Lasagne

PREPARATION TIME 15 MINUTES

COOKING TIME 20 MINUTES

INGREDIENTS

6 fresh lasagne sheets
6 tbsp pesto
2 balls mozzarella, sliced
6 slices cooked ham

- Preheat the oven to 200°C (180° fan), 390 F, gas 6.
- Layer up the 2 lasagne on a baking tray. Start with 2 sheets of pasta and spread them both with a tablespoon of pesto.
- Top with a quarter of the mozzarella then lay a slice of ham on each one. Make another 2 layers in the same way then top with the last of the mozzarella.
- Bake the lasagne in the oven for 20 minutes or until golden brown and bubbling.

Portabella and Pesto Open Lasagne

787

- Replace the ham with 3 portabella mushrooms that have been sliced in half horizontally.

788

SERVES 2

Spaghetti with Garlic and Rosemary

PREPARATION TIME 2 MINUTES

COOKING TIME 12 MINUTES

INGREDIENTS

200 g / 7 oz / 2 cups spaghetti
4 tbsp olive oil
3 cloves garlic, crushed
2 tbsp fresh rosemary
2 tbsp Parmesan, freshly grated

- Cook the spaghetti in boiling salted water according to the packet instructions or until al dente.
- Heat the oil in a sauté pan and stir-fry the garlic and rosemary for 2 minutes.
- Reserve a couple of ladles of pasta water and drain the rest.
- Stir the pasta into the garlic pan with 3 tablespoons of the pasta water and shake to emulsify with the oil. If it looks a bit dry, add some more pasta water.
- Divide between 2 warm bowls and sprinkle over the Parmesan.

Spaghetti with Garlic and Rosemary Cream

789

- Stir 150 ml double cream into the frying pan and bring to a simmer before adding the spaghetti.

790

MAKES 8

Smoked Haddock Potato Cakes

Haddock and Chorizo Potato Cakes

791

- Add 100 g of chorizo in small cubes to the potato cake mixture.

Haddock and Pesto Potato Cakes

792

- Replace the parsley and lemon zest with 2 tbsp of pesto.

PREPARATION TIME 15 MINUTES

COOKING TIME 25 MINUTES

INGREDIENTS

450 g / 1 lb / 2 cups potatoes, peeled and cubed
600 ml / 1 pint / 2 ½ cups whole milk
450 g / 1 lb / 2 ¼ cups smoked haddock
1 lemon, zest finely grated
4 tbsp flat leaf parsley, finely chopped
3 tbsp plain (all purpose) flour
3 tbsp butter, melted

- Preheat the grill to its highest setting.
- Cook the potatoes in boiling salted water for 15 minutes or until tender. Drain well.
- Meanwhile, bring the milk to a simmer then pour it over the smoked haddock. Cover the dish with clingfilm and leave to steep for 10 minutes.
- Drain off and reserve the milk and flake the haddock, discarding any skin and bones.
- Mash the potatoes and mix in the haddock, lemon zest and parsley. Shape the mixture into 8 patties.
- Dust the patties with flour and brush with melted butter then grill for 4 minutes on each side or until golden brown.
- Serve with a mixed green salad.

793

SERVES 2

Tagliatelle with Spring Vegetables

PREPARATION TIME 2 MINUTES

COOKING TIME 12 MINUTES

INGREDIENTS

200 g / 7 oz / 2 cups tagliatelle
1 carrot, sliced
6 asparagus spears, trimmed
75 g / 2 ½ oz / ¾ cup mange tout
75 g / 2 ½ oz / ½ cup fresh peas
4 tbsp olive oil
3 cloves garlic, crushed
75 g / 2 ½ oz / ½ cup fresh goats'
cheese

- Cook the tagliatelle in boiling salted water according to the packet instructions or until al dente.
- Meanwhile, blanch the vegetables in boiling salted water for 3 – 4 minutes or until just tender. Drain well.
- Heat the oil in a sauté pan and fry the garlic for 2 minutes. Add the drained vegetables and cook, stirring occasionally, for 3 minutes so that they take on the flavour from the oil. Season to taste with salt and pepper.
- Reserve a couple of ladles of pasta water and drain the rest.
- Stir the pasta into the sauté pan with 3 tablespoons of the pasta water and shake to emulsify with the oil. If it looks a bit dry, add some more pasta water.
- Divide between 2 warm bowls and crumble over the goats' cheese.

Tagliatelle with Goats' Cheese and Lemon

794

- Replace the vegetables with a sauce made from 200 ml double cream and the zest and juice of a lemon, heated together in a small pan.

795

SERVES 2

Lemon and Asparagus Risotto

PREPARATION TIME 5 MINUTES

COOKING TIME 25 MINUTES

INGREDIENTS

1 litre / 1 pint 15 fl. oz / 4 cups good
quality vegetable stock
2 tbsp olive oil
1 onion, finely chopped
2 cloves of garlic, crushed
1 lemon, zest finely pared
150 g / 5 ½ oz / ¾ cup risotto rice
100 g / 3 ½ oz / 1 cup asparagus
spears, cut into short lengths
2 tbsp butter

- Heat the stock in a saucepan.
- Heat the olive oil in a sauté pan and gently fry the onion for 5 minutes without colouring.
- Add the garlic and lemon zest and cook for 2 more minutes then stir in the rice.
- When it is well coated with the oil, add the asparagus, followed by 2 ladles of the hot stock.
- Cook, stirring occasionally, until most of the stock has been absorbed before adding the next 2 ladles.
- Continue in this way for around 15 minutes or until the rice is just tender.
- Stir in the butter, then cover the pan and take off the heat to rest for 4 minutes.
- Uncover the pan and season well with salt and pepper, then spoon into warm bowls.

Lemon and Pea Risotto

796

- Replace the Asparagus with 100 g of mange tout and 75 g of defrosted frozen peas.

797

SERVES 2

Tomato, Mushroom and Pepper Risotto

- Heat the stock and chopped tomatoes together in a saucepan.
- Heat the olive oil in a sauté pan and gently fry the onion and peppers for 5 minutes without colouring.
- Add the garlic and cook for 2 more minutes then stir in the mushrooms and rice.
- When they are well coated with the oil, add 2 ladles of the hot stock.
- Cook, stirring occasionally, until most of the stock has been absorbed before adding the next 2 ladles.
- Continue in this way for around 15 minutes or until the rice is just tender.
- Stir in the butter, then cover the pan and take off the heat to rest for 4 minutes.
- Uncover the pan and season well with salt and pepper, then spoon into warm bowls.

PREPARATION TIME 5 MINUTES

COOKING TIME 15 MINUTES

INGREDIENTS

500 ml / 17 ½ fl. oz / 2 cups vegetable stock
500 ml / 17 ½ fl. oz / 2 ¼ cups canned tomatoes, chopped
2 tbsp olive oil
1 onion, finely chopped
1 yellow pepper, sliced
2 cloves of garlic, crushed
100 g / 3 ½ oz / 1 cup mushrooms, sliced
150 g / 5 ½ oz / ¾ cup risotto rice
2 tbsp butter
basil leaves to garnish

Tomato, Mushroom and Sausage Risotto

798

- Replace the pepper with 4 skinned pork sausages, broken into chunks.

799

SERVES 2

Pesto Risotto

- Heat the stock in a saucepan.
- Heat the olive oil in a sauté pan and gently fry the onion for 5 minutes without colouring.
- Add the garlic and cook for 2 more minutes then stir in the rice.
- When it is well coated with the oil, add 2 ladles of the hot stock.
- Cook, stirring occasionally, until most of the stock has been absorbed before adding the next 2 ladles.
- Continue in this way for around 15 minutes or until the rice is just tender.
- Stir in the pesto and Parmesan, then cover the pan and take off the heat to rest for 4 minutes.
- Uncover the pan and season well with salt and pepper, then spoon into warm bowls.
- Garnish with rocket leaves and serve immediately.

PREPARATION TIME 5 MINUTES

COOKING TIME 25 MINUTES

INGREDIENTS

1 litre / 1 pint 15 fl. oz / 4 cups good quality vegetable stock
2 tbsp olive oil
1 onion, finely chopped
2 cloves of garlic, crushed
150 g / 5 ½ oz / ¾ cup risotto rice
100 g / 3 ½ oz / ½ cup pesto
50 g / 1 ¾ oz / ½ cup Parmesan, finely grated
a handful of rocket (arugula) leaves

Pesto and Artichoke Risotto

800

- Add 200 g of preserved baby artichokes in oil, 4 minutes before the end of the cooking time.

SERVES 4 # Leek and Ham Gratin

Chicory and Ham Gratin

802

- Replace the leeks with 6 small heads of chicory.

Asparagus and Ham Gratin

803

- Replace the leeks with asparagus, wrapping 3 spears inside each sheet of ham and omitting the initial baking stage.

PREPARATION TIME 5 MINUTES

COOKING TIME 35 MINUTES

INGREDIENTS

6 leeks, trimmed and washed
2 tbsp olive oil
600 ml / 1 pint / 2 ½ cups whole milk
3 tbsp butter
1 tbsp plain (all purpose) flour
75 g / 2 ½ oz / ¾ cup Cheddar, grated
6 slices ham

- Preheat the oven to 190°C (170° fan), 375 F, gas 5
- Rub the leeks with oil and bake them in the oven for 10 minutes.
- Meanwhile, bring the milk to a simmer.
- Heat the butter in a small saucepan then stir in the flour and cook for 1 minute.
- Gradually incorporate the hot milk, stirring continuously to avoid any lumps forming.
- Continue to stir until it starts to bubble then stir in the cheese and season with salt and pepper.
- Take the leeks out of the oven and wrap each one with a piece of ham.
- Return the leeks to the baking dish in a double layer and pour over the sauce, then season with plenty of black pepper.
- Return the dish to the oven and cook for 20 minutes or until the leeks are soft and the sauce has browned at the edges.

804

SERVES 2 Strawberry Risotto

- Heat the milk in a saucepan with 500 ml water.
- Heat the butter in a sauté pan and stir in the rice.
- When it is well coated with butter, add 2 ladles of the hot milk.
- Cook, stirring occasionally, until most of the milk has been absorbed before adding the next 2 ladles.
- Continue in this way for around 15 minutes or until the rice is just tender.
- Stir in the strawberries and crème fraîche, then cover the pan and take off the heat to rest for 4 minutes.
- Spoon into warm bowls and serve immediately.

PREPARATION TIME 5 MINUTES

COOKING TIME 25 MINUTES

INGREDIENTS

500 ml / 18 fl. oz / 2 cups milk
4 tbsp butter
150 g / 5 ½ oz / ¾ cup risotto rice
150 g / 5 ½ oz / ¾ cup strawberries, sliced
2 tbsp crème fraîche

Mango Risotto   805

- Replace the strawberries with a ripe mango, cut into chunks.

806

SERVES 2 Vegetable Risotto with Parmesan Tuiles

- Preheat the oven to 200⁰C (180⁰ fan), 390 F, gas 6 and heat the stock in a saucepan. Fry the courgette in the oil for 5 minutes.
- Add the garlic, peas and mange tout and cook for 2 minutes then stir in the rice. When it is well coated with the oil, add 2 ladles of hot stock.
- Cook, stirring occasionally, until most of the stock has been absorbed before adding the next 2 ladles.
- Continue in this way for 15 minutes. Meanwhile, space out tablespoons of Parmesan on a large baking tray.
- Bake in the oven for 5 – 10 minutes until golden brown.
- Leave the tuiles to set on the tray before removing.
- When the rice is just tender, stir in the butter and spring onions, then cover the pan and take off the heat to rest for 4 minutes.
- Season well, then spoon into warm bowls and serve with the Parmesan tuiles.

PREPARATION TIME 5 MINUTES

COOKING TIME 30 MINUTES

INGREDIENTS

1 litre / 1 pint 15 fl. oz / 4 cups good quality vegetable stock
1 courgette
2 tbsp olive oil
2 cloves of garlic, crushed
100 g / 3 ½ oz / ⅔ cup fresh peas
100 g / 3 ½ oz / 1 cup mange tout, sliced into thin strips
150 g / 5 ½ oz / ¾ cup risotto rice
2 tbsp butter
2 spring onions, thinly sliced

FOR THE TUILES

200 g / 7 oz / 2 cups Parmesan, grated

Parmesan Tuiles   807

- Space out tablespoons of grated Parmesan on a baking tray and bake at 200⁰C for 5 minutes or until golden brown and lacy.

808

SERVES 2

Asparagus Risotto with Grilled Bream

PREPARATION TIME 5 MINUTES

COOKING TIME 25 MINUTES

INGREDIENTS

1 litre / 1 pint 15 fl. oz / 4 cups good
quality vegetable stock
2 tbsp olive oil
1 onion, finely chopped
2 cloves of garlic, crushed
150 g / 5 ½ oz / ¾ cup risotto rice
100 g / 3 ½ oz / 1 cup asparagus
spears, cut into short lengths
2 tbsp butter

FOR THE BREAM

1 sea bream, filleted and pin-boned
2 tbsp olive oil
1 tbsp chives, chopped

- Heat the stock in a saucepan and preheat the grill to its highest setting.
- Heat the olive oil in a sauté pan and gently fry the onion for 5 minutes. Add the garlic and cook for 2 more minutes then stir in the rice.
- When it is well coated with the oil, add the asparagus, followed by 2 ladles of the hot stock.
- Cook, stirring occasionally, until most of the stock has been absorbed before adding the next 2 ladles.
- Continue in this way for around 15 minutes.
- Meanwhile, grill the bream for 3 minutes on each side then leave to rest somewhere warm.
- Stir in the butter into the risotto, then cover the pan and take off the heat to rest for 4 minutes.
- Season well, then spoon into warm bowls and top with the bream and a sprinkling of chives.

Broad Bean Risotto with Bream   809

- Replace the asparagus with 200 g of podded fresh broad beans.

810

SERVES 4

Chicken, Carrot and Leek Gratin

PREPARATION TIME 5 MINUTES

COOKING TIME 25 MINUTES

INGREDIENTS

450 g / 1 lb / 3 cups large carrots,
sliced
600 ml / 1 pint whole milk
3 tbsp butter
1 leek, halved and sliced
1 tbsp plain (all purpose) flour
2 tbsp flat leaf parsley, chopped
450 g / 1 lb / 3 ½ cups cooked chicken
75 g / 2 ½ oz / ¾ cup Red Leicester,
grated

- Cook the carrots in boiling salted water for 12 minutes or until tender. Drain well.
- Meanwhile, bring the milk to a simmer.
- Heat the butter in a small saucepan and fry the leek for 5 minutes.
- Stir in the flour then gradually incorporate the hot milk, stirring continuously to avoid any lumps forming.
- Continue to stir until it starts to bubble then stir in the chicken and season with salt and white pepper.
- Preheat the grill to its highest setting.
- Pour the chicken mixture into a baking dish and top with the carrot slices.
- Sprinkle over the cheese then grill for 5 minutes or until the top is golden and bubbling.

Ham, Carrot and Leek Gratin   811

- Replace the chicken with an equal weight of cooked ham in slices.

812

SERVES 4

Potato and Chorizo Crustless Quiche

Chorizo and Pea Crustless Quiche

813

- Replace the sundried tomatoes with 100 g of defrosted frozen peas.

Pepper and Tomato Crustless Quiche

814

- Replace the chorizo with a jar of roasted peppers in oil that have been drained and chopped.

PREPARATION TIME 5 MINUTES

COOKING TIME 25-30 MINUTES

INGREDIENTS

4 boiled potatoes, cooled and cubed
½ chorizo sausage, cubed
½ jar sundried tomatoes in oil, drained and chopped
2 tbsp olive oil
6 free-range eggs
pea shoots to garnish

- Preheat the oven to 180°C (160° fan), 355 F, gas 4.
- Fry the potatoes and chorizo in the oil for 5 minutes then stir in the sundried tomatoes.
- Lightly beat the eggs and stir in the chorizo and potatoes.
- Pour the mixture into a non-stick cake tin and bake in the oven for 20 – 25 minutes or until just set in the centre.
- Garnish with pea shoots and serve warm or at room temperature.

815

SERVES 8

Savoury Pork and Apple Crumble

PREPARATION TIME 5 MINUTES

COOKING TIME 45 MINUTES

INGREDIENTS

2 tbsp butter
1 onion, sliced
450 g / 1 lb / 3 cups pork shoulder, cubed
2 apples, chopped
250 ml / 9 fl. oz / 1 cup cider

FOR THE CRUMBLE MIXTURE
75 g / 2 ½ oz / ⅓ cup butter
50 g / 1 ¾ oz / ⅓ cup plain (all purpose) flour
25 g / 1 oz ground almonds

- Preheat the oven to 180°C (160° fan), 355 F, gas 4.
- Heat the butter in a sauté pan and fry the onion and pork with plenty of salt and pepper for 5 minutes or until starting to brown.
- Add the apples and cider and bring to a simmer then pour the mixture into a baking dish.
- Meanwhile, rub the butter into the flour and stir in the ground almonds, then season with salt and pepper.
- Take a handful of the topping and squeeze it into a clump, then crumble it over the pork.
- Repeat with the rest of the crumble mixture then press down with your fingertips into an even layer. Bake the crumble for 35 minutes or until the topping is golden brown.

816

MAKES 12

Beef Tartare and Sundried Tomato Bites

PREPARATION TIME 20 MINUTES

INGREDIENTS

350 g / 12 oz / 2 cups beef fillet
1 shallot, finely chopped
100 g / 3 ½ oz / ½ cup sundried tomatoes in oil, drained and chopped
1 tbsp grain mustard
2 tbsp tarragon, finely chopped

TO SERVE
12 little gem lettuce leaves
6 cherry tomatoes, halved

- Cut the beef into very thin slices with a sharp knife, then cut each slice into a fine julienne.
- Cut across the julienne strips into tiny squares then mix with the rest of the ingredients.
- Season the tartare to taste with salt and black pepper then roll the mixture into bite-sized balls.
- Serve each tartare bite inside a little gem leaf, garnished with tomato.

817

SERVES 2

Baked Chicken with Camembert

- Preheat the oven to 200⁰C (180⁰ fan), 390 F, gas 6.
- Thinly slice the green ends of the onions then set aside and reserve. Cut the base of the onions in half and mix with the carrots and oil in a baking dish.
- Lay the chicken breasts on top, skin side up, and season well with salt and pepper.
- Bake for 30 minutes then lay the Camembert on top of the chicken and cook for another 5 minutes or until the chicken is cooked through.
- Divide between 2 warm bowls and sprinkle with the reserved onion tops.

PREPARATION TIME 5 MINUTES

COOKING TIME 35 MINUTES

INGREDIENTS

8 salad onions
8 baby carrots, peeled and halved lengthways
2 tbsp olive oil
2 chicken breasts, skin on
2 slices Camembert

Pot-Roasted Marsala Chicken

818

SERVES 6

PREPARATION TIME 5 MINUTES

COOKING TIME 40 MINUTES

INGREDIENTS

700 ml / 1 pint 5 oz / 3 ½ cups chicken stock
300 ml / 10 ½ fl. oz / 1 ½ cups marsala
2 tbsp plain (all purpose) flour
1 tsp mustard powder
1 chicken, jointed
2 tbsp olive oil
2 tbsp butter
100 g / 3 ½ oz / ½ cup sultanas
2 tbsp thyme leaves
2 tbsp flaked (slivered) almonds

- Preheat the oven to 200⁰C (180⁰ fan), 390 F, gas 6.
- Put the stock and marsala in a saucepan and bring to the boil as you prepare the chicken.
- Mix the flour with the mustard powder and a pinch of salt and pepper and dust it over the chicken pieces.
- Heat the oil and butter in a large cast iron casserole pan then brown the chicken pieces all over in 2 batches.
- Arrange them all in the pot and add the sultanas and thyme, then pour over the hot marsala and chicken stock.
- Transfer the dish to the oven and cook uncovered for 35 – 40 minutes.
- Pierce the thickest part of one of the chicken pieces – if the juices run clear, the meat is ready.
- Sprinkle over the almonds and serve.

Marinated Squid Salad

819

SERVES 2

PREPARATION TIME 40 MINUTES

INGREDIENTS

8 baby squid tubes
1 lemon, juiced
2 tbsp balsamic vinegar
1 tsp sesame seeds
1 tsp black sesame seeds
1 red chilli, finely chopped
2 tbsp basil leaves, shredded
1 jar roasted red peppers in oil, drained
3 tbsp olive oil
a handful rocket (arugula) leaves
a handful baby spinach leaves

- Score a diamond pattern all over the squid then put the in a shallow bowl.
- Mix together the lemon juice, vinegar, sesame seeds, chilli and basil then pour it over the squid.
- Leave to stand for 30 minutes for the acid in the marinade to cure and 'cook' the squid.
- Stir the peppers and oil into the squid mixture and season with salt and pepper.
- Toss with the salad with the leaves and serve immediately.

820

SERVES 4

Chilli Con Carne

PREPARATION TIME 10 MINUTES

COOKING TIME 40 MINUTES

....

INGREDIENTS

2 tbsp olive oil
2 shallots, finely chopped
1 red chilli, finely chopped
2 cloves of garlic, crushed
½ tsp Cayenne pepper
450 g / 1 lb / 2 cups minced beef
400 g / 14 oz / 2 cups canned
tomatoes, chopped
200 ml / 7 fl. oz / 1 cup beef stock
400 g / 14 oz / 2 cups canned kidney
beans, drained
a few sprigs coriander (cilantro)
(cilantro)and boiled rice to serve

- Heat the oil in a large saucepan and fry the shallot and chilli for 3 minutes, stirring occasionally.
- Add the garlic and Cayenne and cook for 2 minutes, then add the mince.
- Fry the mince until it starts to brown then add the chopped tomatoes, stock and kidney beans and bring to a gentle simmer.
- Cook the chilli con carne for 30 minutes, stirring occasionally, until the mince is tender and the sauce has thickened a little.
- Taste for seasoning and add salt and freshly ground black pepper as necessary.
- Serve with boiled rice and garnish with coriander (cilantro).

Chilli No Carne

821

- For a vegetarian version of this dish, replace the minced beef with Quorn mince.

822

SERVES 4

Kidney Bean Pate

PREPARATION TIME 15 MINUTES

COOKING TIME 5 MINUTES

....

INGREDIENTS

2 tbsp olive oil
1 red onion, finely chopped
2 cloves of garlic, crushed
½ tsp ground cumin
½ tsp ground coriander (cilantro)
400 g / 14 oz / 2 cups canned kidney
beans, drained
2 tbsp soured cream
1 spring onion, chopped
tortilla chips to serve

- Heat the oil in a frying pan and fry the onion and garlic for 5 minutes, stirring occasionally.
- Scrape it into a food processor and add the spices, kidney beans and soured cream then season with salt and pepper.
- Pulse the machine until the ingredients are finely chopped and well mixed, then spoon the pate into a serving bowl and sprinkle with spring onion.
- Serve with tortilla chips for dipping.

Spicy Kidney Bean Pate

823

- Add 1 finely chopped green chilli and ½ tsp of Cayenne pepper to the mixture before processing.

824
SERVES 2

Cod with Beetroot and Baby Chard

- Steam the cod for 8 minutes or until just cooked in the centre.
- Meanwhile, put half the beetroot in a liquidiser with the oil and a pinch of salt and pepper and blend to a smooth sauce.
- Arrange the rest of the beetroot with the baby chard on 2 plates and put the cod in the middle.
- Top with beetroot shoots and drizzle some of the sauce over the plate.

PREPARATION TIME 5 MINUTES

COOKING TIME 8 MINUTES

INGREDIENTS

2 large cod steaks
100 g / 3 ½ oz / ½ cup cooked beetroot, sliced
2 tbsp olive oil
50 g / 1 ¾ oz / 2 cups baby chard leaves
beetroot shoots to garnish

Steamed Cod with Roast Beetroot
825

- Alternatively, wrap whole raw beetroot tightly in foil and roast for 45 minutes at 190°C.

826
SERVES 4

Fish Fingers

- Cut the fish into 16 evenly sized fingers.
- Put the flour, egg and panko breadcrumbs in 3 separate bowls.
- Dip the fish fingers first in the flour, then in the egg, then in the breadcrumbs.
- Heat the oil in a deep fat fryer, according to the manufacturer's instructions, to a temperature of 180°C.
- Lower the fish fingers in the fryer basket and cook for 4 – 5 minutes or until crisp and golden brown. You may need to cook them in 2 batches to avoid overcrowding the fryer, in which case keep the first batch warm in a low oven.
- Line a large bowl with a thick layer of kitchen paper and when they are ready, tip them into the bowl to remove any excess oil.
- Sprinkle with sea salt to taste and serve immediately.

PREPARATION TIME 15 MINUTES

COOKING TIME 4-5 MINUTES

INGREDIENTS

800 g / 1 lb 12 oz / 4 cups line-caught pollock fillet
4 tbsp plain (all purpose) flour
1 egg, beaten
75 g / 2 ½ oz / ½ cup panko breadcrumbs
2 - 3 litres / 3 ½ pints – 5 pints / 8-12 cups sunflower oil

Tofu Fingers
827

- Replace the pollock with an equal quantity of firm tofu.

828

SERVES 4

Stir-Fried Tofu with Vegetables

Tofu in Black Bean Sauce

829

- Replace the cornflour, sherry and sugar with ½ jar of black bean sauce.

Tofu in Oyster Sauce

830

- Replace the cornflour, sherry and sugar with 4 tbsp of oyster sauce.

PREPARATION TIME 5 MINUTES

COOKING TIME 8 MINUTES

....

INGREDIENTS

2 tbsp vegetable oil
2 cloves garlic, finely chopped
1 tbsp root ginger, finely chopped
200 g / 7 oz / 1 ¼ cups firm tofu, cubed
75 g / 2 ½ oz / ¾ cup baby sweetcorn, halved lengthways
75 g / 2 ½ oz / ¾ cup mange tout
½ tsp cornflour
2 tbsp rice wine or dry sherry
1 tsp caster (superfine) sugar
1 tbsp light soy sauce
75 g / 2 ½ oz / 1 ½ cups alfalfa sprouts
boiled rice to serve

- Heat the oil in a large wok and fry the garlic and ginger for 30 seconds.
- Add the tofu and stir-fry for 2 minutes then add the baby corn and mange tout and stir-fry for another 2 minutes.
- Mix the cornflour with the rice wine, sugar and soy and add it to the wok.
- Stir-fry for 2 more minutes then serve immediately, garnished with the alfalfa sprouts on a bed of rice.

831

SERVES 4

Macaroni Cheese with Bacon

- Preheat the oven to 180°C (160° fan), gas 4.
- Cook the macaroni in boiling, salted water according to the packet instructions or until al dente. Drain well.
- Meanwhile, melt the butter in a medium saucepan then fry the bacon and courgettes for 2 minutes.
- Remove the bacon and courgettes from the pan with a slotted spoon, then the flour into the pan.
- Gradually whisk in the milk a little at a time until it is all incorporated. Cook the sauce over a low heat, stirring constantly, until the mixture thickens.
- Take the pan off the heat and stir in the bacon and courgettes and half the cheese. Season to taste.
- Stir the macaroni into the cheese sauce and scrape it into a baking dish.
- Sprinkle over the remaining cheese then bake for 25 minutes or until the cheese is bubbling.

PREPARATION TIME 5 MINUTES

COOKING TIME 40 MINUTES

INGREDIENTS

400 g / 14 oz / 4 cups dried macaroni
25 g / 1 oz butter
4 rashers streaky bacon, chopped
2 courgettes, sliced
25 g / 1 oz / ¼ cup plain (all purpose) flour
600 ml / 1 pint / 2 ½ cups milk
150 g / 5 ½ oz / 1 ½ cups Cheddar cheese, grated

Chorizo Macaroni Cheese · 832

- Omit the courgettes and replace the bacon with small cubes of chorizo.

833

SERVES 4

Tuna and Courgette Tortilla

- Heat half the oil in a non-stick frying pan and fry the courgettes for 5 minutes.
- Meanwhile, gently beat the eggs in a jug to break up the yolks. When the courgettes are ready, stir them into the eggs with the tuna and season with salt and pepper.
- Heat the rest of the oil in the frying pan then pour in the egg mixture.
- Cook over a gentle heat for 6 – 8 minutes or until the egg has set round the outside, but the centre is still a bit runny.
- Turn it out onto a plate, then slide it back into the pan and cook the other side for 4 – 6 minutes.
- Leave to cool for 5 minutes then cut into wedges and serve, garnished with oregano.

PREPARATION TIME 10 MINUTES

COOKING TIME 20 MINUTES

INGREDIENTS

4 tbsp olive oil
1 courgette, quartered and sliced
6 free-range eggs
200 g / 7 oz / 1 cup canned tuna, drained and flaked
oregano to garnish

Courgette and Dill Tortilla · 834

- Omit the tuna and stir 2 tbsp of chopped dill into the egg mixture.

835

SERVES 2

Chicken Enchiladas

PREPARATION TIME 10 MINUTES

COOKING TIME 20 MINUTES

INGREDIENTS

2 tbsp vegetable oil
2 chicken breasts, diced
200 g / 7 oz / 2 cups button
mushrooms, quartered
2 tbsp soured cream
150 g / 5 ½ oz / 1 ½ cups mild cheese,
grated
4 corn tortillas
50 g / 1 ¾ oz / ⅓ cup Jalapenos, sliced

- Preheat the oven to 200°C (180° fan), 390 F, gas 6.
- Heat the oil in a frying pan and fry the chicken and mushrooms for 5 minutes or until cooked through.
- Stir in the soured cream and half of the cheese, then divide the mixture between the 4 tortillas.
- Fold them round and arrange in a snugly fitting baking dish.
- Sprinkle over the rest of the cheese and arrange the jalapenos in a line on top then bake for 10 – 15 minutes or until the cheese has melted and the edges are toasted.

Chilli Enchiladas

836

- Replace the chicken filling with chilli con carne.

837

SERVES 4

Sticky Sesame Chicken

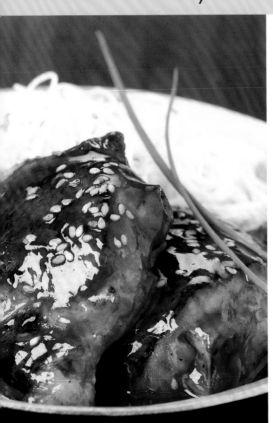

PREPARATION TIME 5 MINUTES

COOKING TIME 35-40 MINUTES

INGREDIENTS

8 chicken thighs
2 tbsp runny honey
2 tbsp soy sauce
½ orange, juiced
2 tbsp oyster sauce
½ tsp Chinese five spice powder
2 tsp sesame oil
2 tbsp sesame seeds
rice noodles and chives to serve

- Preheat the oven to 200°C (180° fan), 390 F, gas 6.
- Arrange the chicken thighs in a single layer in a snugly-fitting baking dish.
- Mix the honey, soy, orange juice, oyster sauce, five spice and sesame oil together and pour it over the chicken.
- Sprinkle with sesame seeds and bake for 35 – 40 minutes or until the chicken is cooked through.
- If it starts to colour too quickly, cover the dish with foil.
- Serve the chicken with rice noodles, garnished with chives.

Sticky Sesame Pork

838

- Replace the chicken thighs with pork spare rib chops.

839

SERVES 1

White Asparagus Omelette

Preserved Artichoke Omelette

840

- Replace the asparagus with a jar of preserved baby artichokes.

Antipasti Omelette

841

- Replace the asparagus with a jar of mixed antipasti in oil.

PREPARATION TIME 2 MINUTES

COOKING TIME 4 MINUTES

INGREDIENTS

3 large eggs
10 g butter
1 tbsp flat leaf parsley, finely chopped
75 g / 2 ½ oz / ¾ cup canned white asparagus, drained

- Break the eggs into a jug with a pinch of salt and pepper and beat them gently to break up the yolks.
- Heat the butter in a non-stick frying pan until sizzling then pour in the eggs.
- Cook over a medium heat until the eggs start to set around the outside. Use a spatula to draw the sides of the omelette into the centre and tilt the pan to fill the gaps with more liquid egg.
- Sprinkle with parsley and arrange the asparagus on top then continue cooking until the top of the omelette is just set.
- Shake the omelette out onto a plate, folding it over as you go.

842

SERVES 2

Penne with Spicy Tomato Sauce

PREPARATION TIME 2 MINUTES

COOKING TIME 25 MINUTES

INGREDIENTS

4 tbsp olive oil
2 cloves of garlic, crushed
2 red chillies, finely chopped
1 tsp smoked paprika
100 g / 3 ½ oz / ½ cup canned tomatoes, chopped
200 g / 7 oz / 2 cups penne

- Heat the oil in a frying pan and fry the garlic and chillies for 2 minutes.
- Stir in the smoked paprika then add the canned tomatoes and simmer for 20 minutes.
- Meanwhile, cook the penne in boiling salted water according to the packet instructions or until al dente.
- Taste the sauce for seasoning, adding plenty of freshly ground black pepper.
- Drain the pasta and stir it into the sauce then divide between 2 warm bowls and serve immediately.

Penne with Spicy Tomato and Tuna Sauce

843

- Add a can of tuna to the sauce 2 minutes before the end of cooking time.

844

SERVES 4

Rigatoni with Meatballs

PREPARATION TIME 10 MINUTES

COOKING TIME 15 MINUTES

INGREDIENTS

6 good quality sausages, skinned
400 g / 14 oz / 4 cups rigatoni pasta
4 tbsp olive oil
2 cloves garlic, crushed
300 ml / 10 ½ fl. oz / 1 ½ cups tomato passata
50 g / 1 ¾ oz / ½ cup Parmesan, finely grated
Greek basil leaves to garnish

- Roll the sausagemeat into small meatballs.
- Cook the rigatoni in boiling salted water according to the packet instructions or until al dente.
- Meanwhile, heat the oil in a frying pan and fry the meatballs for 6 minutes or until golden on all sides.
- Add the garlic to the pan and cook for 1 minute, then pour in the passata and a sprinkle of salt and pepper and simmer for 5 minutes.
- Drain the pasta and stir it into the frying pan. Let it absorb some of the sauce for a minute then spoon it onto 4 warm plates.
- Sprinkle liberally with Parmesan and garnish with basil leaves.

Rigatoni with Mozzarella Meatballs

845

- Cut 150 g of mozzarella into small cubes and press into the centre of each meatball, making sure it is fully encased with the sausagemeat.

846

SERVES 2

Ravioli with Garlic and Parsley Cream

- Cook the ravioli in boiling salted water according to the packet instructions or until al dente.
- Meanwhile, heat the butter in a small saucepan and fry the garlic for 2 minutes without colouring.
- Stir in the parsley then pour in the cream and bring to a simmer. Season to taste with salt and pepper.
- Drain the ravioli and split between 2 warm bowls then spoon over the garlic and parsley cream and garnish with extra parsley.

PREPARATION TIME 2 MINUTES

COOKING TIME 10 MINUTES

INGREDIENTS

250 g / 9 oz fresh ravioli
1 tbsp butter
2 cloves of garlic, crushed
2 tbsp flat leaf parsley, chopped
175 ml / 6 fl. oz / ⅔ cup double cream
parsley sprigs to garnish

Ravioli with Garlic and Dill Cream   847

- Replace the parsley with fresh dill.

848

SERVES 2

Penne with Pesto and Clams

- Cook the penne in boiling salted water according to the packet instructions or until only just al dente.
- While the pasta is cooking, bring the wine to the boil in a saucepan then add the clams, put on the lid and steam for 5 minutes or until they have all opened.
- Drain the pasta, tip it into the clam pan and stir in the pesto.
- Divide the pasta between 2 warm bowls and use a vegetable peeler to shave over some Parmesan.
- Garnish with oregano sprigs.

PREPARATION TIME 5 MINUTES

COOKING TIME 14 MINUTES

INGREDIENTS

200 g / 7 oz penne
50 ml / 1 ¾ fl. oz / ¼ cup dry white wine
250 g / 9 oz / 1 ½ cuplive clams, scrubbed
4 tbsp pesto
30 g / 1 oz / ¼ cup Parmesan
oregano to garnish

Penne with Sundried Tomatoes and Clams   849

- Replace the parsley with fresh dill.

850

SERVES 6-8

Leek, Tomato and Cheese Quiche

Quiche Lorraine

851

- Replace the tomatoes with smoked bacon lardons.

Tomato and Chorizo Quiche

852

- Replace the leeks with a chopped onion and add 150 g of cubed chorizo when you add the tomatoes.

PREPARATION TIME 5 MINUTES

COOKING TIME 40 MINUTES

INGREDIENTS

2 leeks, sliced
2 tbsp butter
3 large eggs, beaten
225 ml / 8 fl. oz / 1 cup double cream
100 g / 3 ½ oz / ¾ cup cherry tomatoes, quartered
150 g / 5 ½ oz / 1 ½ cups Gruyere, grated
1 readymade pastry case

- Preheat the oven to 150°C (130° fan), 300 F, gas 2
- Fry the leeks in the butter with a pinch of salt for 5 minutes or until starting to soften.
- Whisk the eggs with the double cream until smoothly combined then stir in the leeks, tomatoes and half of the Gruyere. Season generously with salt and pepper.
- Pour the filling into the pastry case and scatter the rest of the cheese on top.
- Bake for 35 minutes or until just set in the centre.

853

Smoked Chicken Risotto

SERVES 2

- Heat the stock in a saucepan.
- Heat the olive oil in a sauté pan and gently fry the onion for 5 minutes without colouring.
- Add the garlic and cook for 2 more minutes then stir in the rice.
- When it is well coated with the oil, add 2 ladles of the hot stock.
- Cook, stirring occasionally, until most of the stock has been absorbed before adding the next 2 ladles.
- Continue in this way for around 15 minutes or until the rice is just tender.
- Stir in the Parmesan and season with salt and pepper. Cover the pan and take off the heat to rest for 4 minutes.
- Spoon the risotto into warm bowls and lay the smoked chicken slices on top.

PREPARATION TIME 5 MINUTES

COOKING TIME 25 MINUTES

INGREDIENTS

1 litre / 1 pint 15 fl. oz / 4 cups good quality chicken stock
2 tbsp olive oil
1 onion, finely chopped
2 cloves of garlic, crushed
150 g / 5 ½ oz / ¾ cup risotto rice
50 g / 1 ¾ oz / ½ cup Parmesan, finely grated
1 smoked chicken breast, sliced

Smoked Chicken and Broad Bean Risotto

854

- Add 200 g of fresh baby broad beans to the risotto, 8 minutes before the end of cooking time.

855

Curried Leek and Potato Quiche

SERVES 6-8

- Preheat the oven to 150°C (130° fan), 300 F, gas 2
- Fry the leeks in the butter with a pinch of salt for 5 minutes or until starting to soften then stir in the curry powder and potatoes. Warm through for 2 minutes.
- Whisk the eggs with the double cream until smoothly combined then stir in the leeks, potatoes and half of the Emmental. Season generously with salt and pepper.
- Pour the filling into the pastry case and scatter the rest of the cheese on top.
- Bake for 35 minutes or until just set in the centre.

PREPARATION TIME 5 MINUTES

COOKING TIME 40 MINUTES

INGREDIENTS

2 leeks, sliced
2 tbsp butter
2 tsp mild curry powder
4 boiled potatoes, cooled and cubed
3 large eggs, beaten
225 ml / 8 fl. oz / 1 cup double cream
150 g / 5 ½ oz / 1 ½ cups Emmental, grated
1 readymade pastry case

Curried Leek and Chicken Quiche

856

- Replace the boiled potatoes with 150 g of cooked, cubed chicken breast.

857

SERVES 4

Leek and Mince Hot Pot

PREPARATION TIME 5 MINUTES

COOKING TIME 40 MINUTES

....

INGREDIENTS

400 g / 14 oz / 2 ¼ cups maris piper
potatoes, peeled and sliced
4 tbsp butter
2 leeks, sliced
200 g / 7 oz / 1 cup minced lamb
200 ml / 7 fl. oz / 1 cup white wine
1 tbsp flat leaf parsley, finely
chopped
75 g / 2 ½ oz / ½ cup Red Leicester,
grated

- Preheat the oven to 220°C (200° fan), 430 F, gas 7 and put a baking dish in to heat
- Cook the potatoes in boiling salted water for 10 minutes or until tender. Drain well.
- Meanwhile, heat the oil in a frying pan and cook the leeks with a pinch of salt for 5 minutes.
- Add the mince and stir-fry for 3 minutes then stir in the wine and bring to a simmer.
- Spoon the mince into the preheated baking dish and arrange the potatoes on top.
- Sprinkle over the parsley, followed by the cheese, then bake for 30 minutes or until the potatoes are golden.

Mince and Pea Hot Pot   858

- Replace the leeks with 200 g of defrosted frozen peas.

859

SERVES 8

Savoury Leek and Stilton Crumble

PREPARATION TIME 5 MINUTES

COOKING TIME 45 MINUTES

....

INGREDIENTS

2 tbsp butter
3 leeks, chopped
4 boiled potatoes, cooled and cubed
150 g / 5 ½ oz / 1 cup Stilton, cubed

FOR THE CRUMBLE MIXTURE
75 g / 2 ½ oz / ⅓ cup butter
50 g / 1 ¾ oz / ⅓ cup plain (all
purpose) flour
25 g / 1 oz / ¼ cup ground almonds

- Preheat the oven to 180°C (160° fan), 355 F, gas 4.
- Heat the butter in a sauté pan and fry the leeks with plenty of salt and pepper for 5 minutes or until starting to soften.
- Mix in the potatoes and Stilton then spoon the mixture into a baking dish.
- While the leeks are cooking, rub the butter into the flour and stir in the ground almonds, then season with salt and pepper.
- Take a handful of the topping and squeeze it into a clump, then crumble it over the leeks.
- Repeat with the rest of the crumble mixture then press down with your fingertips into an even layer. Bake the crumble for 35 minutes or until the topping is golden brown.

Parsnip and Stilton Crumble   860

- Replace the boiled potatoes with boiled parsnips.

861

SERVES 4

Thai Red Chicken Curry

Thai Red Aubergine Curry

862

- Replace the chicken with a cubed aubergine (eggplant).

Thai Red Salmon Curry

863

- Replace the chicken with an equal weight of cubed salmon fillet, but add it right at the end and heat through for 2 minutes or until just opaque inside.

PREPARATION TIME 2 MINUTES

COOKING TIME 10 MINUTES

INGREDIENTS

2 tbsp vegetable oil
2 tbsp Thai red curry paste
2 fresh or frozen kaffir lime leaves
2 skinless chicken breasts, cut into chunks
400 ml / 14 fl. oz / 2 cups coconut milk
1 tsp caster (superfine) sugar
1 tbsp fish sauce
2 tbsp coriander (cilantro) (cilantro) leaves, chopped

- Heat the oil in a wok and fry the curry paste and lime leaves for 2 minutes.
- Add the chicken to the wok and stir-fry for 4 minutes then add the coconut milk and bring to a simmer.
- Season to taste with the caster (superfine) sugar and fish sauce before serving in warm bowls, garnished with coriander (cilantro).
- Serve with jasmine rice.

864

SERVES 4

Smoked Haddock and Leek Pie

PREPARATION TIME 10 MINUTES

COOKING TIME 35 MINUTES

....

INGREDIENTS

450 g / 1 lb / 2 ½ cups maris piper
potatoes, peeled and cubed
600 ml / 1 pint / 2 ½ cups whole milk
450 g / 1 lb / 2 ¼ cups smoked
haddock
3 tbsp butter
1 leek, chopped
1 tbsp plain (all purpose) flour
1 tsp Dijon mustard
75 g / 2 ½ oz / ¾ cup Emmental,
grated

- Cook the potatoes in boiling salted water for 15 minutes or until tender. Drain well.
- Meanwhile, bring the milk to a simmer then pour it over the smoked haddock. Cover the dish with clingfilm and leave to steep for 10 minutes.
- Drain off and reserve the milk and flake the haddock, discarding any skin and bones.
- When the potatoes are ready, mash them until smooth with 1 tablespoon of the butter and a little of the haddock milk.
- Heat the rest of the butter in a saucepan and fry the leeks for 5 minutes.
- Stir in the flour then gradually incorporate the rest of the haddock milk, stirring continuously to avoid any lumps forming.
- Continue to stir until it starts to bubble then stir in the mustard and flaked haddock.
- Preheat the grill to its highest setting.
- Pour the haddock mixture into a baking dish and top with the mashed potato.
- Sprinkle over the Emmental and grill for 5 minutes or until the top is golden and bubbling.

865

SERVES 4

Tartiflette

PREPARATION TIME 5 MINUTES

COOKING TIME 40 MINUTES

....

INGREDIENTS

800 g / 1 lb 12 oz / 4 ½ cups maris
piper potatoes, peeled and cubed
2 tbsp olive oil
1 onion, thinly sliced
150 g / 5 ½ oz / 1 cup smoked lardons
4 tbsp crème fraîche
200 g / 7 oz / 2 cups Reblochon,
sliced

- Boil the potatoes in salted water for 12 minutes or until tender then drain well.
- Meanwhile, heat the oil in a sauté pan and fry the onion and lardons for 5 minutes.
- Stir in the crème fraîche and drained potatoes, then spoon the mixture into a baking dish.
- Lay the cheese on top and bake for 25 minutes or until golden brown.

Penne with Smoked Trout

866

SERVES 4

- Preheat the oven to 220°C (200° fan), 430 F, gas 7.
- Cook the penne in boiling salted water according to the packet instructions or until al dente. Drain well.
- Mix the crème fraîche with the trout and watercress then stir in the pasta and season with salt and pepper.
- Spoon it into a baking dish and sprinkle with Emmental then bake for 15 minutes or until the top is golden.

PREPARATION TIME 5 MINUTES

COOKING TIME 30 MINUTES

INGREDIENTS

400 g / 14 oz / 4 cups penne
300 ml / 10 ½ oz / 1 ¼ cups crème fraîche
150 g / 5 ½ oz / 1 cup smoked trout, chopped
50 g / 1 ¾ oz / 2 cups watercress
50 g / 1 ¾ oz / ½ cup Emmental, grated

Cheese and Leek Crustless Quiche

867

SERVES 4

PREPARATION TIME 5 MINUTES

COOKING TIME 30-35 MINUTES

INGREDIENTS

3 leeks, chopped
2 tbsp butter
5 free-range eggs
2 tbsp crème fraîche
75 g / 2 ½ oz / ¾ cup Gruyere, grated

- Preheat the oven to 180°C (160° fan), 355 F, gas 4.
- Fry the leeks in the butter with plenty of salt and pepper for 10 minutes or until softened.
- Lightly beat the eggs with the crème fraîche then stir in the leeks.
- Pour the mixture into a baking dish and sprinkle over the cheese then bake in the oven for 20 – 25 minutes or until just set in the centre.
- Serve warm or at room temperature.

Red Pepper and Asparagus Paella

868

SERVES 4

PREPARATION TIME 5 MINUTES

COOKING TIME 30 MINUTES

INGREDIENTS

1 litre / 1 pint 15 fl. oz / 4 cups good quality vegetable stock
4 tbsp olive oil
1 onion, finely chopped
2 cloves of garlic, crushed
100 g / 3 ½ oz / 1 cup asparagus spears, cut into short lengths
1 courgette, sliced
200 g / 7 oz / 1 cup paella rice
1 red pepper, sliced
2 tbsp flat leaf parsley, chopped

- Heat the stock in a saucepan.
- Heat the olive oil in a paella pan and gently fry the onion for 5 minutes without colouring.
- Add the garlic and cook for 2 more minutes then stir in the vegetables and rice and season with salt and pepper.
- Stir well to coat with the oil, then pour in the stock and stir once more.
- Arrange the pepper slices on top and bring to a simmer, then cook without stirring for 10 minutes.
- Cover the pan with foil or a lid, turn off the heat and leave to stand for 10 minutes.
- Uncover the pan and sprinkle over the parsley before serving.

DESSERTS

869 · SERVES 4

Pear Kebabs with Toffee Sauce

PREPARATION TIME 20 MINUTES

COOKING TIME 6 MINUTES

INGREDIENTS

4 pears, cored and cubed
2 tbsp butter, melted

FOR THE TOFFEE SAUCE
100 g / 3 ½ oz / ½ cup butter
100 g / 3 ½ oz / ½ cup muscovado sugar
100 g / 3 ½ oz / ½ cup golden syrup
100 ml / 3 ½ fl. oz / ½ cup double cream

- Soak 12 wooden skewers in cold water for 20 minutes then preheat the grill to its highest setting.
- Thread the pears onto the skewers and brush with melted butter.
- Grill the kebabs for 3 minutes on each side or until the pears are golden brown.
- Meanwhile, put the toffee sauce ingredients in a small saucepan and stir over a low heat until the butter melts and the sugar dissolves.
- Bring the toffee sauce to the boil then take it off the heat.
- Divide the kebabs between 4 warm plates and drizzle with toffee sauce.

Toffee Apple Kebabs 870

- Replace the pears with apples.

871 · SERVES 4

Strawberry and Kumquat Salad

PREPARATION TIME 5 MINUTES

INGREDIENTS

200 g / 7 oz / 1 cup strawberries, halved
100 g / 3 ½ oz / ¾ cup kumquats, sliced
1 tsp coriander (cilantro) (cilantro) seeds, crushed
1 tsp runny honey
1 tbsp lemon juice
2 tbsp extra virgin olive oil
4 sprigs mint

- Mix the strawberries with the kumquats and divide between 4 bowls.
- Put the coriander (cilantro) (cilantro)seeds, honey, lemon juice and oil in a jar and shake together to emulsify.
- Pour the dressing over the salad and garnish with a sprig of mint.

Plum and Kumquat Salad 872

- Replace the strawberries with 6 plums that have been stoned and cut into eighths.

873

SERVES 4 Spiced Pear and Pineapple Kebabs

- Soak 8 wooden skewers in cold water for 20 minutes.
- Meanwhile, put the honey in a small saucepan with the spices and heat gently. Leave to infuse for 15 minutes.
- Preheat the grill to its highest setting.
- Thread alternate chunks of pear and pineapple onto the skewers and brush with the spiced honey.
- Grill the kebabs for 3 minutes on each side or until the edges of the fruit start to caramelise.
- Transfer the kebabs to 4 warm plates and garnish with star anise and mint sprigs.

PREPARATION TIME 20 MINUTES

COOKING TIME 6 MINUTES

INGREDIENTS

4 tbsp runny honey
1 star anise, plus extra to garnish
4 cloves
2 pears, quartered, cored and sliced
½ pineapple, peeled, cored and cut into large chunks
a few sprigs of mint

Spiced Pineapple and Mango Kebabs

874

- Replace the pear with chunks of fresh mango.

875

SERVES 4 Mango, Banana and Lime Crumble

- Preheat the oven to 180°C (160° fan), 355 F, gas 4.
- Mix the fruit with the lime juice and zest and tip it into a baking dish.
- Rub the butter into the flour and stir in the ground almonds and brown sugar.
- Take a handful of the topping and squeeze it into a clump, then crumble it over the fruit.
- Repeat with the rest of the crumble mixture then bake for 40 minutes or until the topping is golden brown.

PREPARATION TIME 5 MINUTES

COOKING TIME 40 MINUTES

INGREDIENTS

1 mango, peeled, stoned and cubed
2 bananas, peeled and cut into chunks
1 lime, juiced and zest finely grated
75 g / 2 ½ oz / ⅓ cup butter
50 g / 1 ¾ oz / ⅓ cup plain (all purpose) flour
25 g / 1 oz / ¼ cup ground almonds
40 g / 1 ½ oz / ¼ cup light brown sugar

Tropical Coconut Crumble

876

- Replace the ground almonds in the crumble topping with desiccated coconut.

877

SERVES 4

Peaches with Mascarpone and Honey

PREPARATION TIME 5 MINUTES

COOKING TIME 10 MINUTES

INGREDIENTS

6 peaches, halved and stoned
250 g / 9 oz / 1 cup mascarpone
50 g / 1 ¾ oz / ½ cup flaked (slivered)
almonds
4 tbsp runny honey

- Preheat the oven to 180°C (160° fan), 355 F, gas 4.
- Arrange the peaches in a large baking dish and top each one with a spoonful of mascarpone.
- Sprinkle the peaches with flaked (slivered) almonds and drizzle with honey then grind over a little black pepper.
- Bake the peaches for 10 minutes or until the flesh is soft and the almonds are toasted.

Baked Apricots with Pistachios

878

- Replace the peaches with apricots and substitute the almonds with pistachio nuts.

879

SERVES 4

Marinated Strawberries and Kumquats

PREPARATION TIME 35 MINUTES

COOKING TIME 5 MINUTES

INGREDIENTS

200 g / 7 oz / 1 cup strawberries,
halved
100 g / 3 ½ oz / ¾ cup kumquats,
sliced
3 tbsp runny honey
1 tbsp Cointreau
4 dried lemon verbena leaves
1 tbsp granulated sugar

- Mix the strawberries with the kumquats in a shallow bowl.
- Put the honey, Cointreau and lemon verbena in a small saucepan with 3 tablespoons of water and bring to a simmer.
- Pour the marinade over the fruit and leave to macerate for 35 minutes.
- Sprinkle with granulated sugar just before serving.

Marinated Pineapple and Kumquats

880

- Replace the strawberries with half a fresh pineapple, cut into cubes.

SERVES 4

Raspberry Eton Mess

Classic Eton Mess 882

- Replace the raspberries with sliced strawberries, but use a food processor rather than a sieve to make the sauce.

Raspberry Fool 883

- Omit the meringue and replace half of the whipped cream with readymade chilled custard.

PREPARATION TIME 5 MINUTES

COOKING TIME 35-40 MINUTES

....

INGREDIENTS

300 g / 10 ½ oz / 2 ¼ cups raspberries
600 ml / 1 pint / 2 ½ cups double cream
4 meringue nests, crushed

- Press half the raspberries through a sieve to make a smooth sauce and discard the pips.
- Whip the cream until it forms soft peaks then fold in the meringue pieces and all but 4 of the whole raspberries.
- Swirl through the raspberry sauce and divide it between 4 sundae glasses then top each one with a raspberry.

884

SERVES 2

Baked, Spiced Bananas

PREPARATION TIME 5 MINUTES

COOKING TIME 15 MINUTES

INGREDIENTS

3 bananas, peeled
150 ml / 5 ½ fl. oz / ⅔ cup coconut milk
½ tsp ground cinnamon
½ tsp ground ginger
2 tbsp muscovado sugar
2 tbsp flaked (slivered) almonds

- Preheat the oven to 180°C (160° fan), 355 F, gas 4.
- Arrange the bananas in a small baking dish and pour over the coconut milk.
- Mix the spices with the brown sugar and sprinkle over the top then scatter over the flaked (slivered) almonds.
- Bake in the oven for 15 minutes or until the bananas are soft and the liquid has thickened.

Baked, Spiced Mango

885

- Replace the bananas with very ripe mango halves that have been peeled and stoned.

886

SERVES 4

Summer Fruit Crêpes

PREPARATION TIME 5 MINUTES

COOKING TIME 20 MINUTES

INGREDIENTS

150 g / 5 ½ oz / 1 cup plain (all purpose) flour
1 large egg
325 ml / 11 ½ fl. oz / 1 ½ cups whole milk
30 g / 1 oz butter, melted

FOR THE FILLING

3 tbsp redcurrant jelly (jello)
200 g / 7 oz / 1 cup mixed summer berries

- To make the filling, melt the redcurrant jelly in a small saucepan and stir in the fruit. Leave to macerate.
- Sieve the flour into a bowl and make a well in the centre. Break in the egg and pour in the milk then use a whisk to gradually incorporate all of the flour from round the outside.
- Melt the butter in a small frying pan then whisk it into the batter.
- Put the buttered frying pan back over a low heat. Add a small ladle of batter and swirl the pan to coat the bottom.
- When it starts to dry and curl up at the edges, turn the pancake over with a spatula and cook the other side until golden brown and cooked through.
- Repeat with the rest of the mixture then serve each crepe rolled up with a big spoonful of summer fruits inside.

Winter Fruit Crepes

887

- Use a mixture of dried figs, dried pears and prunes and leave them to macerate in 300 ml of hot earl grey tea for 30 minutes.

SERVES 4

Chocolate Dip with Soldiers

- Chop the chocolate and put it in a bowl.
- Bring the cream to simmering point then pour it over the chocolate and stir until smooth.
- Put the kumquats and hazelnuts in a food processor and pulse until finely chopped.
- Spread the pain d'epices with honey and dip it in the kumquat mixture then cut it into soldiers.
- Put the bowl of chocolate dip on the table and serve the soldiers alongside.

PREPARATION TIME 10 MINUTES

COOKING TIME 4 MINUTES

INGREDIENTS

100 g / 3 ½ oz / ¾ cup milk chocolate
150 ml / 3 ½ fl. oz / ⅔ cup double cream

FOR THE SOLDIERS

50 g / 1 ¾ oz / ⅓ cup candied kumquats
50 g / 1 ¾ oz / ½ cup hazelnuts (cob nuts)
4 slices pain d'epices (spiced bread)
2 tbsp runny honey

White Chocolate Dip with Soldiers

889

- Replace the milk chocolate with white chocolate.

890

SERVES 4

Chocolate Fondue

- Chop the chocolate and put it in a fondue bowl.
- Bring the cream and brandy to simmering point then pour it over the chocolate and stir until smooth.
- Serve with the clementine segments and strawberries for dipping.

PREPARATION TIME 2 MINUTES

COOKING TIME 4 MINUTES

INGREDIENTS

100 g / 3 ½ oz / ¾ cup milk chocolate
150 ml / 3 ½ fl. oz / ⅔ cup double cream
2 tbsp brandy
3 clementines, peeled
200 g / 7 oz / 1 cup strawberries, hulled and halved

Black Forest Fondue

 891

- Replace the brandy with kirsch and stir 3 tbsp of sieved cherry jam into the fondue at the end. Serve with chocolate brownie bites and fresh cherries for dipping.

892

SERVES 4

Natillas

Banana Custard

893

- Add a sliced banana to the bottom of each bowl and replace the cinnamon with a sprinkle of desiccated coconut.

Blancmange Bowls

894

- Increase the quantity of cornflour to 4 tsp and chill the bowls in the fridge after filling.

PREPARATION TIME 10 MINUTES

COOKING TIME 15 MINUTES

INGREDIENTS

450 ml / 12 ½ fl. oz / 1 ¾ cup whole milk
4 large egg yolks
75 g / 2 ½ oz / ⅓ cup caster (superfine) sugar
2 tsp cornflour
1 tsp ground cinnamon

- Pour the milk into a saucepan and bring to simmering point.
- Meanwhile, whisk the egg yolks with the sugar and cornflour until thick.
- Gradually incorporate the hot milk, whisking all the time, then scrape the mixture back into the saucepan.
- Stir the custard over a low heat until it thickens then divide it between 4 bowls.
- Sprinkle the tops with cinnamon and leave for 10 minutes or a skin to form.

895
SERVES 4
Griddled Pineapple with Vanilla and Honey

- Put the honey in a small saucepan with the vanilla and infuse over a low heat for 5 minutes.
- Pour the honey over the pineapple slices and leave to marinate for 20 minutes.
- Heat a griddle pan until smoking hot.
- Griddle the pineapple slices for 2 minutes on each side or until nicely marked, then divide between 4 warm plates and serve.

PREPARATION TIME 25 MINUTES

COOKING TIME 5-8 MINUTES

INGREDIENTS

100 g / 3 ½ oz / ½ cup runny honey
1 vanilla pod, halved lengthways
1 pineapple, peeled, cored and sliced

Griddled Pineapple with Chilli and Honey
896

- Replace the vanilla pod with ½ tsp of dried chilli flakes.

897
SERVES 4
Brioche and Apricot Pudding

- Preheat the oven to 180°C (160° fan), 355 F, gas 4.
- Spread the brioche with butter and arrange the slices in a baking dish with the apricot pieces scattered throughout.
- Whisk the milk, cream, eggs and sugar together and pour it over the top, then press down on the brioche to help it soak up the liquid.
- Bake for 35 – 40 minutes or until the top is golden brown.

PREPARATION TIME 5 MINUTES

COOKING TIME 35-40 MINUTES

INGREDIENTS

1 brioche loaf, sliced
3 tbsp butter, softened
75 g / 2 ½ oz / ⅓ cup dried apricots, chopped
250 ml / 9 fl. oz / 1 cup whole milk
200 ml / 7 oz / ¾ cup double cream
4 large egg yolks
75 g / 2 ½ oz / ⅓ cup caster (superfine) sugar

Apricot Croissant and Butter Pudding
898

- Replace the brioche with 4 croissants that have been halved horizontally and omit the butter.

899

SERVES 6

Marmalade Baguette and Butter Puddings

PREPARATION TIME 10 MINUTES

COOKING TIME 15-20 MINUTES

INGREDIENTS

1 baguette, thinly sliced
3 tbsp butter, softened
250 ml / 9 fl. oz / 1 cup whole milk
200 ml / 7 oz / ¾ cup double cream
4 large egg yolks
75 g / 2 ½ oz / ⅓ cup caster
(superfine) sugar
4 tbsp marmalade

- Preheat the oven to 180°C (160° fan), 355 F, gas 4.
- Spread the baguette with butter and arrange the slices in 6 small baking dishes.
- Whisk the milk, cream, eggs and sugar together and pour it over the top, then press down on the baguette to help it soak up the liquid.
- Melt the marmalade in a small saucepan then spoon it over the puddings.
- Bake for 15 – 20 minutes or until the tops are golden brown.

Ginger Baguette and Butter Puddings

900

- Replace the marmalade with ginger jam or finely chopped stem ginger in syrup.

901

SERVES 4

Meringues with Cream and Raspberries

PREPARATION TIME 10 MINUTES

COOKING TIME 30 MINUTES

INGREDIENTS

75 g / 2 ½ oz / ½ cup dark chocolate
(minimum 60 % cocoa solids)
16 small meringues
300 ml / 10 ½ fl. oz / 1 ¼ cups double cream
200 g / 7 oz / 1 ¾ cup raspberries
mint sprigs to garnish

- Melt the chocolate in a microwave or bain marie. Dip the base of each meringue in the chocolate then leave to set on a non-stick baking mat for 30 minutes.
- Whip the double cream until thick then use it to sandwich the meringues together in pairs.
- Arrange on a serving plate and scatter over the raspberries.
- Garnish with fresh mint.

Meringues with Orange Cream and Blueberries

902

- Replace the raspberries with blueberries and add the grated zest of an orange to the cream.

903

MAKES 6

Summer Fruit Compote with Meringue

- Preheat the oven to 200°C (180° fan), 390 F, gas 6.
- Put the fruit in a saucepan with the sugar and vanilla and cover with a lid.
- Cook it over a medium heat for 5 minutes, stirring occasionally, then discard the vanilla pod and spoon the compote into 6 oven-proof glasses or bowls.
- Whisk the egg whites until stiff, then gradually add the sugar and whisk until the mixture is thick and shiny.
- Spoon the meringue into a piping bag, fitted with a large star nozzle, and pipe a big swirl of meringue on top of each compote.
- Bake for 10 minutes or until the tops are golden brown.

PREPARATION TIME 20 MINUTES

COOKING TIME 15 MINUTES

INGREDIENTS

450 g / 1 lb / 2 cups frozen summer fruits, defrosted
2 tbsp caster (superfine) sugar
1 vanilla pod, halved lengthways

FOR THE MERINGUE

4 large egg whites
110g / 4 oz / ½ cup caster (superfine) sugar

Apple Compote with Meringue

904

- Replace the summer fruits with 2 peeled and cubed cooking apples and increase the cooking time to 8 minutes.

905

SERVES 8

Lemon Meringue Pie

- Preheat the oven to 200°C (180° fan), 390 F, gas 6.
- Fill the pastry case with lemon curd and smooth the top with a palette knife.
- Whisk the egg whites until stiff, then gradually add the sugar and whisk until the mixture is thick and shiny.
- Spoon the meringue on top of the lemon curd, making peaks with the spoon.
- Bake for 10 minutes or until golden brown.

PREPARATION TIME 15 MINUTES

COOKING TIME 10 MINUTES

INGREDIENTS

1 pastry case
1 jar lemon curd
4 large egg whites
110g / 4 oz / ½ cup caster (superfine) sugar

Passion Fruit Meringue Pie

906

- Press the pulp from 4 fresh passion fruit through a sieve to remove the seeds and stir it into the lemon curd.

907

SERVES 8

Apricot Upside-Down Cake

PREPARATION TIME 10 MINUTES

COOKING TIME 35 MINUTES

....

INGREDIENTS

300 g / 10 ½ oz / 2 cups self-raising
flour
2 tsp baking powder
250 g / 9 oz / 1 ¼ cups caster
(superfine) sugar
250 g / 9 oz / 1 ¼ cups butter,
softened
5 large eggs
4 tbsp raspberry jam
6 apricots, halved and stoned

- Preheat the oven to 170°C (150° fan), 340 F, gas 3 and butter a 23 cm round cake tin.
- Sieve the flour and baking powder into a mixing bowl and add the sugar, butter and eggs.
- Beat the mixture with an electric whisk for 4 minutes or until smooth and well whipped.
- Spread the jam over the base of the cake tin and arrange the apricots on top.
- Spoon in the cake mixture and bake for 35 minutes or until a skewer inserted comes out clean.
- Turn the cake out of the tin and serve warm or at room temperature.

Peach Melba Upside Down Cake **908**

- Replace the apricots with peaches.

909

SERVES 4

Coconut Crème Brulee

PREPARATION TIME 35 MINUTES

COOKING TIME 10 MINUTES

....

INGREDIENTS

450 ml / 12 ½ fl. oz / 1 ¾cup whole
milk
4 large egg yolks
75 g / 2 ½ oz / ⅓ cup caster
(superfine) sugar
2 tsp cornflour
4 tbsp desiccated coconut
4 tsp Demerara sugar

- Pour the milk into a saucepan and bring to simmering point.
- Meanwhile, whisk the egg yolks with the caster (superfine) sugar, cornflour and coconut until thick.
- Gradually incorporate the hot milk, whisking all the time, then scrape the mixture back into the saucepan.
- Stir the custard over a low heat until it thickens then divide it between 4 ramekins.
- Chill in the fridge for 25 minutes.
- Sprinkle the tops with Demerara sugar then caramelise with a blow torch or under a hot grill.

Coconut Banana Crème Brulee **910**

- Divide 2 sliced bananas between the ramekin dishes before pouring the custard on top.

911

SERVES 8

Lemon Tart

Lime Tart
912

- Replace the lemons with 5 limes.

Pink Grapefruit Tart
913

- Replace the lemons with a large grapefruit.

PREPARATION TIME 5 MINUTES

COOKING TIME 25-30 MINUTES

INGREDIENTS

3 lemons, juiced
175 g / 6 oz / ¾ cup caster (superfine) sugar
2 tsp cornflour
4 large eggs, beaten
225 ml / 8 fl.oz / ¾ cup double cream
1 pastry case
lemon zest to garnish

- Preheat the oven to 170°C (150° fan), 340 F, gas 3.
- Stir the lemon juice into the caster (superfine) sugar and cornflour to dissolve, then whisk in the eggs and cream.
- Strain the mixture into the pastry case and bake for 25 – 30 minutes or until just set in the centre.
- Garnish with lemon zest and serve warm or at room temperature.

914

SERVES 4

Apple Crumble Tatin

PREPARATION TIME 10 MINUTES

COOKING TIME 35 MINUTES

INGREDIENTS

50 g / 1 ¾ oz / ¼ cup granulated sugar
450 g / 1 lb / 4 ¼ cup eating apples, peeled, cored and cut into wedges
75 g / 2 ½ oz / ⅓ cup butter
50 g / 1 ¾ oz / ⅓ cup plain (all purpose) flour
30 g / 1 oz / ½ cup ground almonds
30 g / 1 oz / ¼ cup blanched almonds, chopped
40 g / 1 ½ oz / ¼ cup light brown sugar

- Preheat the oven to 180°C (160° fan), 355 F, gas 4.
- Put the granulated sugar in a saucepan and heat gently without stirring until it starts to turn to caramel round the edges.
- Continue to cook, swirling the pan occasionally, until it is all liquid, then pour the caramel into a buttered spring-form cake tin.
- Arrange the apples on top.
- Rub the butter into the flour and stir in the ground almonds, flaked (slivered) almonds and brown sugar.
- Take a handful of the topping and squeeze it into a clump, then crumble it over the fruit.
- Repeat with the rest of the crumble mixture then bake for 30 minutes or until the topping is golden brown.
- Leave to cool for 5 minutes then carefully turn the crumble out onto a serving plate.

Pear Crumble Tatin   915

- Replace the apples with pears.

916

SERVES 4

Plum and Almond Crumble

PREPARATION TIME 5 MINUTES

COOKING TIME 40 MINUTES

INGREDIENTS

450 g / 1 lb / 4 ½ cups plums, halved and stoned
2 tbsp caster (superfine) sugar
75 g / 2 ½ oz / ⅓ cup butter
50 g / 1 ¾ oz / ⅓ cup plain (all purpose) flour
30 g / 1 oz / ¼ cup ground almonds
30 g / 1 oz / ¼ cup flaked (slivered) almonds
40 g / 1 ½ oz / ¼ cup light brown sugar

- Preheat the oven to 180°C (160° fan), 355 F, gas 4.
- Toss the plums with the caster (superfine) sugar and arrange in a baking dish.
- Rub the butter into the flour and stir in the ground almonds, flaked (slivered) almonds and brown sugar.
- Take a handful of the topping and squeeze it into a clump, then crumble it over the fruit.
- Repeat with the rest of the crumble mixture then bake for 40 minutes or until the topping is golden brown.

Cherry and Marzipan Crumble   917

- Replace the plums with the same weight of stoned cherries and add 150 g of marzipan in small cubes to the crumble topping.

918
SERVES 4
Apple and Raspberry Crumble

- Preheat the oven to 180°C (160° fan), 355 F, gas 4.
- Mix the fruit with the caster (superfine) sugar and tip it into a baking dish.
- Rub the butter into the flour and stir in the ground almonds and brown sugar.
- Take a handful of the topping and squeeze it into a clump, then crumble it over the fruit.
- Repeat with the rest of the crumble mixture then bake for 40 minutes or until the topping is golden brown.

PREPARATION TIME 5 MINUTES

COOKING TIME 40 MINUTES

INGREDIENTS

1 bramley apple, peeled and chopped
200 g / 7 oz / 1 ¾ cup raspberries
4 tbsp caster (superfine) sugar
75 g / 2 ½ oz / ⅓ cup butter
50 g / 1 ¾ oz / ⅓ cup plain (all purpose) flour
25 g / 1 oz / ¼ cup ground almonds
40 g / 1 ½ oz / ¼ cup light brown sugar

Pear and Blueberry Crumble
919

- Replace the apples with pears and substitute blueberries for the raspberries.

920
SERVES 4
Crêpes with Honey

- Sieve the flour into a bowl and make a well in the centre. Break in the egg and pour in the milk then use a whisk to gradually incorporate all of the flour from round the outside.
- Melt the butter in a small frying pan then whisk it into the batter.
- Put the buttered frying pan back over a low heat. Add a small ladle of batter and swirl the pan to coat the bottom.
- When it starts to dry and curl up at the edges, turn the pancake over with a spatula and cook the other side until golden brown and cooked through.
- Repeat with the rest of the mixture then serve the crepes drizzled with honey.

PREPARATION TIME 5 MINUTES

COOKING TIME 20 MINUTES

INGREDIENTS

150 g / 5 ½ oz / 1 cup plain (all purpose) flour
1 large egg
325 ml / 11 ½ fl. oz / 1 ⅓ cup whole milk
30 g / 1 oz butter, melted
6 tbsp runny honey

Crepes with Honey and Lemon
921

- Stir the zest and juice of a lemon into the honey before drizzling it over the crepes.

922

SERVES 4

Chocolate Crêpes

Chocolate and Banana Crepes

923

- Stir 2 chopped bananas into the chocolate filling at the last minute and omit the garnish.

Black Forest Crepes

924

- Stir 100 g of stoned maraschino cherries in syrup into the chocolate filling at the last minute.

PREPARATION TIME 5 MINUTES

COOKING TIME 20 MINUTES

INGREDIENTS

150 g / 5 ½ oz / 1 cup plain (all purpose) flour
1 large egg
325 ml / 11 ½ fl. oz / 1 ⅓ cup whole milk
30 g / 1 oz butter, melted

FOR THE FILLING
100 ml / 3 ½ fl. oz / ½ cup double cream
100 g / 3 ½ oz / ¾ cup dark chocolate (minimum 60 % cocoa solids), chopped

TO SERVE
1 tsp cocoa powder
1 orange, segmented and cubed
a few sprigs mint

- To make the filling, heat the cream to simmering point then pour it over the chocolate and stir to emulsify. Leave to cool and thicken slightly while you make the crepes.
- Sieve the flour into a bowl and make a well in the centre. Break in the egg and pour in the milk then use a whisk to gradually incorporate all of the flour from round the outside.
- Melt the butter in a small frying pan then whisk it into the batter.
- Put the buttered frying pan back over a low heat. Add a small ladle of batter and swirl the pan to coat the bottom.
- When it starts to dry and curl up at the edges, turn the pancake over with a spatula and cook the other side until golden brown and cooked through.
- Repeat with the rest of the mixture then serve each crêpe rolled up with a big spoonful of chocolate ganache inside.
- Sprinkle over a little cocoa powder and arrange some orange and mint on the side.

Amaretti Fool

925

SERVES 4

- Crush half of the biscuits and set aside.
- Divide the rest of the biscuits between 4 fool glasses and pour over the liqueur and orange juice.
- Whip the cream until thick but not stiff, then fold in most of the crushed biscuits.
- Spoon the cream into the fool glasses and sprinkle over the remaining biscuits and the toasted almonds.

PREPARATION TIME 10 MINUTES

INGREDIENTS

100 g / 3 ½ oz / 1 cup amaretti biscuits
4 tbsp amoretto liqueur
4 tbsp orange juice
600 ml / 1 pint / 2 ½ cups double cream
2 tbsp flaked (slivered) almonds, toasted

Amaretti and Cherry Fool

926

- Fold 200 g of stoned maraschino cherries in syrup into the cream with the crushed biscuits.

Raspberry and Orange Fool

927

SERVES 4

- Press half of the raspberries through a sieve into a bowl and discard the seeds.
- Add the icing (confectioners') sugar and orange juice and stir to dissolve.
- Add the cream to the bowl and whip it all together until thick.
- Spoon the fool into 4 bowls and sprinkle over the remaining raspberries and the pared orange zest.

PREPARATION TIME 10 MINUTES

INGREDIENTS

150 g / 5 ½ oz / 1 ¼ cups raspberries
50 g / 1 ¾ oz / ½ cup icing (confectioners') sugar
1 orange, juiced and zest finely pared
600 ml / 1 pint / 2 ½ cups double cream

Raspberry and Lime Fool

928

- Replace the orange juice and zest with the zest and juice of 2 limes.

929

SERVES 4

Crêpes with Chocolate Dipping Sauce

PREPARATION TIME 5 MINUTES

COOKING TIME 20 MINUTES

INGREDIENTS

150 g / 5 ½ oz / 1 cup plain (all purpose) flour
1 large egg
325 ml / 11 ½ fl. oz / 1 ⅓ cup whole milk
30 g / 1 oz butter, melted

FOR THE DIPPING SAUCE

100 ml / 3 ½ fl. oz / ½ cup double cream
1 tbsp brandy
100 g / 3 ½ oz / ¾ cup dark chocolate (minimum 60 % cocoa solids), chopped

- To make the dipping sauce, heat the cream and brandy to simmering point then pour it over the chocolate and stir to emulsify. Spoon into 4 serving glasses.
- Sieve the flour into a bowl and make a well in the centre. Break in the egg and pour in the milk then use a whisk to gradually incorporate all of the flour from round the outside.
- Melt the butter in a small frying pan then whisk it into the batter.
- Put the buttered frying pan back over a low heat. Add a small ladle of batter and swirl the pan to coat the bottom.
- When it starts to dry and curl up at the edges, turn the pancake over with a spatula and cook the other side until golden brown and cooked through.
- Repeat with the rest of the mixture then fold the crepes into quarters and serve with the dipping sauce.

930

SERVES 4

Cherry Fool

PREPARATION TIME 10 MINUTES

INGREDIENTS

150 g / 5 ½ oz / ¾ cup cherries, stoned
2 tbsp kirsch
50 g / 1 ¾ oz / ½ cup icing (confectioners')sugar
600 ml / 1 pint / 2 ½ cups double cream

- Put the cherries, kirsch and icing (confectioners') sugar in a food processor and pulse until finely chopped.
- Whip the cream until thick then fold through the cherry mixture.
- Spoon the mixture into 4 fool glasses and serve.

931
SERVES 4

Milk Chocolate Crumble Pots

- Preheat the oven to 180°C (160° fan), 355 F, gas 4.
- Heat the cream to simmering point then pour it over the chocolate and stir until smooth.
- Divide the mixture between 4 ramekins and chill for 35 minutes.
- Rub the butter into the flour and stir in the ground almonds, flaked (slivered) almonds and brown sugar.
- Crumble the mixture onto a baking tray and bake for 25 minutes or until golden and crisp.
- Leave the crumble to cool for 5 minutes then sprinkle it over the chocolate pots.

PREPARATION TIME 20 MINUTES

COOKING TIME 40 MINUTES

INGREDIENTS

200 ml / 7 fl. oz / ¾ cup double cream
200 g / 7 oz / 1 ½ cups milk chocolate, chopped

FOR THE CRUMBLE
75 g / 2 ½ oz / ⅓ cup butter
50 g / 1 ¾ oz / ⅓ cup plain (all purpose) flour
30 g / 1 oz / ¼ cup ground almonds
30 g / 1 oz / ¼ cup blanched almonds, chopped
40 g / 1 ½ oz / ¼ cup brown sugar

Chocolate and Banana Puddings

932
SERVES 4

933
SERVES 4

Coconut Fool

PREPARATION TIME 40 MINUTES

COOKING TIME 5 MINUTES

INGREDIENTS

100 ml / 3 ½ fl. oz / ½ cup double cream
100 g / 3 ½ oz / ¾ cup milk chocolate, chopped
14 biscuits
1 banana, chopped

- Heat the cream to simmering point then pour it over the chocolate and stir until smooth.
- Put 6 of the biscuits into a food processor and blend to fine crumbs.
- Pour in the chocolate mixture then add the banana and blend again until smooth.
- Divide the mixture between 4 bowls and press 2 biscuits into the top of each one.
- Chill in the fridge for 30 minutes or until firm.

PREPARATION TIME 10 MINUTES

COOKING TIME 2 MINUTES

INGREDIENTS

75 g / 2 ½ oz / ¾ cup desiccated coconut
300 ml / 10 ½ fl. oz / 1 ¼ cups double cream
300 g / 10 ½ oz / 1 ¼ cups coconut flavoured yoghurt

- Preheat the grill to its highest setting.
- Spread the coconut out on a baking sheet and toast under the hot grill until golden brown. Leave to cool.
- Whip the cream until thick but not stiff, then fold in the yoghurt and half of the toasted coconut.
- Spoon the cream into 4 fool glasses and sprinkle over the remaining coconut.

934

SERVES 4

Crêpes with Chocolate Drizzle

PREPARATION TIME 5 MINUTES

COOKING TIME 20 MINUTES

INGREDIENTS

150 g / 5 ½ oz / 1 cup plain (all purpose) flour
1 large egg
325 ml / 11 ½ fl. oz / 1 ⅓ cup whole milk
30 g / 1 oz butter, melted

FOR THE DRIZZLE
100 ml / 3 ½ fl. oz / ½ cup double cream
1 tbsp brandy
100 g / 3 ½ oz / ¾ cup dark chocolate (minimum 60 % cocoa solids), chopped

FOR THE TOPPINGS
1 orange, zest finely grated
1 tbsp desiccated coconut
1 tbsp crystallised ginger, chopped
1 tbsp chocolate honeycomb, crushed

- To make the chocolate drizzle, heat the cream and brandy to simmering point then pour it over the chocolate and stir to emulsify. Set aside.
- Sieve the flour into a bowl and make a well in the centre. Break in the egg and pour in the milk then use a whisk to incorporate all of the flour from round the outside.
- Melt the butter in a frying pan then whisk it into the batter. Put the buttered frying pan back over a low heat. Add a small ladle of batter and swirl to coat the bottom.
- When it starts to dry and curl up at the edges, turn the pancake over with a spatula and cook the other side until golden brown and cooked through.
- Repeat with the rest of the mixture then roll up the crepes and arrange them on a serving platter.
- Drizzle over the chocolate sauce and sprinkle with the toppings of your choice.

Crêpes with White Chocolate Drizzle

935

- Replace the dark chocolate with white chocolate and cook the same way.

936

SERVES 2

Sweet French Toast

PREPARATION TIME 5 MINUTES

COOKING TIME 4 MINUTES

INGREDIENTS

1 orange, zest finely grated
2 large eggs
75 ml / 2 ½ fl. oz / ⅓ cup milk
25 g butter
8 slices baguette
4 tbsp runny honey

- Whisk the orange zest into the eggs with the milk.
- Heat the butter in a large frying pan until sizzling.
- Dip the baguette slices in the egg mixture on both sides until evenly coated then fry them for 2 minutes on each side or until golden brown. Divide the toast between 2 plates.
- Drizzle the toasts with honey and serve immediately.

Marmalade French Toast

937

- Replace the honey with marmalade and heat it in a small pan until runny.

938

SERVES 2

Baked Bananas with Rum and Raisins

- Preheat the oven to 180°C (160° fan), 355 F, gas 4.
- Arrange the bananas in a small baking dish.
- Scrape the seeds out of the vanilla pod into a small bowl and mix with the honey and rum.
- Spoon over the bananas and scatter over the raisins and sultanas.
- Bake in the oven for 10 minutes or until the bananas are soft and the liquid has thickened.

PREPARATION TIME 5 MINUTES

COOKING TIME 10 MINUTES

INGREDIENTS

2 bananas, halved lengthways
1 vanilla pod, halved lengthways
2 tbsp runny honey
2 tbsp dark rum
3 tbsp raisins and sultanas

Baked Bananas with Chocolate

939

- Omit the raisins and sultanas. Break 100 g of milk chocolate into squares and use them to stud the bananas before baking.

940

SERVES 6

Baked Spiced Apples

- Preheat the oven to 180°C (160° fan), 355 F, gas 4.
- Arrange the apples in a baking dish.
- Beat together the butter and powdered spices and spread it over the apples, then scatter over the whole spices.
- Bake in the oven for 25 minutes or until the apples are soft.

PREPARATION TIME 10 MINUTES

COOKING TIME 25 MINUTES

INGREDIENTS

6 small eating apples, peeled
2 tbsp butter, softened
2 tbsp brown sugar
½ tsp ground ginger
½ tsp ground cinnamon
1 vanilla pod
1 cinnamon stick
1 orange, zest peeled

Mincemeat Stuffed Apples

941

- Core the apples and stuff each cavity with a heaped teaspoon of mincemeat.

942

SERVES 4

Cherry and Chocolate Fool

PREPARATION TIME 10 MINUTES

INGREDIENTS

300 ml / 10 ½ fl. oz / 1 ¼ cups double cream
50 g / 1 ¾ oz / ½ cup icing (confectoners')sugar
300 g / 10 ½ oz / 1 ¼ cups natural yoghurt
150 g / 5 ½ oz / ¾ cup cherries, stoned
4 tbsp grated dark chocolate

- Whip the cream with the icing (confectioners') sugar until thick then fold through the yoghurt.
- Arrange the cherries in the bottom of 4 fool glasses and spoon the fool mixture on top.
- Sprinkle with grated chocolate and serve.

Strawberry and Chocolate Fool   943

- Replace the cherries with strawberries.

944

SERVES 4

Baked Apples with Honey and Almonds

PREPARATION TIME 10 MINUTES

COOKING TIME 25 MINUTES

INGREDIENTS

4 small eating apples, halved
2 tbsp butter
4 tbsp runny honey
2 tbsp blanched almonds

- Preheat the oven to 180°C (160° fan), 355 F, gas 4.
- Arrange the apples, cut side up, in a baking dish.
- Dot over the butter then bake for 20 minutes or until the apples are soft.
- Drizzle with honey and sprinkle over the almonds then return the apples to the oven for 5 minutes to glaze.

Baked Apples with Honey and Pistachios   945

- Replace the almonds with pistachio nuts and add a pinch of ground cardamom to the honey.

946

SERVES 2

Banana Split

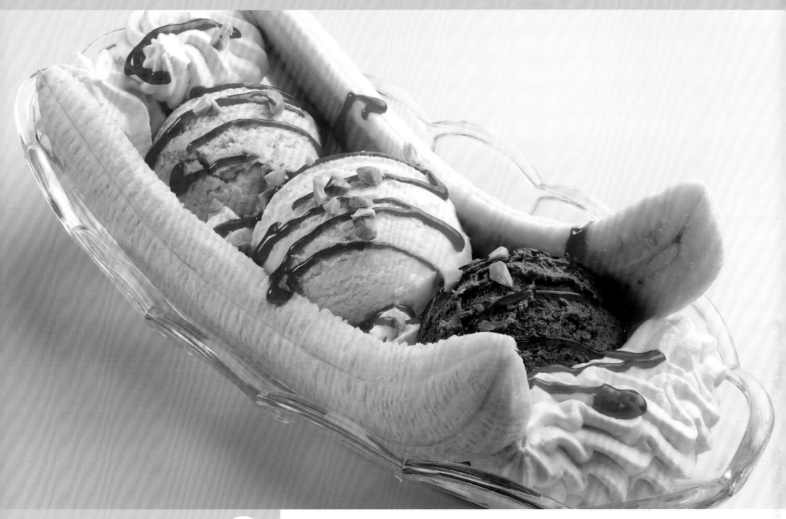

Dairy-Free Banana Split 947

- Omit the cream and replace the ice cream with mango sorbet, lime sorbet and pineapple sorbet.

Banana and Chocolate Split 948

- Replace the strawberry ice cream with a scoop of chocolate ice cream and replace the strawberry sauce with chocolate sauce. Use chocolate flakes instead of the chopped hazelnuts.

PREPARATION TIME 10 MINUTES

INGREDIENTS

150 ml / 5 ½ fl. oz / ¾ cup double cream
2 scoops of chocolate ice cream
2 scoops of vanilla ice cream
2 scoops of strawberry ice cream
2 bananas, peeled and halved lengthways
1 tbsp hazelnuts (cob nuts), chopped
strawberry ice cream sauce

- Whip the cream until thick then spoon it into a piping bag fitted with a large star nozzle.
- Scoop the ice cream into 2 banana split bowls and pipe a swirl of cream at either end.
- Tuck the banana halves down the sides and sprinkle with hazelnuts then drizzle over some strawberry sauce.

949

SERVES 6

Fresh Fruit Sponge Pudding

PREPARATION TIME 10 MINUTES

COOKING TIME 30-35 MINUTES

INGREDIENTS

110 g / 4 oz / ⅔ cup self-raising flour, sifted
110 g / 4 oz / ½ cup caster (superfine) sugar
110 g / 4 oz / ½ cup butter, softened
2 large eggs
1 tsp vanilla extract
2 plums, cut into eighths
55 g / 1 oz / ½ cup raspberries
55 g / 1 oz / ½ cup seedless black grapes

- Preheat the oven to 190°C (170° fan), 375 F, gas 5 and butter a small baking dish.
- Combine the flour, sugar, butter, eggs and vanilla extract in a bowl and whisk together for 2 minutes or until smooth.
- Arrange half of the fruit in the baking dish and spoon in the cake mixture.
- Top with the rest of the fruit then bake for 30 – 35 minutes.
- Test with a wooden toothpick, if it comes out clean, the cake is done.
- Serve warm with custard or cream.

Blueberry Sponge Pudding

950

- Replace the fruit with 200 g of fresh blueberries and add the grated zest of an orange to the cake batter.

951

SERVES 2

Coffee Ice Cream Sundae

PREPARATION TIME 10 MINUTES

INGREDIENTS

150 ml / 5 ½ fl. oz / ⅔ cup double cream
2 shots fresh espresso
2 scoops of vanilla ice cream
2 scoops of coffee ice cream
4 Mikado biscuits
chocolate sprinkles and cocoa powder to garnish

- Whip the cream until thick then spoon it into a piping bag fitted with a large star nozzle.
- Put an espresso shot in the bottom of 2 glass mugs and top with a scoop of vanilla ice cream.
- Scoop in some coffee ice cream then pipe a swirl of cream on top of each one.
- Garnish the sundaes with 2 Mikado biscuits, chocolate sprinkles and a dusting of cocoa powder.

Tiramisu Sundae

952

- Break 8 sponge fingers in pieces and divide between the mugs before topping with the espresso and a shot of Tia Maria.

Summer Fruit Crumble

953

SERVES 4

- Preheat the oven to 180°C (160° fan), 355 F, gas 4.
- Mix the fruit with the sugar and tip it into a baking dish.
- Rub the butter into the flour and stir in the ground almonds and brown sugar.
- Take a handful of the topping and squeeze it into a clump, then crumble it over the fruit.
- Repeat with the rest of the crumble mixture then bake for 40 minutes or until the topping is golden brown.

PREPARATION TIME 5 MINUTES

COOKING TIME 40 MINUTES

INGREDIENTS

300 g / 10 ½ oz mixed summer fruit
4 tbsp caster (superfine) sugar
75 g / 2 ½ oz / ⅓ cup butter
50 g / 1 ¾ oz / ⅓ cup plain (all purpose) flour
25 g / 1 oz / ¼ cup ground almonds
40 g / 1 ½ oz / ¼ cup light brown sugar

Summer Fruit Cobbler

954

- Add enough milk to the crumble mixture to bring it together into a soft dough. Shape it into small discs and arrange them round the outside of the baking dish before baking.

Raspberry and Vanilla Trifle Pots

 955

SERVES 6

- Scrape the seeds out of the vanilla pod and put them in a small saucepan with the milk. Bring to a simmer then turn off the heat and leave to infuse for 5 minutes.
- Whisk the egg yolks, sugar and cornflour together then gradually whisk in the milk.
- Scrape the mixture back into the saucepan then cook over a medium heat until the mixture thickens, stirring constantly. Remove from the heat and plunge the base of the pan into cold water .
- Mash a third of the raspberries with a fork then stir in the rest of the whole raspberries.
- Put a spoonful of the raspberry mixture in the bottom of 6 glasses and crumble over half of the cake.
- Top with half the custard, then add half of the remaining raspberries. Top with the rest of the cake, then the rest of the custard and finish each glass with a ring of raspberries.

PREPARATION TIME 20 MINUTES

COOKING TIME 15-20 MINUTES

INGREDIENTS

200 g / 7 oz / 1 ¾ cup raspberries
1 small Madeira loaf cake

FOR THE CUSTARD

1 vanilla pod, split lengthways
450 ml / 16 fl. oz / 1 ¾ cup whole milk
4 large egg yolks
75 g / 2 ½ oz / ½ cup caster (superfine) sugar
2 tsp cornflour

Strawberry and Vanilla Trifle Pots

956

- Replace the raspberries with strawberries.

957

SERVES 8

Pineapple Tarte Tatin

Apricot Tarte Tatin   958

- Replace the pineapple with canned apricot halves.

Mandarin Tarte Tatin   959

- Replace the pineapple with canned mandarin segments.

PREPARATION TIME 10 MINUTES

COOKING TIME 25 MINUTES

INGREDIENTS

2 tbsp butter, softened and cubed
3 tbsp dark brown sugar
400 g / 14 oz / 2 cups canned pineapple rings, drained
250 g / 9 oz all-butter puff pastry

- Preheat the oven to 220°C (200° fan), 430 F, gas 7.
- Dot the butter over the base of a large ovenproof frying pan and sprinkle over the sugar.
- Arrange the pineapple rings on top.
- Roll out the pastry on a floured surface and cut out a circle the same size as the frying pan.
- Lay the pastry over the pineapple and tuck in the edges, then transfer the pan to the oven and bake for 25 minutes or until the pastry is golden brown and cooked through.
- Using oven gloves, put a large plate on top of the frying pan and turn them both over in one smooth movement to unmold the tart.

960

SERVES 4

Summer Fruits with Mint Cream

- Mix the strawberries with the raspberries in a shallow bowl.
- Put the honey, lemon juice and mint in a small saucepan with 2 tablespoons of water and bring to a simmer.
- Pour the marinade over the fruit and leave to macerate for 35 minutes.
- Meanwhile, whip the cream with the icing (confectioners') sugar until thick then spoon it into a piping bag fitted with a large star nozzle.
- Discard the mint sprigs and divide the fruit between 4 sundae glasses.
- Pipe a swirl of cream on top of each one and sprinkle over the mint.

PREPARATION TIME 35 MINUTES

COOKING TIME 5 MINUTES

INGREDIENTS

200 g / 7 oz / 1 cup strawberries
100 g / 3 ½ oz / ⅔ cup raspberries
2 tbsp runny honey
2 tbsp lemon juice
2 sprigs mint

FOR THE CREAM

300 ml / 10 ½ fl. oz / 1 ¼ cups double cream
2 tbsp icing (confectioners') sugar
1 tbsp mint, finely chopped

Summer Fruits with Basil and Lime Cream

961

- Replace the mint with fresh basil and replace the lemon juice with lime juice.

962

SERVES 4

Pineapple and Raspberry Salad

- Put the honey, rum and peppercorns in a small saucepan with 4 tbsp water and infuse over a low heat for 5 minutes.
- Arrange the pineapple in a serving bowl and pour over the mixture, then leave to marinate for 20 minutes.
- Scatter the raspberries over the pineapple and garnish with mint leaves and a dusting of icing (confectioners') sugar.

PREPARATION TIME 25 MINUTES

COOKING TIME 5 MINUTES

INGREDIENTS

4 tbsp honey
2 tbsp dark rum
½ tsp Szechwan peppercorns
1 pineapple, peeled, cored and cut into chunks
150 g / 5 ½ oz / 1 ¼ cups raspberries
mint leaves and icing (confectioners') sugar to garnish

Pineapple and Blueberry Salad

 963

- Replace the raspberries with blueberries.

964

SERVES 8

Apple and Lemon Tarte Tatin

PREPARATION TIME 10 MINUTES

COOKING TIME 25 MINUTES

INGREDIENTS

2 tbsp butter, softened and cubed
3 tbsp dark brown sugar
1 lemon, juiced and zest finely grated
4 bramley apples, peeled and thinly sliced
250 g / 9 oz all-butter puff pastry
whipped cream and finely pared lemon zest to serve

- Preheat the oven to 220°C (200° fan), 430 F, gas 7.
- Beat together the butter, sugar and lemon zest and juice then mix in the apple slices.
- Spread the mixture out inside an oven proof frying pan.
- Roll out the pastry on a floured surface and cut out a circle the same size as the frying pan.
- Lay the pastry over the apples and tuck in the edges, then transfer the pan to the oven and bake for 25 minutes or until the pastry is golden brown and cooked through.
- Using oven gloves, put a large plate on top of the frying pan and turn them both over in one smooth movement to unmold the tart.
- Cut into slices and serve with a spoonful of whipped cream and a sprinkling of lemon zest.

Apple and Lavender Tarte Tatin

965

- Add ½ tsp of dried lavender flowers to the butter and sugar mixture.

966

SERVES 4

Pink Grapefruit with Mint and Gin

PREPARATION TIME 30 MINUTES

COOKING TIME 4 MINUTES

INGREDIENTS

3 tbsp runny honey
3 tbsp gin
1 tbsp mint, finely chopped
2 pink grapefruit, cut into segments

- Put the honey, gin and mint in a small saucepan with 3 tbsp water and bring to a simmer.
- Pour the mixture over the grapefruit segments and leave to marinate for 30 minutes.
- Divide the grapefruit between 4 glasses and serve chilled or at room temperature.

Pink Grapefruit and Gin Sorbet

967

- Blend the grapefruit and gin syrup in a food processor until smooth, then churn in an ice cream machine for 25 minutes or until firm.

968

SERVES 4

Chocolate Risotto

- Heat the milk in a saucepan with 500 ml water.
- Heat the butter in a sauté pan and stir in the rice, cocoa and sugar.
- When it is well coated with the butter, add 2 ladles of the hot milk.
- Cook, stirring occasionally, until most of the milk has been absorbed before adding the next 2 ladles.
- Continue in this way for around 15 minutes or until the rice is just tender.
- Stir in the chocolate and crème fraîche, then cover the pan and take off the heat to rest for 4 minutes.
- Stir well then spoon into glass mugs and serve immediately.

PREPARATION TIME 5 MINUTES

COOKING TIME 25 MINUTES

INGREDIENTS

500 ml / 18 fl. oz / 2 cups milk
4 tbsp butter
150 g / 5 ½ oz / ¾ cup risotto rice
3 tbsp unsweetened cocoa powder
4 tbsp caster (superfine) sugar
50 g / 1 ¾ oz / ⅓ cup dark chocolate
(minimum 60 % cocoa solids), grated
2 tbsp crème fraîche

Chocolate and Almond Risotto

969

- Cut 200 g of marzipan into small cubes and stir it into the risotto with the chocolate and crème fraîche.

970

SERVES 4

Vanilla Baked Peaches

- Preheat the oven to 180°C (160° fan), 355 F, gas 4.
- Arrange the peaches, cut side up, in 4 small baking dishes.
- Scrape the seeds out of the vanilla pod and put them in a small saucepan with the honey and orange juice. Bring to a simmer then pour the liquid over the peaches.
- Bake in the oven for 25 minutes or until the peaches are soft.
- Serve garnished with the empty vanilla pod.

PREPARATION TIME 10 MINUTES

COOKING TIME 25-30 MINUTES

INGREDIENTS

6 peaches, halved and stoned
1 vanilla pod, split lengthways
2 tbsp runny honey
1 orange, juiced

Lavender Baked Peaches

971

- Replace the vanilla pod with 2 sprigs of dried lavender.

972

SERVES 4

White Chocolate Fondue

PREPARATION TIME 5 MINUTES

COOKING TIME 4 MINUTES

INGREDIENTS

100 g / 3 ½ oz / ⅔ cup white chocolate
150 ml / 3 ½ fl. oz / ⅔ cup double cream
2 tbsp Cointreau
raspberries and brownie squares for dipping

- Chop the chocolate and put it in a fondue bowl.
- Bring the cream and Cointreau to simmering point then pour it over the chocolate and stir until smooth.
- Serve with the raspberries and brownie squares for dipping.

White Chocolate Espresso Fondue

973

- Replace the Cointreau with Tia Maria and add 2 shots of espresso to the cream.

974

SERVES 6

Lemon Curd Ice Cream Tart

PREPARATION TIME 45 MINUTES

INGREDIENTS

1 jar lemon curd
1 readymade pastry case
450 g / 1 lb / 1 ¾ cup lemon curd ice cream, slightly softened
candied lemon peel, to garnish

- Spoon the lemon curd into the pastry case and level the surface.
- Scoop in the ice cream and level the top with a palette knife, then transfer the tart to the freezer for 40 minutes.
- Meanwhile, cut the candied peel into long thin strips, then cut half of it across into tiny cubes.
- Take the tart out of the freezer and sprinkle with candied peel, then serve immediately.

Strawberry Ice Cream Tart

975

- Replace the lemon curd with strawberry jam and substitute strawberry ice cream for the lemon curd ice cream.

976

SERVES 4

Mulled Wine Pears

Mulled Cider Pears

977

- Replace the wine with cider.

Mulled Port Pears

978

- Replace half of the wine with port.

PREPARATION TIME 5 MINUTES

COOKING TIME 40 MINUTES

INGREDIENTS

700 ml / 1 pint 4 fl. oz / 3 ½ cups red wine
100 g / 3 ½ oz / ½ cup caster (superfine) sugar
1 orange, juiced
2 cinnamon sticks
4 cloves
a few sprigs thyme, plus extra to garnish
8 small ripe pears, peeled

- Put the wine, sugar, orange juice, spices and thyme in a large saucepan and bring to the boil, stirring to dissolve the sugar.
- Boil for 5 minutes then add the pears and simmer for 30 minutes, or until tender.
- Arrange the pears in a serving dish then strain the sauce through a sieve to remove the spices and pour it over the top.
- Garnish the pears with fresh thyme sprigs and serve hot or cold.

979

SERVES 4

Crêpes Suzette

PREPARATION TIME 5 MINUTES

COOKING TIME 30 MINUTES

INGREDIENTS

150 g / 5 ½ oz / 1 cup plain (all purpose) flour
1 large egg
325 ml / 11 ½ fl. oz / 1 ¼ cups whole milk
30 g / 1 oz butter, melted
2 oranges, juiced and zest finely pared
1 lemon, juiced
4 tbsp caster (superfine) sugar
2 tbsp Cointreau

- Sieve the flour into a bowl and make a well in the centre. Break in the egg and pour in the milk then use a whisk to incorporate all of the flour from round the outside.
- Melt the butter in a frying pan then whisk it into the batter. Put the buttered frying pan back over a low heat. Add a small ladle of batter and swirl to coat the bottom.
- When it starts to dry and curl up at the edges, turn the pancake over with a spatula and cook the other side until golden brown and cooked through.
- Repeat with the rest of the mixture then fold the crêpes into quarters. Put the rest of the ingredients in the pan and heat until bubbling, stirring to dissolve the sugar.
- Arrange the folded pancakes in the pan and cook for 30 seconds, then turn them over and cook for another 30 seconds so that they soak up some of the sauce.
- Transfer the crêpes to warm plates and spoon over any leftover sauce.

Lemon Crepes

980

- Replace the oranges with lemons and the Cointreau with Limoncello.

981

MAKES 6

Muesli Biscuits

PREPARATION TIME 10 MINUTES

COOKING TIME 20-25 MINUTES

INGREDIENTS

100 g / 3 ½ oz / ¼ cup butter
100 g / 3 ½ oz / ½ cup light brown sugar
300 g / 10 ½ oz / 2 ½ cups fruit and nut muesli

- Preheat the oven to 170°C (150° fan), 340 F, gas 3
- Put the butter and sugar in a small saucepan and heat together until melted, stirring to dissolve the sugar. Stir in the muesli.
- When the mixture is cool enough to handle, press it into 6 patties with your hands and space them out on a baking tray.
- Bake for 20 – 25 minutes or until the biscuits are firm and lightly golden on top.

Oat and Marzipan Biscuits

982

- Replace the muesli with porridge oats and add 100 g of marzipan in small cubes.

983

SERVES 4

Apple and Cinnamon Bread Pudding

- Preheat the oven to 180°C (160° fan), 355 F, gas 4.
- Spread the bread with butter and cut it into triangles.
- Mix the Demerara sugar with the cinnamon then stir in the apple and Calvados.
- Spread the apple mixture over the bread triangles then arrange them in a baking dish.
- Whisk the milk, cream, eggs and caster (superfine) sugar together and pour it over the top, then press down on the bread to help it soak up the liquid.
- Bake for 35 – 40 minutes or until the top is golden brown.

PREPARATION TIME 5 MINUTES

COOKING TIME 35-40 MINUTES

....

INGREDIENTS

1 loaf white bread, sliced and crusts removed
3 tbsp butter, softened
2 tbsp Demerara sugar
1 tsp ground cinnamon
1 bramley apple, grated
1 tbsp Calvados
250 ml / 9 fl. oz / 1 cup whole milk
200 ml / 7 oz / ¾ cup double cream
4 large egg yolks
75 g / 2 ½ oz / ⅓ cup caster (superfine) sugar

Apple and Almond Bread and Butter Pudding

984

- Replace the calvados with amaretto and sprinkle the pudding with 50 g of flaked almonds before baking.

985

SERVES 2

Caramalised Spiced Mangoes

- Preheat the oven to 180°C (160° fan), 355 F, gas 4.
- Arrange the mango wedges in a small baking dish.
- Mix the honey with the rum, melted butter and star anise and pour it over the top.
- Bake in the oven for 15 minutes or until the mango is soft and starting to caramelise at the edges.

PREPARATION TIME 5 MINUTES

COOKING TIME 15 MINUTES

....

INGREDIENTS

2 mangoes, peeled, stoned and cut into wedges
3 tbsp runny honey
2 tbsp dark rum
1 tbsp butter, melted
2 star anise

Spiced Mango Sorbet.

986

- Spoon the finished mangoes onto a food processor and blend until smooth then churn in an ice cream machine for 25 minutes or until firm.

987

SERVES 6-8

Watermelon Salad

Tropical Fruits with Chilli Salt

988

- Put ½ tsp of chilli flakes and 2 tsp sea salt crystals in a pestle and mortar and crush to a powder. Serve with the fruit for dipping.

Watermelon Sorbet Bowl

989

- Use the hollowed out watermelon as a bowl for serving scoops of tropical fruit sorbet.

PREPARATION TIME 25 MINUTES

INGREDIENTS

½ seedless watermelon
2 tbsp caster (superfine) sugar
2 limes, juiced
2 peaches, cubed
2 apples, cubed
2 pears, cubed
lemon verbena leaves to serve

- Scoop the centre out of the watermelon and cut the flesh into cubes.
- Combine the sugar and lime juice in a small bowl and stir to dissolve.
- Mix the watermelon cubes with the rest of the fruit then toss with the lime juice and pack back into the watermelon shell.
- Garnish with lemon verbena and serve with wooden skewers to eat the fruit with.

990

SERVES 4

Espresso Risotto

- Heat the milk in a saucepan with 500 ml water and the vanilla extract.
- Heat the butter in a sauté pan and stir in the sugar and rice.
- When it is well coated with the butter, add 2 ladles of the hot milk.
- Cook, stirring occasionally, until most of the milk has been absorbed before adding the next 2 ladles.
- Continue in this way for around 15 minutes or until the rice is just tender.
- Stir in the crème fraîche, then cover the pan and take off the heat to rest for 4 minutes.
- Spoon into 4 glasses and pour an espresso shot over each one. Serve immediately.

PREPARATION TIME 5 MINUTES

COOKING TIME 25 MINUTES

INGREDIENTS

500 ml / 18 fl. oz / 2 cups milk
1 tsp vanilla extract
4 tbsp butter
50 g / 1 ¾ oz / ¼ cup caster (superfine) sugar
150 g / 5 ½ oz / ¾ cup risotto rice
2 tbsp crème fraîche
4 shots espresso

Chocolate and Espresso Risotto **991**

- Add 1 tbsp of cocoa powder to the rice and stir in 75 g of grated chocolate with the crème fraîche at the end.

992

SERVES 4

Chocolate and Almond Sponge Pudding

- Preheat the oven to 190°C (170° fan), 375 F, gas 5 and butter a small baking dish.
- Combine the flour, cocoa, sugar, butter, eggs and almond extract in a bowl and whisk together for 2 minutes or until smooth.
- Spoon it into the baking dish and sprinkle with flaked (slivered) almonds then bake for 30 – 35 minutes.
- Test with a wooden toothpick, if it comes out clean, the cake is done.
- Serve warm with custard or cream.

PREPARATION TIME 10 MINUTES

COOKING TIME 30-35 MINUTES

INGREDIENTS

110 g / 4 oz / ⅔ cup self-raising flour, sifted
3 tbsp unsweetened cocoa powder
110 g / 4 oz / ½ cup caster (superfine) sugar
110 g / 4 oz / ½ cup butter, softened
2 large eggs
1 tsp almond extract
2 tbsp flaked (slivered) almonds

Chocolate and Orange **993**
Sponge Pudding

- Omit the almonds and almond extract and replace with the grated zest of an orange and 1 tbsp Cointreau.

994

SERVES 4

Summer Fruit Cheesecake Pots

PREPARATION TIME 40 MINUTES

COOKING TIME 5 MINUTES

....

INGREDIENTS

200 g / 7 oz / ¾ cup cream cheese
200 g / 7 oz / 1 cup condensed milk
2 lemons, juiced
200 g / 7 oz / 1 cup mixed summer
berries

FOR THE CHOCOLATE SAUCE
100 ml / 3 ½ fl. oz / ½ cup double
cream
1 tbsp brandy
75 g / 2 ½ oz / ¾ cup dark chocolate
(minimum 60 % cocoa solids),
chopped

- Beat the cream cheese with an electric whisk until smooth then whisk in the condensed milk.
- Whisk in the lemon juice until the mixture starts to thicken, then fold in the berries and spoon into 4 glasses.
- Leave to chill in the fridge for 30 minutes to firm up.
- Meanwhile, make the chocolate sauce.
- Heat the cream and brandy to simmering point then pour it over the chocolate and stir to emulsify.
- When the pots have set, drizzle over some of the sauce and serve immediately.

995

SERVES 6

Chocolate Ice Cream Biscuits

PREPARATION TIME 30 MINUTES

COOKING TIME 4 MINUTES

....

INGREDIENTS

200 g / 7 oz / 2 cups dark chocolate
(minimum 60 % cocoa solids),
chopped
6 ginger nut biscuits
6 scoops vanilla ice cream

- Line a small baking tray with a non-stick making mat.
- Melt the chocolate in a microwave or bain marie.
- Dip the biscuits in the chocolate and space them out, chocolate side down, on the baking tray.
- Freeze for 5 minutes to set the chocolate.
- Take the tray out of the freezer and add a big scoop of ice cream to the top of each biscuit.
- Spoon over the slightly cooled chocolate to cover the ice cream completely, then put the tray back in the freezer for 15 minutes.

996

SERVES 6

Chocolate and Raspberry Parfaits

- Line 6 mini pudding basins with clingfilm.
- Mix the softened ice cream with the raspberries and pistachio nuts and pack the mixture into the pudding basins.
- Freeze the parfaits for 30 minutes or until firm.
- Turn the parfaits out onto serving plates and peel off the clingfilm then garnish with extra raspberries and pistachios.

PREPARATION TIME 45 MINUTES

INGREDIENTS

450 g / 1 lb / 1 ¾ cup chocolate ice cream, softened slightly
100 g / 3 ½ oz / ¾ cup raspberries
50 g / 2 ½ oz / ½ cup pistachio nuts, chopped

997

Mini Pavlovas with Fruit Coulis

SERVES 4

PREPARATION TIME 35 MINUTES

COOKING TIME 5 MINUTES

INGREDIENTS

250 g / 10 ½ oz / 1 ¼ cups mixed summer berries
2 tbsp caster (superfine) sugar
1 tbsp kirsch

250 ml / 9 fl. oz / 1 cup double cream
4 meringue nests
mint leaves to garnish

- Reserve some of the berries for a garnish and put the rest in a saucepan with the sugar and kirsch.
- Cook over a low heat for 5 minutes or until the berries start to burst.
- Pour the mixture into a liquidiser and blend to a smooth sauce then chill in the fridge for 25 minutes.
- Whisk the cream until softly whipped and spoon it onto the meringue nests.
- Arrange the mini pavlovas on a serving plate and drizzle the coulis over and around.
- Scatter over the berries and garnish with mint leaves.

998

Blueberry Yoghurt Pots

SERVES 4

PREPARATION TIME 5 MINUTES

INGREDIENTS

400 g / 14 oz / 1 ⅔ cups blueberry yoghurt
100 g / 3 ½ oz / 1 cup granola
4 tbsp condensed milk
50 g / 1 ¾ oz / ⅓ cup blueberries

- Divide half the yoghurt between 4 glasses and top with the granola.
- Top with the rest of the yoghurt, then add a tablespoon of condensed milk to each one and sprinkle over the blueberries.

999

SERVES 4

Passion Fruit and Lemon Cheesecake Pots

PREPARATION TIME 40 MINUTES

COOKING TIME 5 MINUTES

....

INGREDIENTS

200 g / 7 oz / ¾ cup cream cheese
200 g / 7 oz / 1 cup condensed milk
2 lemons, juiced
1 tbsp poppy seeds
4 passion fruit, halved

- Beat the cream cheese with an electric whisk until smooth then whisk in the condensed milk.
- Whisk in the lemon juice and poppy seeds until the mixture starts to thicken, then spoon into 4 glasses.
- Leave to chill in the fridge for 30 minutes to firm up.
- When the pots have set, spoon over the passion fruit pulp and seeds and serve.

Kiwi Cheesecake Pots

1000

- Replace the passion fruit with 3 finely chopped kiwi fruits.

1001

SERVES 4

Peach Crumble

PREPARATION TIME 5 MINUTES

COOKING TIME 40 MINUTES

....

INGREDIENTS

3 peaches, peeled, stoned and cubed
75 g / 2 ½ oz / ⅓ cup butter
50 g / 1 ¾ oz / ⅓ cup plain (all purpose) flour
25 g / 1 oz / ¼ cup ground almonds
40 g / 1 ½ oz / ¼ cup light brown sugar

- Preheat the oven to 180°C (160° fan), 355 F, gas 4.
- Arrange the cubed peaches in a baking dish.
- Rub the butter into the flour and stir in the ground almonds and brown sugar.
- Take a handful of the topping and squeeze it into a clump, then crumble it over the fruit.
- Repeat with the rest of the crumble mixture then bake for 40 minutes or until the topping is golden brown.

Mango Crumble

1002

- Replace the peaches with 3 peeled, stoned mangoes, cut into cubes.

1003

SERVES 4

Stewed Mirabelles

- Put the wine, sugar, lemon and spices in a saucepan and add 200 ml water.
- Bring to the boil, stirring to dissolve the sugar then stir in the mirabelles.
- Simmer gently for 15 minutes or until they are soft.
- Serve warm or chilled.

PREPARATION TIME 5 MINUTES

COOKING TIME 20 MINUTES

INGREDIENTS

200 ml / 7 fl. oz / ¾ cup white wine
75 g / 2 ½ oz / ⅓ cup caster (superfine) sugar
1 lemon, zest finely pared
1 vanilla pod, slit lengthways
1 cinnamon stick
450 g / 1 lb / 2 ⅔ cup mirabelles

Stewed Cherries 1004

- Replace the mirabelles with cherries and use orange zest instead of lemon zest.

1005

SERVES 4

Nectarine and Apricot Crumble

- Preheat the oven to 180°C (160° fan), 355 F, gas 4.
- Arrange the nectarines and dried apricots in a baking dish.
- Rub the butter into the flour and stir in the ground almonds and brown sugar.
- Take a handful of the topping and squeeze it into a clump, then crumble it over the fruit.
- Repeat with the rest of the crumble mixture then bake for 40 minutes or until the topping is golden brown.

PREPARATION TIME 5 MINUTES

COOKING TIME 40 MINUTES

INGREDIENTS

3 nectarines, peeled, stoned and cubed
50 g / 1 ¾ oz / ¼ cup dried apricots, chopped
75 g / 2 ½ oz / ⅓ cup butter
50 g / 1 ¾ oz / ⅓ cup plain (all purpose) flour
25 g / 1 oz / ¼ cup ground almonds
40 g / 1 ½ oz / ¼ cup light brown sugar

Double Apricot Crumble 1006

- Replace the nectarines with fresh apricots.

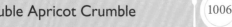

SERVES 6

Chocolate Samosas with Pineapple

PREPARATION TIME 25 MINUTES

COOKING TIME 12-15 MINUTES

INGREDIENTS

225 g / 8 oz filo pastry
100 g / 3 ½ oz / ½ cup butter, melted
200 g / 7 oz / 2 cups dark chocolate
(minimum 60 % cocoa solids), finely
chopped
1 pineapple, peeled and thinly sliced

- Preheat the oven to 180°C (160° fan), 355 F, gas 4 and grease a large baking tray.
- Cut the pile of filo sheets in half then take one halved sheet and brush it with melted butter.
- Arrange a tablespoon of chopped chocolate at one end and fold the corner over, then triangle-fold it up.
- Transfer the samosa to the baking tray and repeat with the rest of the filo and chocolate, then brush with any leftover butter.
- Arrange the pineapple slices alongside the samosas and roast for 12 – 15 minutes or until the pastry is crisp and the pineapple is caramelised at the edges.
- Serve warm.

Chocolate Orange Samosas   1008

- Add the grated zest of an orange to the chopped chocolate and add 1 tbsp of Cointreau to the melted butter.

SERVES 6

Fig and Raspberry Compote

PREPARATION TIME 10 MINUTES

COOKING TIME 8 MINUTES

INGREDIENTS

250 g / 5 oz / 2 cups raspberries
4 figs, quartered
1 orange, juiced and zest finely
grated
2 tbsp light brown sugar
200 ml / 7 fl. oz / ¾ cup double
cream
2 tbsp icing (confectioners') sugar
1 tsp vanilla extract

- Preheat the oven to 200°C (180° fan), 390 F, gas 6.
- Put the fruit in a saucepan with the orange juice and zest and brown sugar.
- Cover with a lid and cook over a medium heat for 8 minutes, stirring occasionally, then spoon the compote into 6 bowls or glasses.
- Whip the cream with the icing (confectioners') sugar and vanilla extract until thick then spoon on top of the compotes.

Fig and Rhubarb Compote   1010

- Replace the raspberries with 3 chopped rhubarb stems.

1011

SERVES 4

Natural Yoghurt with Summer Fruit Coulis

Natural Yoghurt with Lemon Sauce

1012

- Make a simple sauce by mixing 2 tbsp of limoncello with 4 tbsp of lemon curd. Drizzle over the yoghurts and garnish with fresh raspberries.

Fromage Frais with Summer Fruit Coulis

1013

- Replace the yoghurt with unsweetened fromage frais and add the grated zest of an orange to the fruits before cooking.

PREPARATION TIME 30 MINUTES

COOKING TIME 5 MINUTES

INGREDIENTS

250 g / 10 ½ oz / 2 ¼ cups mixed summer berries
2 tbsp caster (superfine) sugar
1 tbsp kirsch
4 pots set natural yoghurt
2 tbsp pistachio nuts, chopped

- Reserve some of the berries for a garnish and put the rest in a saucepan with the sugar and kirsch.
- Cook over a low heat for 5 minutes or until the berries start to burst.
- Pour the mixture into a liquidiser and blend to a smooth sauce then chill in the fridge for 25 minutes.
- Remove the lids from the yoghurt pots and turn them out onto 4 plates.
- Spoon over the cooled coulis and garnish with the rest of the berries and a sprinkling of pistachio nuts.

1014

MAKES 4

Banana and Sultana Bread Puddings

Apricot Bread Puddings 1015

- Replace the sultanas with chopped dried apricot and substitute the bananas with halved fresh apricots.

Banana and Rum Puddings 1016

- Omit the sultanas and stir 3 tbsp of dark rum into the cream mixture.

PREPARATION TIME 5 MINUTES

COOKING TIME 35-40 MINUTES

INGREDIENTS

250 ml / 9 fl. oz / 1 cup whole milk
200 ml / 7 fl. oz / ¾ cup double cream
4 large egg yolks
75 g / 2 ½ oz / ⅓ cup caster (superfine) sugar
1 loaf white bread, cubed
4 tbsp sultanas
1 tsp mixed spice
2 bananas, quartered
4 tbsp runny honey

- Preheat the oven to 180°C (160° fan), 355 F, gas 4.
- Whisk the milk, cream, eggs and caster (superfine) sugar together then stir in the bread, sultanas and spice.
- Divide the mixture between 4 small buttered baking dishes and press 2 pieces of banana into the top of each.
- Bake for 35 – 40 minutes or until the tops are golden brown, then drizzle over the honey.

1017

SERVES 4

Quick Chocolate Mousse

- Heat the cream to simmering point then pour it over the chocolate and stir until smooth.
- Leave to cool for 10 minutes.
- Whip the egg whites until stiff then whisk in the sugar.
- Stir a big spoonful of the egg white into the cooled chocolate mixture then fold in the rest with a big metal spoon, keeping as many of the air bubbles intact as possible.
- Spoon the mousse into 4 glasses and chill for 20 minutes.
- Decorate with chocolate sugar balls before serving.

PREPARATION TIME 5 MINUTES

COOKING TIME 40 MINUTES

INGREDIENTS

200 g / 7 fl. oz / ¾ cup double cream
200 g / 7 oz / 2 cups milk chocolate, chopped
2 egg whites
4 tbsp caster (superfine) sugar
chocolate sugar balls, to decorate

Quick White Chocolate Mousse   1018

- Replace the milk chocolate with white chocolate and add the finely grated zest of half an orange.

1019

SERVES 6

Warm Yoghurt Cake with Blueberry Jam

- Preheat the oven to 190°C (170° fan), 375 F, gas 5 and butter a small baking dish.
- Combine the flour, sugar, yoghurt, eggs and vanilla extract in a bowl and whisk together for 2 minutes or until smooth.
- Spoon the mixture into the baking dish then bake for 30 – 35 minutes.
- Test with a wooden toothpick, if it comes out clean, the cake is done.
- Towards the end of the cooking time, heat the blueberry jam in a small saucepan with 2 tbsp water until runny.
- Cut the cake into wedges and serve drizzled with the warm jam.

PREPARATION TIME 10 MINUTES

COOKING TIME 30-35 MINUTES

INGREDIENTS

110 g / 4 oz / ⅔ cup self-raising flour, sifted
110 g / 4 oz / ½ cup caster (superfine) sugar
110 g / 4 oz / ½ cup Greek yoghurt
2 large eggs
1 tsp vanilla extract
1 jar blueberry jam

Warm Citrus Yoghurt Cake   1020

- Add the grated zest of a lemon, a lime and an orange to the cake mixture. Heat 3 tbsp each of lemon curd and marmalade together until runny and drizzle over the cake to serve.

Index

Index

Index

Index